CITIES AND CIVILIZATIONS

CITIES AND CIVILIZATIONS
CHRISTOPHER HIBBERT

WEIDENFELD & NICOLSON
LONDON

AUTHOR'S NOTE

The purpose of this book is far more modest than that of Lewis Mumford's brilliant survey, The City in History, *which dealt with the forms and functions of the city in general and with its mission in furthering 'man's conscious participation in the cosmic and the historic process'. I have merely attempted to give impressions of the appearance and social life of twenty-one of the world's greatest cities at crucial periods in their development, to glimpse at their origins and to indicate the nature of the civilizations in which they emerged and whose ethos they reflected.*

For his help in the research for the book I am deeply grateful to my friend, the Hon. Edmund Howard, whose copious notes on most of the chapters have been invaluable. I want also to thank Mrs Phyllis McDougall for having compiled the index, my helpful editors Johanna Awdry and Denny Hemming, Mrs Sheila Kidd, Mrs Tessa Street, Mrs Margaret Lewendon, Mrs Nonie Rae, my wife, and Major J. T. Cooper.

Christopher Hibbert

For Francis and Elizabeth
with love

First published in Great Britain in 1987

This 1996 paperback edition published by
George Weidenfeld & Nicolson Ltd.
The Orion Publishing Group,
Orion House,
5, Upper St. Martin's Lane,
London WC2H 9EA.

A catalogue record for this book is available from the British Library

ISBN 0-297-82176-8

Filmset in the United Kingdom
Printed and bound in Italy
Designed by Joy FitzSimmons

CONTENTS

Author's Note   4

Prologue   6

PART I: THE ANCIENT CITY

1 Thebes in the Days of the Pharoahs, 2000 BC–1200 BC   8

2 Jerusalem in the Days of David and Herod, 1000 BC–AD 60   20

3 Athens in the Days of Pericles, 480 BC–404 BC   32

4 Rome in the Days of the Emperor Trajan, AD 53–117   44

PART II: THE DEVELOPING CITY

5 Constantinople in the Days of Constantine and Justinian, 330–565   56

6 Hangzhou in the Days of the Sung Emperors, 1138–1279   67

7 Cuzco in the Days of the Incas, 1300–1533   78

8 Florence in the Days of the Medici, 1389–1492   90

9 Toledo in the Days of Philip II and El Greco, 1556–1598   104

10 Amsterdam in the Days of Rembrandt, 1606–1669   116

11 Paris in the Days of Louis XIV, 1651–1715   124

12 London in the Days of Pepys and Wren, 1666–1723   136

13 St Petersburg in the Days of Peter the Great, 1703–1725   152

14 Venice in the Days of Canaletto and Casanova, 1697–1798   162

15 Vienna in the Days of Franz Josef, 1848–1916   174

PART III: THE MODERN CITY

16 New Orleans: 'The Crescent City'   186

17 Tokyo: 'City of the Rising Sun'   196

18 Berlin: 'The Babylon of the World'   205

19 Moscow: 'A Model Communist City'   216

20 New York: 'A Stroke of Genius'   228

21 Sydney: 'The Finest Harbour in the World'   240

Photographic Acknowledgements   249

Sources   250

Index   253

PROLOGUE

At the beginning of 1881 a rich American sailed up the Nile as far as Luxor, the site of the lost city of Thebes, in search of antiquities to add to his growing collection. Believing that he could find better bargains in the dark houses of the back streets than in the shops of recognized dealers, he made his way into the bazaar where he was soon offered a papyrus in remarkably good condition. He bought it, packed it in his trunk, and, evading police and customs alike, took it back with him to Europe. Proudly and openly he showed it to friends and experts, telling them how it had come into his possession, describing his visit by night to the house of the Egyptian who had sold it to him, and how he had smuggled it across the Mediterranean. Concerned by the American's story, one of the experts regaled with it wrote to Professor Gaston Maspero, the French egyptologist in Cairo, who had recently been appointed Director General of Excavation and Antiquities by the Egyptian government.

From its description, Maspero considered that the papyrus might well be a mortuary gift from the tomb of a pharaoh of the Twenty-First Dynasty, all traces of which had disappeared and had been presumed lost for ever. So, having examined the records of other antiquities which had mysteriously surfaced within the past few years, Maspero decided to send one of his assistants to Luxor, in the guise of a collector, to uncover what secrets he could. The young man booked a room in the hotel where the American had stayed, and became a familiar figure in the bazaar, obviously rich but also discerning: the dealers soon realized it was a waste of time offering him the sort of fakes and copies which might tempt more gullible foreigners. One day he was beckoned into a house and shown a statuette of superb craftsmanship. He recognized it immediately from its inscription as a work of art of the Twenty-First Dynasty. Concealing his excitement, however, he contrived to give the man the impression that he was only mildly interested, and that he was really looking for something finer and larger. He was accordingly introduced to one Abd-el-Rassul, an Arab of commanding height and forceful personality who over the next few days presented for his inspection so extraordinary a variety of mortuary objects that Maspero's assistant had no hesitation in informing the police and having the man arrested as a tomb robber.

It transpired that the tall, imposing Arab was the head of a large family much respected in their village, Kurna, where their forebears had lived for generations. A procession of witnesses spoke highly of them before the Mudir who conducted their examination. No evidence could be found to incriminate them; and, while the frustrated young man from Cairo fell ill with fever, the hearing continued in its desultory fashion before being abandoned altogether. But the Mudir was a formidable as well as a patient man; and, although he could get nothing from Abd-el-Rassul himself, he did eventually manage to extract a confession from one of his numerous relations. At a renewed hearing it gradually emerged that the inhabitants of the village of Kurna were tomb robbers almost to a man, that they had been so for centuries past, and that, as recently as 1875, Abd-el-Rassul had come by chance upon a mass of treasure in a mortuary chamber whose small entrance was concealed beneath the tumbled rocks. He had seen enough to convince him that the treasure was more than enough to keep his family and their descendants in comfort for as long as the secret could be kept; and little by little he had been extracting objects for sale in Luxor. Yet, as was discovered by another young museum official from Cairo who had arrived to take the place of his feverish colleague, there were still left in the tomb, lying beside the mummies and the sarcophagi, countless objects of incalculable worth which had lain undisturbed for three thousand years. The mysteries of the Valley of the Kings had at last been revealed to the world.

Gold pectoral, inlaid with precious stones, from the tomb of Queen Meret, wife of Ammenemes III (1842–1797 BC)

PART I

THE
ANCIENT
CITY

1
Thebes
in the Days of the Pharaohs
2000 BC—1200 BC

'At the sight of its scattered ruins,' recalled Vivant Denon, the artist and archaeologist who accompanied Bonaparte's expedition to Egypt in 1798, 'the army halted of its own accord at Luxor and, by one spontaneous impulse, the soldiers grounded their arms.' Twenty-three centuries earlier, the Greek historian Herodotus, who made a tour of Egypt in the fifth century BC, had been equally impressed. There were, he considered, 'wonders more in number than those of any other land, and works beyond expression great'. Over two thousand years before his time, a great civilization had been established here. Beside the banks of the Nile its monuments survived – vast pyramids of innumerable stone blocks each weighing as much as fifteen tons; huge temples with doorways flanked by monumental statues; obelisks covered with strange hieroglyphs of birds and insects, human figures, eyes and abstract symbols; and gigantic stone lions with the heads of men gazing inscrutably across the sand of the desert.

It was the Nile that had made this civilization possible. Worshipped as a god at its source in Ethiopia, the Blue Nile flows north to meet the White Nile which itself rises in what is now Uganda. The two rivers converge at Khartoum in

The Great Pylon of Rameses II at the Amon-Mut-Khons temple, Luxor (1290–1224 BC).

the Sudan and thence their intermingled waters flow on for nearly two thousand miles, tumbling over six cataracts in their course, leaving the Red Lands of the desert, then entering the Black Land of Upper Egypt, before fanning out into tributaries of the Delta that take them into the Mediterranean.

Every year, in the season known as Inundation, the river, swollen by the torrential African rains, flooded across the valley. Four months or so later the waters receded, and in the season called Emergence, men planted their seeds in the rich mud. During the third season, the Drought, they harvested the crops and awaited the next Inundation. Sometimes the floods were so high that whole villages were washed away in the rushing waters; in other years they covered so much less of the parched land that seed could not be sown and families went hungry.

The unpredictability of the river rendered the organization of society essential if starvation were not constantly to threaten much of Egypt's large population. Dikes had to be built, canals and irrigation trenches dug, wells sunk, catch-basins created and storehouses constructed; and for these purposes an immense labour force was required. This force was conscripted and organized under the pharaohs, rulers of a civilization that lasted for almost three thousand years.

The first ruler emerged in about 3100 BC when the lands known as Upper Egypt, where the river flows between towering cliffs, and Lower Egypt, where it approaches the more fertile country of the Delta, were united under one king. Thereafter, under thirty successive dynasties, the Egyptians, formerly scattered tribesmen, became a prosperous and unified people, farmers and traders, exporters of grain, linen and papyrus, the reed which grew so thickly in the mud flats of the Delta and was used not only as a writing material but also for ropes and in the manufacture of boats, baskets, mats and furniture. They were protected from invasion by the wastelands and desert to the east and west and, to the north, by the readily

ABOVE LEFT *Harvesting and measuring the fields : a wall-painting in the tomb of Menena at Thebes.*

CENTRE LEFT *Grape-picking : a wall-painting from the Eighteenth-Dynasty tomb of Nakht at Thebes.*

BELOW LEFT *Treading the grapes : a wall-painting from the tomb of Nakht at Thebes.*

The Step Pyramid of Djoser, first Pharaoh of the Third Dynasty, built at Sakkarah by the architect Imhotep in c.2686 BC.

defensible Mediterranean coast; they were surrounded by such limitless quantities of hard stone that the building programmes of the most ambitious pharaohs could all be realized; and they were favoured by rich deposits of semi-precious stones and, in the Eastern Desert and Nubia, by mines of gold.

The earliest main era of Egyptian civilization is known as that of the Old Kingdom. This lasted from about 2700 BC to 2200 BC and during this time the great monumental tombs, the pyramids, were built, not by tens of thousands of slaves, as Herodotus had supposed, but by more modest numbers of Egyptian workmen, conscripted in villages during the season of Inundation, issued with tools and clothing, and trained in gangs of eighteen or twenty to use wedges, rollers, ramps and sledges to haul the vast stone blocks from the quarries – where they had been laboriously cut and chiselled into shape – to drag and lever them onto barges, and then to work them into the precise places indicated by the pharaoh's architects.

The first of the tombs to be completed was the Step Pyramid (*c.*2686 BC) at Sakkarah, the necropolis of Memphis where the founder of the First Dynasty had established his capital. It was built for Djoser, the first pharaoh of the Third

Dynasty, and designed by his gifted architect, Imhotep. Previously the Egyptians' principal building material had been sun-dried brick, but the Step Pyramid was made entirely of stone and was the first large structure of this material that the world had seen. It stood some 200 feet high above its underground chambers and measured 413 feet by 344 feet at its base; but even so, it was soon to be dwarfed by other stone pyramids built for Djoser's successors, pharaohs of the Fourth Dynasty, at Giza, west of Memphis, on the outskirts of modern Cairo. The first and largest of these was completed in about 2600 BC for the pharaoh, Khufu, and was probably about 450 feet high before the capstone and outer facing were removed for other buildings, thus reducing its height by 30 feet. Beside it stand the pyramids of Menkaure and of Khafre, whose features are said to have served as a model for the sculptors of the Great Sphinx at Giza whose face was carved in his reign.

The cost of these pyramids, of which over seventy more were to be built on a smaller scale, was enormous and so was the cost of the objects

The temple complex and sacred lake at Karnak. On the
left is the first pylon, in the centre is the hypostyle hall,
and on the right the obelisk.

with which they were filled for the use and
pleasure of the pharaoh in the life of the other
world. Their building and embellishment led to
economic troubles which – combined with a
growth in the power of the pharaoh's noble
officials and of the priests of the sun god of whom
the pharaoh was an incarnation – led in turn to the
breakdown of centralized rule, the failure of the
system that had made the Nile the 'gift of Egypt',
the assumption of power by local governors who
set themselves up as petty pharaohs, and the
eventual disintegration of the Old Kingdom. An
anarchic age known as the First Intermediate
Period ensued and lasted for two hundred years
until, in Thebes, a town far upstream in Upper
Egypt below the First Cataract, a family established themselves as the Eleventh Dynasty,

spread their rule into Lower Egypt, and inaugurated the age know as the Middle Kingdom.

In about 2000 BC the two parts of Egypt were
united once more under a Theban family who
inaugurated the Twelfth Dynasty. Although the
capital was moved from Thebes to Lower Egypt,
the pharaohs of the Twelfth Dynasty continued to
lavish money upon the embellishment of Thebes,
home of their ancestors; and it was largely upon
Theban families that they relied in administering
their kingdom, in extending its frontiers south
into Nubia beyond the Second Cataract, in establishing Egyptian influence in Palestine and large
parts of Syria, and in promoting trade with these
and other countries through ports along the
Mediterranean and the Red Sea.

The great days of Thebes seemed, however, to
be coming to an end when the last pharaoh of the
Twelfth Dynasty died; and, under the pharaohs
of the Thirteenth Dynasty in the seventeenth
century BC, Egypt entered upon another era of

disruption and decline known as the Second Intermediate Period. Egypt once again split into two; Asiatic tribesmen armed with weapons unknown to the Egyptians, wearing armour and driving chariots, came down from the north and occupied much of the lands of the Delta; and the Thebans were forced back into straitened territories in the arid lands between their capital and the First Cataract. But then, in the middle of the sixteenth century BC, another energetic and ambitious family rose to prominence in Thebes, founded the Eighteenth Dynasty under the pharaoh Ahmose I, and established the period know as the New Kingdom.

Adopting the weapons introduced into Egypt by the Asiatic conquerors of the north, they drove them out of the Delta, advanced through Palestine and Syria across the Euphrates, and extended their dominion far south beyond the Eastern Desert into Africa. Ahmose I was succeeded by his son, Amenophis I, who continued his father's expansion of the Egyptian empire which was still further enlarged by Tuthmosis I, Amenophis's son by a woman of the royal harem. He had strengthened his claim to the throne by marrying his father's fully royal daughter and his son, Tuthmosis II, had for the same reason also married his half-sister, Hatshepsut. It was she who ruled the empire after her sickly husband's death in about 1503 BC.

She was a remarkable woman, wearing not only the double white and red crown which signified the pharaoh's rule over both Upper and Lower Egypt, but also donning the robes of a king and even the narrow false beard which, traditionally worn by the pharaohs, can be seen on the beaten gold mask of the mummy of Tutankhamen in the Egyptian Museum in Cairo. In the words of one of her courtiers, she 'directed the affairs of the whole land according to her wishes'. Forsaking war and conquest for the peaceful pursuit of profitable trade, Hatshepsut sent delegations of merchants to the African coast whence they returned with shiploads of ebony and gold and living myrrh trees. She also received immense quantities of tribute from Libya and Asia as well as from Nubia, and with the money and precious cargoes thus earned or exacted she undertook an astonishingly ambitious building programme in and around Thebes both in honour of herself and her family and of the god Amun, father of the pharaoh, the invisible spirit whose rays reached out to the far corners of the earth where the mountains supported the sky.

By the time of Hatshepsut's coronation in about 1503 BC, the pharaoh was no longer glorified as a god in his own right but in company with the other gods of the Egyptians; and pyramids had accordingly given way to funerary complexes of halls and temples, porticoes and courtyards, chapels, terraces and groups of statues and obelisks, often approached by way of a monumental gateway of two truncated pyramids known as a pylon and provided with all the additional buildings necessary for the communities that served the god, living quarters, storerooms, workshops, schools and sacred pools of water.

Hatshepsut's father had built for himself a memorial hall in the Temple of Karnak near Thebes; and this she herself renovated and decorated with four obelisks, each almost a hundred feet high, adding a chapel, terrace and court. And for herself she built near Thebes the magnificent temple beneath the cliffs at Deir el Bahari, a complex of colonnaded shrines depicting the achievements of her reign in nearly two hundred statues and reliefs along the porticoes. She is shown being born, the child of the god Amun, being divinely chosen as pharaoh, and being crowned. Her expedition to the African coast of Somalia is illustrated in fascinating detail; so is the transportation by water of the four immense obelisks for her earthly father's temple. This great temple was designed under her direction by her trusted architect and minister of public works, Senmut, who, in order to share her lustre and to ease his path to greatness in the nether world, had images of himself carved in not too obtrusive places on the walls. But as soon as his mistress heard of his insolence she had all the carvings effaced, his tomb desecrated and his sarcophagus destroyed. When it came to her own turn to die, twenty years after her assumption of power, the

pharaoh, her stepson, whose dignities she had usurped, had his revenge by treating her own memorials in the same way, and, towards the end of his own reign, having her name chipped off the walls with which she had attempted to perpetuate her glory.

This new pharaoh was Tuthmosis III (ruled 1490–1436 BC), a vigorous, farsighted ruler whom his stepmother, who was also his aunt and officially co-regent with him, had tried to relegate to the shadows by having him appointed a priest of the god Amun. The son of a court concubine, he had been betrothed at the age of ten to his half-sister Neferu, Hatshepsut's daughter. He was small, no more than five feet three inches tall, according to the evidence of his mummy which was discovered in 1889 in a place where it had been hidden for safety after the looting of his tomb. But he was an athletic man of formidable strength and resolution who was to prove himself an exceptionally gifted soldier. In a total of seventeen campaigns he enlarged and consolidated the Egyptian Empire and those territories the Egyptians administered through native princes and governors; and with the growth of empire came an increase in wealth and in the sums available for the building of temples to the glory of the gods who smiled so favourably on Egypt's fortunes.

The Temple at Karnak, approached through rows of massive columns thirty-three feet in circumference and sixty-nine feet high, was enlarged and embellished with several new obelisks, one of which, originally weighing eight hundred tons, is now to be seen in Istanbul in the square in front of the Blue Mosque, the site of the Byzantine Hippodrome; the other is in Rome where it was found lying in three pieces in the Circus Maximus in 1587 and later erected in Piazza San Giovanni in Laterano. Two further obelisks which were made in Tuthmosis's reign for the temple of the sun-god at Heliopolis have also been transported overseas, one to New York's Central Park, the other, known as Cleopatra's Needle – her name was inscribed upon it later – to Victoria Embankment, London.

As well as furnishing the Temple of Amun at Karnak with obelisks, Tuthmosis III provided it with a splendid Festival Hall decorated with pictures and reliefs of the animals and plants he had brought back with him from his campaigns:

giraffes, bears, elephants and all kinds of birds and exotic flowers. Originating as a small shrine of the Twelfth Dynasty, it had been added to by pharaoh after pharaoh and was to be further enlarged by pharaohs of the Nineteenth Dynasty, notably Seti I and his son, Rameses II, father of more than a hundred children and builder of grandiose monuments, whose mortuary temple at Thebes was to be dominated by a thousand-ton statue of himself fifty-seven feet tall and whose four colossal statues on the façade of his temple at Abu Simbel below the Second Cataract are even more massive than this, being sixty-seven feet high from his feet to the summit of his majestic crown. At his feet stand statues of members of his family, reaching less than half-way to his knees.

While the vast structure of the Temple of Amun at Karnak was the work of many architects over hundreds of years, from 2000 BC to the days of the Nubian King Taharqa of the Twenty-Fifth Dynasty, who died in 664 BC, another temple to that god, two miles away near the modern town of Luxor, was largely constructed to please one man, Amenophis III, known as Amenophis the Magnificent, who came to the throne in 1417 BC. During his peaceful and prosperous reign the architects, artists and craftsmen of Egypt attained new skills and heightened talents in design and execution while retaining the fundamental traditions by which Egyptian art was bound.

In the time of the Old Kingdom, as Professor Lionel Casson has observed, the basic poses of sculpture were established. 'Egyptian artists did not concern themselves with trying to capture fleeting emotions. The sculptor who was commissioned to make a statue for the god-king's tomb and embody his spirit for eternity attempted to show the essence of the subject and not the wrinkles on his face. Egyptian figures, consequently, are motionless and devoid of passion. If the statues expressed no emotion, however, they did convey character and majesty, and Egyptian sculpture can offer, as a consequence, some of the most impressive portraiture that has ever been wrought in stone. The figure is generally shown seated, with its hands on its knees (in the manner of the gigantic effigy of Rameses II at Abu Simbel), or standing with one foot forward and the hands held straight at the sides (as with the twin statues of Rameses II at Luxor) or folded across the breast – a stately pose intended to

Head of Amenophis III of the Eighteenth Dynasty.

suggest the majesty of the pharaohs.' But, while poses remained fixed, the treatment of the carving did not. The pharaohs of the Old Kingdom were shown with the serene and confident faces of gods; those of the Middle Kingdom, when the pharaoh's power was being circumscribed by priests and provincial governors and the pharaoh himself was beginning to be regarded as human as well as divine, are shown reflecting the characters of men. By the time of the New Kingdom 'growing wealth and luxury led to a softening of severity in art, to sophistication, and finally to a self-conscious seeking after effect. In the time of Amenophis III, when armed conquest had been supplanted by diplomacy and the country was governed from a sumptuous court, the sculpture was given a delicacy and refinement quite different in style from the simple straightforward spareness' of the past.

Jewellers at work : fragment of a wall-painting from an Eighteenth-Dynasty tomb at Sheik Abd el-Qurna.

The same kind of conventions and the same sort of development are apparent in that other form of temple and tomb decoration, carved relief, in which the message to be conveyed was more important than realism and the pharaoh dwarfed the men and women and animals with whom he was depicted. Yet, as the years passed, carving in relief became less conventional and formalized; while painting, in which the Egyptians excelled – using mineral pigments so that their colours have remained wonderfully clear – was no longer confined to the decoration of relief but became an art in its own right, and figures, previously painted in silhouette or shown in stylized groups with, for example, a man's wife clasping him round the waist and a child grasping his leg to indicate a family, became lively and animated. At the same time simple hunting scenes and pictures of men fishing amid the Nile's papyrus reeds, or women dancing, were supplemented by depiction of historical events and court ceremonies, of funerals and banquets in which the mourners and guests seem to be portraits of men and women who had taken part in them.

Amenophis III, in whose reign the arts of ancient Egypt were in full flower, was as ambitious a builder as Rameses II was to be. Before his death in 1379 BC he had not only constructed the main parts of the Temple at Luxor and a huge pylon in the Temple of Karnak, he had also inaugurated the mortuary temple in Thebes (of which the Colossi of Memnon survive), a large temple in Nubia and several other temples in various parts of the empire.

His people seem never to have been more content and prosperous since the days of the Old Kingdom when Egypt, under the pharaohs, gods on earth, lived a life free from all the complications that contact with the outside world was later to bring. The sun shone all day; and even for the very poor, whose children ran about quite naked, there was always enough to eat except in those rare hard seasons when they had to be content with boiled papyrus shoots. In Thebes the poorer people were mostly gathered on the west bank of the Nile where they went out to work every day from their village to excavate and to decorate the tombs in the rock of the Valley of the Kings where all the pharaohs of the Eighteenth, Nineteenth and Twentieth Dynasties had been buried since the time of Tuthmosis I. Their mud-brick dwellings were cramped; but they had whitewashed walls which reflected the sunlight that shone through slits in the roof. Their small rooms, whose floors were covered with matting, contained seats with cushions, wooden chairs and cabinets; and on one of the walls was a shrine containing a stele on which was carved a prayer. Most rooms seem to have been clean and tidy. Fleas were kept in check with fish spawn, while cat grease and gazelle dung were employed to keep rats at bay. A large jar of water stood in the main room, and its contents were used for washing as well as drinking and cooking. Soap was unknown but bodies were scoured with soda and then the skin was rubbed with ointment so that it was not left too dry. Ointment, indeed, as well as food and clothing, was among the payments in kind that the workers at Thebes received instead of money wages; and when they downed tools in about 1170 BC in the first strike known to history, and sat down behind a temple in the necropolis in protest against the witholding of their entitlements, it was not only their rations of food but also of ointment that they demanded. On their death little jars of ointment, together with pieces of food, were placed beside them for their comfort in the life that followed death.

Their corpses were not, of course, placed in the kind of decorated tombs that the richer families could afford to equip with the sandalwood chests, bouquets of flowers, baskets of fruit, vases of oils, statues, and models of boats and chariots which were discovered in the tomb of the pharaoh Tutankhamen. Yet their names might be

THEBES _____ 17

mentioned in the texts that were inscribed on the walls of such tombs, or representations of them might be included in the sculpted scenes; and, while their bodies did not receive the expensive embalming of a pharaoh or a noble, they were embalmed in a crude way before being placed in a common grave either in a coffin or wrapped in cloth and separated from the body beneath by a layer of sand.

The process of embalmment was described by Herodotus accurately enough, though he does not mention the resin with which the body and bandages were smeared and which, usually mixed with sawdust, was stuffed into the abdominal cavity: 'The finest grade of embalming is as follows. First, by means of bent iron instruments inserted in the nostrils they extract the brains ... Next, with a sharp stone knife they make an incision in the flank and empty the whole abdominal cavity, washing it first with palm wine and then rinsing with an infusion of ground spices. They then fill the cavity with pure ground myrrh and cassia and all other spices, except frankincense, and sew up the incision. Having completed this operation, they put the body in natron, keeping it completely covered for seventy days ... Then they wash the body and wrap it all up in bandages of fine linen smeared with gum ... The deceased's relatives then take it over and give orders to make a wooden case in human shape. When this is ready, they put the body in it and, fastening the cover, set it in the tomb chamber standing upright against a wall ... For people with little money they cleanse the abdominal cavity with a purge, put the body in natron for seventy days, and then hand it over to be carried away. Wives of men of standing or women who are beautiful and important are not turned over to the embalmers immediately after death but only after a delay of three to four days. This is done in order to prevent the embalmers from having intercourse with them.'

By the Eighteenth Dynasty mummies were being made to appear more lifelike by the application of resinous pastes to the outside of the body and the addition of artificial eyes; while toes and fingers, complete with their nails, were kept in place with thread.

The cliffs along the west bank at Thebes were honeycombed with elaborately decorated tombs, all long since plundered, but once filled with the mummified bodies of noblemen and their families attended by little pottery or faience figurines of workers and servants equipped with the appropriate tools to perform for the dead all the duties that might be required of them in the other world.

In the living world the rich man was surrounded by servants and slaves accommodated in communal quarters along the plastered brick whitewashed walls which, often decorated with murals, surrounded the garden of his house on the east bank of the river. The walls were pierced by a large gateway which led through gardens, filled with flowering shrubs, with willows, sycamores and palm trees, and shady arbours beside lotus-covered pools, to the columned porch of the house which was usually approached by a ramp from the garden path. Inside, the guest was conducted through a hall, its roof supported perhaps by columns of wood so precious in a country with few trees that they were often transported with the furniture when a family moved house. Beyond the hall was the main room of the villa. This was also embellished with painted and carved wooden or stone columns and lit by grilles set high in the walls. At the far end of the hall, beyond a raised central hearth with a brazier to warm the room in the winter months, was a wide dais covered with cushions from which the family rose to greet their visitors and on which they sat to eat their meals. The ceiling, like the columns, would be painted; there would probably be a patterned frieze around the top of the walls beneath the grilles, and a dado of faience tiles or wooden panelling.

Leading off the living-room were smaller sitting-rooms and bedrooms for the family and guests; a staircase led to the roof where, beneath an awning to shelter them from the sun, guests could look down upon the garden below. There were bathrooms with stone floors, and lavatories with pots, regularly removed and replaced by servants, beneath brick or wooden seats.

There were low boxwood and ebony chairs with carved backs and leather or linen seats in the sitting-rooms; chests for linen and clothes in the bedrooms as well as wooden-framed beds on which mattresses were laid over the cord network. At night lamps burning castor, linseed or sesame oil were lit, and mosquito nets were drawn over the beds. In the dining-room there were several small tables instead of one large one and on these

were placed gold and silver dishes, brilliantly decorated pottery and bronze cups.

After his morning bath, a shave and massage, the noble would have his skin rubbed with oils and scented unguents, apply deodorants to his – often shaven – armpits and between his thighs, have his short hair as carefully dressed as his wives and concubines and, if it was thinning, have his scalp rubbed with a lotion containing the fat of lions, crocodiles, cats, serpents, ibexes and hippopotami. Many men shaved their heads as well as their faces, though on formal occasions they would cover their bare scalps with wigs. Both men and women wore make-up, applying red ochre mixed with vegetable oil to the lips, juice of henna to fingernails and toenails, and green powdered malachite and black powdered galena to the corners of the eyes, the rims and lashes to create that unnaturally large almond shape which was universally admired. Having completed this lengthy toilet, the nobleman dressed himself in loose comfortable linen, 'always freshly washed', so Herodotus said, a short-sleeved shirt, perhaps, and a skirt reaching to knees or ankles according to fancy. He wore sandals of leather or plaited papyrus and what, in later civilization, would be considered an extravagant amount of jewelry – bangles, necklaces, bracelets, rings, magical charms and a collar of beads, faience, jasper or lapis lazuli.

The women of his household also wore loose-fitting clothes about the house, though on formal occasions they were to be seen in gaily coloured, tight-fitting sheaths which were frequently cut so that one breast was exposed. Slaves, like children, went about their duties completely naked, apart from their wigs, their necklaces and the narrow beaded belts which they sometimes wore round their waists, purely for ornamentation and not intended to hide their pubic hairs, which the young daughters of the household were also not ashamed of exposing.

At banquets both men and women, who sat apart from each other on chairs, stools or cushions, wore cones of pomade on their wigs which, as they melted, poured a sweet-smelling grease down the braided locks. Food, placed on the

Funerary model of an offering bearer, a girl carrying a basket of meats and a live duck, from the Eleventh-Dynasty tomb of Meketre.

tables by the serving-maids, was varied and plentiful. The Egyptians had fifteen different words for bread and this was baked in all manner of shapes in the baker's oven in the kitchen. So were pastries, rich in honey and butter. Much beef was eaten, much game from the desert, mainly gazelle and antelope and great quantities of wild fowl, geese, quails, cranes, pigeons and ducks, though not fish, which was considered unclean and a dish suitable only for the poor who netted shoal upon shoal in the Nile. Many of the fruits, oranges and peaches, pears and cherries, which were to be enjoyed later, were not yet grown; but apples and pomegranates were cultivated and so were figs and dates. Vegetables were served at most meals. Beans and lettuce, radishes, spinach, turnips, carrots and onions, leeks, peas and garlic, were all cultivated on farms and in kitchen gardens. Grapes were grown in the Delta; but wine, frequently sweetened with honey and date juice, was served only on the tables of the rich, most people drinking beer, and drinking a lot. 'Drink until you are drunk,' a female guest is advised by a servant in one captioned picture. 'Spend your day in happiness!' 'Give me eighteen measures of wine,' the guest replies. 'Look! I love it wildly.' 'Drink! Drink up!' cries another lady. 'When is the cup coming to me?'

Guests frequently did get drunk or ate so much that they were sick and lay sprawled with their heads on the table, oblivious to the bare-breasted dancers, the somersaults of the acrobats, and the musicians playing their lutes and harps and flutes, tapping their drums and tambourines.

Beneath the table could be seen the family's pets. Animals were held in high regard in Egypt, dogs being under the protection of the great god,

Musicians: detail of a wall-painting from an Eighteenth-Dynasty tomb.

Anubis, cats also being divinely protected and both being mummified and placed in tombs and temples. Living animals associated with gods were also revered and honoured in temples. There were sacred bulls; the white ibis was also sacred; and basking by the waters of the temple pool at Crocodilopolis was a huge, bejewelled crocodile. Gods were represented with the heads of animals, of rams and jackals and baboons. Horus, son of Isis and Osiris, was depicted with the head of a falcon. Osiris himself, the green-skinned god of fertility and ruler of the Underworld, presided over the trial that men underwent before passing from one life into the next. Assisted by the jackal-headed Anubis, Osiris weighed the heart of the dead on a scale balanced by a figure of Truth. Then, passing by Osiris's sacred eye, the dead entered that nether world where all the pleasures of their earthly life could be enjoyed for ever.

It was at the court of Rameses II that Moses, the lawgiver of the Jews who bore an Egyptian name, is supposed to have grown up. His people had long believed themselves to be descendants of Abraham, a partriach who had led the Hebrews from Ur, the Sumerian city of Mesopotamia, the ruins of which are now near Babylon in southern Iraq. Abraham had taken them west from the Euphrates into Syria and into the coastal region then known as Canaan after the first settlers, and later to be called Palestine. His grandson, Jacob, was thought to have taken the branch of the people known as Israelites, south and still further west into Egypt where they had been enslaved by the pharaohs probably during the Eighteenth Dynasty. It was the dream of the Israelites that they would one day return to Canaan, the 'promised land'; and about thirteen hundred years before the birth of Christ the longed-for exodus began.

Ezechielis. v.
Hæc est Ierusalem, Ego eam in medio Gentiu
posui, et in eius circuitu terras.

HIEROSOLYMA VRBS SANC
TA, IVDEAE, TOTIVSQVE
ORIENTIS LONGE CLARIS·
SIMA, QVA AMPLITVDINE AC
MAGNIFICENTIA HOC NOS·
TRO ÆVO CONSPICVA EST.

The City of Jerusalem : sixteenth-century etching by the Flemish artist Hans von Hoghenberg.

2

Jerusalem
in the Days of David and Herod
1000 BC—AD 60

When the long lines of their caravans had passed out of Egypt and through the Sea of Reeds into Palestine, the Israelites found that the Canaanites were established in well-fortified towns but exercised little control over the surrounding countryside. So the newcomers were able to settle without undue difficulty in the lands which their prophets had promised them, and gradually they assimilated much of the culture of the people whose territories they occupied. Especially in the northern and more fertile part of the country, they began to live in houses rather than in the nomadic tents to which they had been accustomed. Formerly most of them had been shepherds, wandering from place to place to pasture their flocks; but now they turned to farming, growing grain, olives and vines. Their religion began to change, too.

Moses, their leader in Egypt, had told them that there was only one God, that they were to have no other gods but Him; and he had, so the Book of Exodus relates, provided his people with laws and commandments preserved in the box known as the Ark of the Covenant. But since Moses' death, the religion of the majority of the Israelite immigrants had become closer to that of the Canaanites, who revered many gods and who believed that the fruitfulness of the soil might be secured by sexual intercourse with sacred prostitutes at the gods' shrines and temples. Indeed, in the course of time most Israelites had become scarcely distinguishable from Canaanites, many of whom were of the same stock. The common enemy of both were the Philistines.

These people were an Indo-Germanic race who seem to have come over the sea from the Aegean. In about 1050 BC they defeated the Israelites in battle and, in a later engagement, succeeded in capturing the Ark of the Covenant. At this critical moment in Hebrew history, there emerged a young peasant leader named Saul, a farmer who was also a *nabi*, a kind of fanatical dervish, though the Hebrew word is translated in the English Bible as 'prophet'. Occasionally seized by frenzied fits of religious fervour, he was as devoted to his people as he was to God; and when he learned that the town of Jabesh-Gilead beyond the river Jordan was being besieged by the Ammonites, a tribe as aggressive as the Philistines, he slaughtered his own oxen in a sudden attack of fury, slashed the corpses to pieces and sent the scraps of flesh throughout the twelve tribes into which the Israelite people had been divided in a military and religious federation. He warned his fellow-tribesmen that, unless they rallied to the national cause and rejected all gods but the one Lord God, they too would be cut to pieces like cattle. Soon afterwards, Jabesh-Gilead was relieved, the Ammonites routed, and, in a subsequent battle, the Philistines too were defeated. After his triumph, Saul was elected the first King of Israel.

For the rest of his life Saul had to face the threat of the Philistines who were determined to avenge their defeat. In about 1000 BC their armies marched upon Israel, and in a savage battle at Gilboa they had their revenge at last. Three of Saul's sons, including the dashing and impulsive Jonathan, were killed and he himself committed suicide. His son-in-law, however, escaped the slaughter.

This was David, a farmer's son and former shepherd-boy who had become one of Saul's most successful generals. He appears to have been a handsome, alert and charming young man and a musician of exceptional talent. He had sung for the King and played for him on his harp; he had been appointed one of his courtiers, had become a close friend of his son, Jonathan, and had married Jonathan's sister, Michal. And, in a battle on the hillside overlooking the vale of Elah, he had made himself a hero to his people by engaging the Philistine, Goliath, in single combat. The story is told in the First Book of Samuel: 'And he took his staff in his hand, and chose him five smooth stones

out of the brook, and put them in a shepherd's bag which he had, even in a scrip: and his sling was in his hand: and he drew near to the Philistine. And the Philistine came on and drew near unto David: and the man that bare the shield went before him. And when the Philistine looked about and saw David, he disdained him: for he was but a youth ... And the Philistine said unto David, "Come to me, and I will give thy flesh unto the fowls of the air, and the beasts of the field." Then said David to the Philistine, "Thou comest to me with a sword, and with a spear, and with a shield: but I come to thee in the name of the Lord of Hosts, the God of the armies of Israel" ... And it came to pass, when the Philistine arose, and came and drew nigh to meet David, that David hasted and ran toward the army to meet the Philistine. And David put his hand in his bag and took hence a stone, and slang it, and smote the Philistine in his forehead: and he fell upon his face to the earth ... Therefore David ran, and stood upon the Philistine, and took his sword and drew it out of the sheath thereof, and slew him, and cut off his head therewith. And when the Philistines saw their champion was dead, they fled.'

In time, however, King Saul had grown jealous of David and, more than once, in the fits of madness that periodically overwhelmed him, he had tried to kill him. So David had fled from the court into the wilderness where, in a cave at Adullam, he had formed a band of warriors who followed his lead in a life of banditry and even of occasional service with the Philistines. He was still an outlaw when the Israelites were overwhelmed and Jonathan killed at the battle of Mount Gilboa.

Soon after this battle, David went up to the highlands of Hebron where the people, to whom he remained a hero, anointed him King of Judah. At the same time, Saul's surviving son, Ishbaal, was proclaimed his father's successor as King of Israel in the south at the instigation of Abner, Commander of the Israelite army. Soon war broke out between the rival factions of north and south; but, after Abner had changed sides and Ishbaal had been murdered by two of his own officers, the issue was no longer in doubt. In due course David, who was now about thirty years old, was elected King of Israel by all the tribes.

Fearing the strength of this union, the Philistines now marched into the plain of Rephaim to

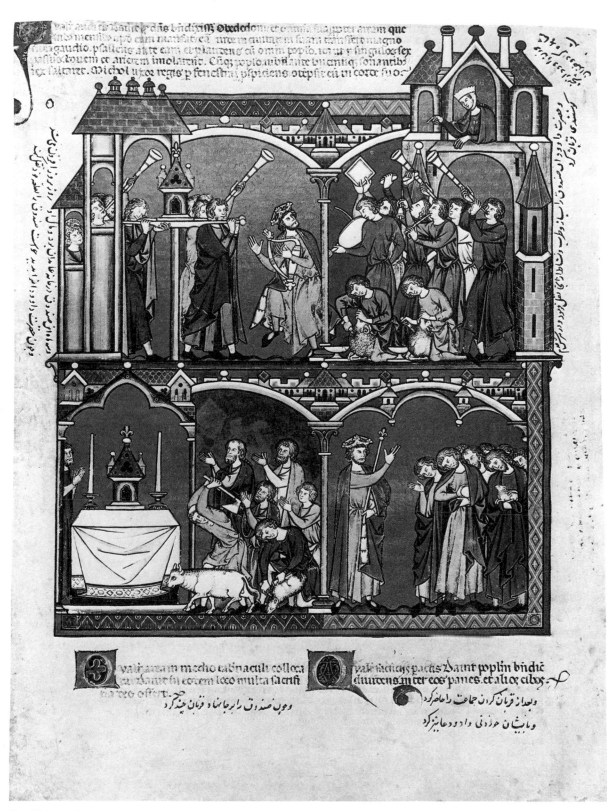

David dancing before the Ark of the Covenant from a
French manuscript of C.I250. ABOVE: *the Ark is brought*
into Jerusalem amid scenes of great rejoicing ;
BELOW: *the Ark is placed in the Tabernacle.*

attack the young King before he could consolidate his position. But they were overwhelmed and the remnants of their army were driven back across the frontier, never again to threaten Israel's existence.

David's task was now to find a capital for his country. Ideally, so as to avoid the renewal of old rivalries, this would have to be in neutral territory between the north and south. His attention was drawn to a city on the crest of a mountain range between the river Jordan and the sea. It was a stronghold of the Jebusites, one of the tribes of Canaan mentioned at the end of the fifteenth chapter of the First Book of Moses called Genesis. Perched on a spur which fell away steeply on three sides into the Valleys of Kidron, Tyropeon and the Hinnom, its only easy access was from the north and this route was no doubt heavily guarded. The Bible gives only a hint as to how the difficult task of capturing the stronghold was accomplished. In the Second Book of Samuel, David is reported as having said, 'Whosoever getteth up the gutter [the Hebrew word is *sinnor* which could also be translated as 'shaft'] and smiteth the Jebusites . . . that are hated of David's soul, he shall be chief and captain.' And in the First Book of Chronicles it is reported merely that 'Joab, the son of Zeruiah [David's sister] went up first and was chief'. But the secret may have been revealed by a British Army officer, Captain Warren, who, while visiting Jerusalem in 1867, found himself with a party of pilgrims by a spring at the foot of the rocks in the Kidron Valley. In the Old Testament this spring is called Gihon ('bubbler') and was the source of Jerusalem's water supply. Traditionally, it was here that Mary washed the swaddling clothes of the baby Jesus, and the spring is therefore also known as the Fountain of the Virgin Mary.

Stepping down into the cavern where the pure water from the spring was gathered, Captain Warren noticed in the dim light that there was a cavity in the roof. He asked the pilgrims and their guide about this, but evidently no one had observed it before, or, if they had, had taken no interest in it. Intrigued, Warren returned next day to the spring with a ladder and a rope. He clambered up towards the cavity where he discovered a long shaft, and, using the experience he had gained climbing in the Alps, he laboriously made his way up the shaft until he came to a narrow passage. Crawling forward in the darkness, he felt steps cut into the rock and came out into a vaulted chamber through which light filtered onto a number of dusty jars. He squeezed his body through the fissure which admitted the glimmer of the sun, and came out suddenly into the very heart of the city of Jerusalem.

The city into which the Israelites had erupted so many centuries before was enlarged and its defences strengthened on David's orders. Its wall was extended northwards and towers and bastions were built throughout its length. A royal palace of stone and cedarwood was constructed by masons and carpenters sent to Jerusalem by David's friend, King Hiram of Tyre; and smaller houses were built for David's wives and concubines, the numerous attendants and officials of his court, and for his powerful bodyguard of Cheresite and Pelethite mercenaries. A large temple was also apparently planned and an extensive threshing floor above the Jebusite citadel bought from one Arunah for its site. And in order to lend sanctity to his new capital, the city of Zion, which was also known as the City of David, the King ordered that the Ark of the Covenant, the sacred symbol of God's favour of the people of Israel which had been recovered from the Philistines, should be brought to Jerusalem and kept there in a tent, a reminder of the nomadic life of the patriarchs.

During the recent wars with the Philistines, the Ark, which had been taken by the Israelites on their desert wanderings and had been carried at the head of the army, had been entrusted to a man called Abinadab in a city of the Gideonites on the frontiers of the territories of the Israelite tribe of Benjamin. It was now reclaimed from him and brought into Jerusalem to serve as a focus of loyalty for the people. The procession was led by David himself, the Ark being carried through the streets to the sound of trumpets and the acclamations of the people.

From his new capital David set out to extend his dominions over the surrounding tribes and he eventually ruled over territories which stretched from the Gulf of Aqaba in the Red Sea northwards to Damascus, and from the Mediterranean eastwards beyond the Jordan into the desert. Yet for all his great gifts and virtuosity, David's political skills were limited and his character flawed. He failed to integrate the two kingdoms,

King Solomon from a fifteenth-century mural by Philip Goul in the Church of St Mammas Louvaras, Cyprus.

own subjects for Egyptian horses and chariots which he disposed of elsewhere. He certainly recruited men into gangs of forced labour and set them to work upon the reconstruction and embellishment of Jerusalem and to repair and extend the city's walls and defences.

For seven years work continued on a temple to enshrine the Ark of the Covenant and for six more years after that labourers and Phoenician craftsmen were at work upon the adjoining royal palace. Both were constructed on the threshing floor which, bought by David, was on the present site of the Mosque of Omar. There are no archaeological remains of the temple or its courts; but it seems to have been about ninety feet long, thirty feet wide and, perhaps, thirty-five feet high. The porch, as wide as the building, was fifteen feet deep and led into the Holy Place which was entirely panelled with cedarwood and was decorated with 'carved figures of cherubim and palm trees and open flowers'. 'And the temple when it was in building [according to the First Book of Kings] was built of stone made ready before it was brought thither: so that there was neither hammer nor axe nor any tool of iron heard

The building of Solomon's Temple in Jerusalem, from a late fifteenth-century French manuscript of the 'Jewish Antiquities' by Flavius Josephus.

Judah and Israel, over which he ruled; and his vain, over-indulged and plausible son, Absalom, rebelled against him and plunged the country into civil war. David was driven from his own palace; and, although he was able to return after Absalom's defeat and death in battle, sorrow at the loss of his wayward and treacherous but beloved son overwhelmed him. He himself died not long afterwards in the 960s BC, having been persuaded by Bathsheba – his favourite wife, whom he had long ago seduced after seeing her bathing from his palace roof – to designate her son, Solomon, his successor.

A wildly extravagant and sensual man, Solomon (ruled *c*.960–*c*.932 BC) was both ruthless and, as a businessman, astute. After assassinating his rivals, he set about increasing the riches of his kingdom by all the means at his disposal: he exploited the iron and copper mines discovered by recent archaeology; he greatly increased the country's trade with foreign customers; he exacted heavy tolls on caravans passing through his territories; he bought horses in Cilicia, in what is now south-east Turkey, and sold them in Syria; he even, so it was said, exchanged some of his

Sennacherib's army fleeing Jerusalem from a sixteenth-century Turkish miniature.

in the temple while it was in building ... And Solomon overlaid the Holy of Holies [in which lay the Ark of the Covenant] with pure gold, and so covered the altar which was of cedar ... And within the Holy Place he made two cherubim of olive trees ... and their wings touched one another in the midst of the temple. And he overlaid the cherubim with gold. And he carved all the walls of the temple round about with carved figures and trees and flowers within and without. And the floor of the temple he overlaid with gold.'

Although a small building, it was undoubtedly impressive; and the inner shrine with its gold and cedar carving, lit by narrow shafts of light from the windows in the morning and evening hours, must have overawed the visitor. So, surely, must have Solomon's palace which was much larger than the temple. No remains of this either have been unearthed by archaeologists. But it was evidently built of big dressed stones surmounted by a course of cedar beams. In addition to Solomon's own residence, that of his harem, and the large house of his most important wife, a daughter of the pharaoh, there was a Throne Room where state visitors were received and justice dispensed, there was a Hall of Pillars whose uses are unknown, and an armoury which contained among other stores three hundred shields of beaten gold. All the rooms of the palace were evidently filled with priceless gold, silver and brass ornaments made by Phoenician craftsmen from Tyre. In the palace compound there must have been workshops and counting-houses, store-rooms and quarters for slaves. There must

also have been quarters for the royal bodyguard and for the many scribes who kept records on clay tablets of foreign trade, taxation, the mobilization of manpower, building programmes and all the business of the extensive empire which was ruled from the city.

Solomon's reign was a time of peace in which vast riches were accumulated. But it was also a time of moral debilitation as the religious unity of the people began to be impaired by the King's introduction of the worship of foreign idols from the various nations of his numerous wives. It was a period, too, of revolts among the subject tribes conquered by David, and of growing discontent among the Israelites themselves, culminating in the rebellion of Jeroboam, Solomon's prefect of forced labour. And after Solomon's death in about 932 BC the northern tribes seceded from Israel and David's empire began to disintegrate. Jerusalem was attacked and sacked by the pharaoh Shishah in about 918 BC. Restoration and repairs were subsequently carried out by Hezekiah, King of Judah, who brought the waters of the Gihon spring to a reservoir so as to ensure the city's water supply; but Hezekiah's son was forced to become a vassal of the Assyrians whose gleaming cohorts under Sennacherib swooped down upon the city which was saved from another sack only by its strong defences and a plague that swept through the Assyrian ranks. A century later, in 587 BC, the Babylonian King, Nebuchadnezzar, captured the city, looted the Temple and carried off most of the inhabitants into captivity where, as the psalmist recorded, ' By the waters of Babylon we sat down and wept when we remembered Zion. We hanged our harps upon the willows. For they that carried us away captive required of us a song; saying, Sing us one of the songs of Zion. How shall we sing the Lord's song in a strange land? If I forget thee, O Jerusalem, let my right hand forget her cunning. If I do not remember thee, let my tongue cleave to the roof of my mouth, if I prefer not Jerusalem above my chief joy.'

The Babylonian captivity lasted some seventy years until 538 BC when the Jews were allowed to return to Jerusalem to rebuild their city. They did not complete the task, however, and the city and its walls were still in disrepair and part of a Persian satrapy when, in about 445 BC, a Jewish exile, Nehemiah, who was cup-bearer to Artaxerxes, King of Persia, told his master, while helping to serve his dinner, how unhappy he was that Jerusalem was still in ruins, its walls demolished and its gates burned down. 'And I said unto him,' so Nehemiah wrote, 'If it please the King and if thy servant have found favour in thy sight, send me to the city of my father's sepulchres that I may build it. And the King said unto me (the Queen also sitting by him), for how long shall thy journey be? And when wilt thou return? So I set him a time and it pleased the King to send me.'

When he arrived in Jerusalem with the authority of a governor of Judah, Nehemiah inspected the walls by night, for he was unsure how his plans would be received there. But he soon convinced the leaders of the community that strong fortifications were essential; he persuaded the rich to lend money without interest; and when the walls had been completed after fifty-two days of intensive work, and towers and gates had been built or reconstructed, he induced the country people beyond the walls to draw lots to choose ten in every hundred families to come to live in the city to make up its depleted population. To prevent further disasters overcoming the city Nehemiah tried to make the people 'separate from all strangers' by restoring their former sense of religious unity, their respect for the observance of the Sabbath and their old religious practices, their insistence on racial purity by the banning of mixed marriages. This revival of the spirit of Judaism was continued and extended by another Hebrew official, Ezra, a priest from Babylon skilled in the Law of Moses, who was authorized by the Persian authorities to preserve and strengthen the religion and customs of the Jews as a means of maintaining order in the empire. Determined to bring the people of Jerusalem firmly under Mosaic Law, Ezra read from the Book of the Laws and the Ten Commandments in a solemn ceremony which lasted for two days. The large retinue of scribes whom he had brought with him then explained to the people the meaning and purpose of the Laws, and the essential need for racial purity. Men who had married foreign wives were persuaded to divorce them, to disown their children and to submit in future to the rule of priests who would impose a strengthened monotheism accompanied by a more rigorous observance of ritual.

The restoration of the early strictness of their religion did not, however, protect the Jews' Holy City from its enemies. It was captured in 332 BC by Alexander the Great who met with no resistance; it was attacked in about 250 BC by Ptolemy the Great who devastated its walls; and in 168 BC it was occupied by Antiochus Epiphanes, one of the Seleucid Kings of Syria, who massacred or enslaved its inhabitants, installed a new fortress known as the Acra in the citadel of David, and left behind a Phrygian governor committed to the task of converting the Jews to the worship of Jove whose image was raised in the Temple. A revolt against the foreign yoke succeeded in clearing Jerusalem of its Syrian overlords; but the subsequent quarrels of the Pharisees, who interpreted Mosaic law in the severest manner, and the Sadducees, who advocated collaboration with foreign rule, disrupted and weakened the leadership. By 65 BC the city was in no condition to resist the power of the Roman Empire when Pompey attacked and captured it, nor when, a few years later, another Roman General, Marcus Crassus, plundered the Holy Places which Pompey – while inflicting a dreadful massacre on the inhabitants – had spared. And it was not until Herod was appointed King of the Jews by the Romans and installed himself in Jerusalem in 37 BC that the city began to recover its former importance.

Herod and Herodias on their throne: detail from a thirteenth-century mosaic in the Baptistry, Florence.

Modern model of Herod's palace in Jerusalem.

Herod was the son of an Idumaean official in Roman service and of an Arabian princess; and, not only on account of his mixed blood, but also because of his allegiance to Rome and his indifference to religion, he was much disliked by the Jews in general. He was, however, a clever man, forceful, energetic, ambitious and astute, and he provided Jerusalem both with the firm government it had lacked and a building programme that was to transform the appearance of the city. He built a theatre and an amphitheatre, he laid out parks and gardens, erected fountains and aqueducts, constructed the great fortress of

Antonia, named after Mark Anthony, in which Pontius Pilate may have lived, and, on the site of the modern Citadel, he created for himself a splendid royal palace. Above all, to placate the religious sensitivies of the Jews, he built a magnificent temple of white stone, increasing the area where Solomon's temple had stood to thirty-five acres by cutting, building up and levelling the solid rock.

To carry out this great work one thousand carts were made for the transportation of stone from the quarries on the north side of the city, and ten thousand masons were recruited, a thousand of these being priests trained in the craft so that no profane hand could afterwards be said to have taken part in the construction of the most holy of places. All these workers were provided with garments that emphasized the special nature of the work upon which they were engaged, long, narrow sleeved cassocks such as those worn by the priests, long girdles the ends of which could be secured over the shoulders when necessary, turbaned skull caps and, since shoes were not allowed on holy ground, leather sandals.

Building began in 19 BC, King Herod sacrificing three hundred oxen at the ceremony of inauguration; and it continued for ten years, the decorations and embellishments taking a further seventy-four years to finish. The completed Temple was a marvellously impressive creation of courts and porticoes, of colonnades, treasuries and sanctuaries, the white limestone ornamented with gold plating and gilded pinnacles, the whole surrounded by a wall pierced by eight gates, the two on the south side leading to the porch of the Temple by way of a vaulted passageway, the four on the west opening on to viaducts that spanned the Valley of the Tyropeon and led down into the city.

The largest of the courts, the Court of the Gentiles, was open to all; but the Court of Israel could be entered only by Jews. Beyond this was the Court of the Priests where burnt offerings were made. From the Court of the Priests twelve

Basalt olive-press from Capernaum.

steps led up to a porch approached through a huge doorway sixty feet wide and thirty feet high. A further large doorway beyond this led to the Holy Place with its altar, the table of the holy shewbread, and the seven-branched candelabrum, the menorah. Separated from the Holy Place by a veil was the Holy of Holies, a chamber of utter darkness entered only once a year by the high priest on the Day of Atonement.

Magnificent though the Temple was, there often hung about it the stench of carrion. For, in addition to the lambs which were sacrificed every morning and every night as silver trumpets blared from the walls, numerous animals were sacrificed in the Court of Israel on the high altar of unhewn stones, pieces of flesh being hung on hooks, entrails and lumps of fat being placed upon tables. There was a big ablution laver in the court supplied by an aqueduct and immense storage cisterns holding ten million gallons or more. Yet the smell of flesh must have lingered in the air long after the carcasses had been carried off by the priests who were allowed to keep them as perquisites, either to give to their families or to sell.

Below the Temple in the city the houses were clustered together in narrow streets. Built of stone and sun-baked brick, their interiors seem to have been brightly coloured though sparsely furnished. Only a few of the rich had beds such as those found in Egyptian palaces. Most people slept on straw mats or on their cloaks spread on the ground. There are, however, references in the Old Testament to guests sitting at tables on couches. The tables appear to have been low, the diners reclining on the couches in the Roman fashion. Poorer people sat on the floor around a mat upon which the food was spread. It was eaten with the fingers, spoons and forks being unknown, though there was a wide variety of dishes and vessels for water and wine. The host would offer choice delicacies to favoured guests by hand. In most households there were two meals a day; but in some there may have been four, the most substantial being at about the ninth hour, between three and four o'clock. It was a lengthy meal, as was Christ's last supper, and sometimes lasted into the night.

Bread was eaten at every meal, either bread made of barley flour or, in the wealthier houses, wheat bread. There were bakeries in the city,

The burning of the Temple at Jerusalem by the Emperor Titus and his troops, as depicted by a seventeenth-century Dutch artist.

though most bread was baked at home either by the housewife or by slaves. At dawn every day the sound of stone hand-mills began to break the stillness of the night, and before the sun had risen far in the sky the noise of grinding and pounding disturbed all rest. The kinds of meat which could be eaten depended upon the strictness of the observance of ancient laws and religious customs. Certain animals were deemed clean, others unclean; and while the Sea of Galilee was well stocked with fish, only those with fins and scales were considered suitable for the table.

Before sitting down to a meal the diners washed their hands, and guests – who would often appear in white robes on festive occasions – would have their feet washed, perhaps in a special stone footbath complete with handles and heel-rest. Washing also took place after meals and upon rising in

the morning. The water seems often to have been scented.

Sweet perfumes and aromatic resins were, indeed, used in all kinds of ways. Sleeping mats and clothes were scented with myrrh, aloes and cinnamon, with cassia, ginger-grass and mastic. Bodies, too, were perfumed and anointed with oil; and women paid much attention to the dressing, scenting and colouring of their hair which they dyed with a yellowish red powder extracted from the bark and leaves of henna. They also dyed their fingernails and toenails with henna, tinted their eyebrows and eyelashes with galena, shadowed their eyelids with powdered lapis-lazuli and reddened their lips with cochineal from dried insects.

Their clothes were as brightly coloured as their faces. They were evidently very fond of green and scarlet; men, too, wore red, also blue and purple as well as yellow and white. Yellow dyes came from pomegranates and saffron, red from madder root, blue from woad, purple from the murex snail. Huge piles of the shells of this mollusc have been found at both Tyre and Sidon.

Women as well as men wore cloaks and tunics, though the clothes of the women were of a different style and the Fifth Book of Moses called Deuteronomy contains a specific injunction against one sex dressing in the clothes of another: 'The women shall not wear that which pertaineth unto a man, neither shall a man put on a woman's garment: for all that do so are an abomination unto the Lord thy God.' A girdle served not only to bind the garments together and to tuck them up for work but was also provided with pockets into which coins and such articles as knives could be kept. Women wore veils as a sign of mourning and at the time of their marriage, and it seems possible that veils were also worn during sexual intercourse.

Strongly as the prophets preached against sexual incontinence, against infractions of the law and the unseemly painting of women's faces, life in Jerusalem appears to have been little con-strained by their strictures. Soon after Herod's death, however, that contented life was suddenly extinguished. In AD 66 the Jews rebelled against Rome and the city was besieged and captured by Roman troops commanded by Titus, son of the Emperor Vespasian and himself to become Emperor in 79. Prisoners were slaughtered wholesale and thrown to wild animals; and the Roman eagle was set up in the Holy of Holies before Herod's Temple was reduced to ashes and the city almost entirely destroyed. The sacred treasures, among them the menorah and the silver trumpets from the Temple, were carried off to Rome and paraded in triumph down the Sacra Via from the Forum to the Temple of Jupiter Capitolinus. And, as Jerusalem lay smouldering in ruins, the Arch of Titus was erected beneath the Capitol and represented in relief upon it, and still to be seen today, are these emblems of the Jewish faith and of a people who were to wait for almost two thousand years before another Jewish state was established.

———————————————————

When Abraham led his people into Canaan, there was already in existence a thriving civilization on the island of Crete where towns and villages were built of stone and where, in about 2000 BC, splendid palaces such as that at Knossos began to appear. The civilization was known as Minoan after a legendary king of the island; and the Cretans who developed it appear to have been a mixture of people whose families had lived there for many generations and of relatively recent immigrants from Asia Minor. This civilization began to decline in about 1500 BC. And soon afterwards there was a catastrophic earthquake. For a short time the rebuilt towns were occupied by people from the Greek mainland; but in about 1400 BC the huge palace at Knossos was almost completely destroyed by fire and the civilization of Crete did not recover from this shock.

The immigrants who came to the island after the earthquake had not been in Greece long. Their ancestors had come from the north only a few centuries before. They were uncivilized compared with the Minoans, though they could ride horses, used chariots, had a written language and built well-designed fortresses. One of their forts was on the site of Athens, a more important one at Mycenae from which the civilization they developed after they had made contact with Asia took its name.

The Mycenaeans were traders as well as warriors with outposts in Asia Minor; but by about 1000 BC their rule began to crumble. Fresh waves of invaders came in from the north; tribes speaking a dialect known as Doric, who settled south of Mycenae at Argos and further south still at Sparta, then advancing into Crete, Rhodes and Cos; and other tribes known as Ionians who occupied territories to the east in the area around Athens known as Attica before moving on to the Cyclades and the coast of Asia Minor which became known as Ionia. Soon the whole of the Aegean area was settled by Greek-speaking and mostly independent communities which developed into little city states each with its citadel or acropolis, its temple to the gods, and its monarch. There were to be twelve of these cities in Attica alone. The largest of them was Athens.

3

Athens
in the Days of Pericles
480 BC–404 BC

The Persian army was the most powerful that had ever invaded Greece. The historian, Herodotus, was so impressed by reports of its immense size that he said it numbered five million men who in their march across the stony tracks drank many a river dry. Commanded by Xerxes, king of kings, the cavalry and spearmen, the chariots of Ahura Mazdā, supreme god of Persia, and the élite infantry known as the Immortals closed upon the Pass of Thermopylae where the heavily armed Greek foot-soldiers, the hoplites, had been drawn up to withstand their advance. The Greeks' position was turned, however, by means of a mountain path; their general was decapitated and his body hung on a cross; and the Persians moved on, trampling over the dead, to Athens.

In the city, preparations for evacuation were immediately put under way. The people were reluctant to leave, for Athens was not only their home, it was also the embodiment of their faith. But the council allayed their apprehension: Athena, the patron goddess of the city, had already fled to the island of Salamis where the Greek fleet lay at anchor; her priestess announced that Athena's serpent on the citadel of the Acropolis had not slithered out as usual to eat its honeycake; moreover, the oracle at Delphi had been consulted and the wisdom of the Council's decision had been confirmed. So the citizens agreed to depart: the able-bodied men were embarked upon the fleet; the rest of the population were taken away to Salamis, to Aegina and to Troezen.

The Acropolis from Philopappus Hill, Athens.

The Persian hosts advanced into Attica through a deserted countryside, ravaging and burning the buildings and crops in their path. 'They found the city forsaken,' Herodotus recorded. 'A few people only remained in the temple, either keepers of the treasures, or men of the poorer sort. These persons, having fortified the citadel with planks and boards, held out against the enemy ... The Persians encamped upon the hill over against the citadel and began the siege of the place, attacking the Greeks with arrows to which pieces of lighted tow were attached, shooting at the wooden barricades. And now those within the citadel found themselves in a most woeful case; for their wooden rampart caught fire. Yet still they

Red-figured Panathenaean amphora depicting Athena, patron goddess of Athens.

continued to resist.' They were offered terms of surrender but, refusing to consider them, they defiantly rolled masses of stone down the hillside as the enemy endeavoured to approach the gates. At length, however, the Persians managed to scale the cliff at a place where 'no watch was kept since no one had thought it possible that any foot of man could climb the steep precipice'. 'As soon as the Athenians saw them upon the summit, some threw themselves headlong from the wall, and so perished, while others fled for refuge to the inner part of the temple. The Persians rushed to the gates and opened them, after which they massacred the suppliants. When all were slain, they plundered the temple, and fired every part of the citadel.' The houses in the lower part of the city were also destroyed, except for a few which were spared for the use of Persian generals, and the whole area around them laid waste.

The Acropolis where these brave Athenians perished in 480 BC had already been occupied by man for two and a half thousand years, as is shown by fragments of pottery which have been found in shallow pits and which indicate a settled population of high artistic attainments. In about 1200 BC an enormous wall of massive blocks, resting upon each other unsecured by mortar, had been built around the citadel; and within this wall, where the temple known as the Erechtheum was later to be constructed, was the palace of the king. Already, it seems, Athens was acknowledged to be supreme among the towns of Attica.

As the centuries passed the city had grown and prospered, safe within its strong walls and defended when necessary by the bravery of its citizens. Buildings had begun to spread beneath the citadel and across the land previously reserved for burials; the civic centre known as the Agora had been developed between the Acropolis and the principal city gate, the Dipylon, in the Potters' Quarter; and in the sixth century BC, in the days when the tyrant Pisistratus and his sons ruled over the city, several new stone temples had been erected, including the Temple of Olympian Zeus, the Temple to Athena, the Hekatompedon, which occupied the site where the Parthenon now stands, and, about fifty years after this, another temple to the Guardian Goddess of the City on the site of the old royal palace. By now the whole of the lower town had been enclosed by a defensive wall so that the fortifications on the Acropolis were no longer so important. The winding path which led up to the summit was, therefore, replaced by a ceremonial ramp, similar to the Cordonata which Michelangelo was later to design for the approach to the Capitol in Rome. At the same time the old Agora was much enlarged and around it were built law courts and shrines, chambers for the Council, a house for the city's chief magistrate and a fountain house which supplied water from beyond the city walls through terracotta pipes. In this new forum the Panathenaic Games were held every four years in honour of Athena. Here, also, the people of Athens assembled on the festivals of the city's other patron gods and goddesses to celebrate the glory of their city.

The Athenians were inordinately proud of their city-state which they believed – as did Aristotle – had originally come into existence for 'the sake of mere life' but which now existed 'for the sake of the good life'. They felt it to be the proper unit for social life, the natural development first from the family and then from the village, the perfect organization under which men could live under just laws, hallowed by custom, laws that protected themselves, their families and property without subjecting them to the caprices of wayward monarchs as barbarians were in other countries.

The Athenians had had no king since King Codrus had been killed defending the Acropolis from an attack by the Dorians who had invaded Greece from the north in about 1000 BC. After his death the rule of the city had been entrusted to three archons, or chief magistrates, the archon *basileus*, who was in charge of religious affairs, the *polemarchos*, commander of the military forces of the city, and the archon *eponymos* who was invested with civil authority. Later the term of office of these archons was limited to ten years, in 683 BC to one year; and, soon after this, six further archons, known as *thesmothetai*, were added to their number and elected by the people. Once they had served their term, former archons joined the Council of the Areopagos, originally a kind of House of Lords. Although power was thus retained in the hands of leading families, democracy was being slowly developed. Before the tyranny of Pisistratus and his successors, the archon Solon, a poet and merchant of noble descent, divided the citizens into four classes and gave each class a measure of political responsibility. The office of

archon and seats on the Council of the Areopagos were limited to the two highest classes, the minor offices to the third; but members of the lowest and poorest class were granted votes in the Assembly and were given the opportunity to serve as jurymen. And after the tyranny had drawn to a close, further democratic reforms were carried out by Cleisthenes, a member of a noble family who was elected archon in 508–7 BC. It was not, however, until the time of Pericles, the great orator, popular leader and military commander, that the archonship was opened to all but the lowest class of citizens, that payment for jurymen was introduced – thus making it practicable for those without private means to serve in the courts – and

Bust of Pericles: a first-century Roman copy from a Greek original of the fifth century BC.

that allowances were made to the poorer citizens of Athens to enable them to attend performances at the theatre.

Pericles's character seemed wholly at variance with that of a democratic leader. Reserved and aloof, on occasions haughty and dismissive, he appeared to regard the common people with distaste. His manner aroused widespread dislike and many were the stories told against him. A few days before his birth his mother had dreamed that she was giving birth to a lion; and, while his physical features were 'almost perfect', his head was unnaturally long and out of proportion. Almost all his portraits consequently depict him in a helmet; and in his lifetime he had to face constant ridicule from the comic poets of Athens, one of whom referred to him as 'squill-head', another maintaining that his skull was 'big enough to hold eleven couches'. The poet Ion said that he had a disdainful and arrogant demeanour and that 'his pride had in it a good deal of superciliousness and contempt for others'. Certainly he was far from gregarious and wholly dedicated to his career and to the city-state of Athens. 'He was never to be seen walking in any street except the one which led to the market-place and the council-chamber,' Plutarch wrote. 'He refused not only invitations to dinner but every kind of friendly or familiar intercourse, so that through all the years of his political career, he never visited a single one of his friends for a meal. The only exception was an occasion when his great-uncle Euryptolemus gave a wedding feast. Pericles sat at table till the libations were poured at the end of the meal, and then at once rose and took his leave.'

Austere as he was, however, no one could doubt the passionate sincerity of his devotion to Athens which found memorable expression in the oration he delivered in 431 BC at the state funeral of his fellow-citizens who had fallen in battle. He spoke movingly of the courage of the dead and of the bravery and virtues of their ancestors who had made Athens great and free, praising the valour of the Athenians, who passed their lives without burdensome restrictions, yet who were just as ready to face danger as were their enemies, the Spartans, who 'are submitted to the most laborious and exacting training'. He spoke, so Thucydides reported, of the virtues of Athenian democracy in which power 'is in the hands not of a minority but of the whole people', in which 'no one, so long as he has it in him to be of service to the state, is kept in political obscurity because of poverty', and in which 'everyone is equal before the law'. 'We are free and tolerant in our private lives,' he said; 'but in public affairs we keep to the law. This is because it commands our deep respect. We freely give our obedience to those whom we put in positions of authority, and we obey the laws themselves, especially those which are for the protection of the oppressed, and those unwritten laws which it is an acknowledged shame to break.'

He went on to speak of the Athenians' love of beauty and 'of the things of the mind': 'When our work is over, we are in a position to enjoy all kinds of recreation for our spirits. There are various kinds of contests and sacrifices held regularly throughout the year; and in our own homes we find a beauty and a good taste which delight us every day and drive away our cares. Then the greatness of our city brings it about that all the good things from all over the world flow in to us.'

'Taking everything together then,' he ended, 'I declare that our city is an education to Greece, and I declare that each single one of our citizens, in all the manifold aspects of life, is able to show himself the rightful lord and owner of his own person, and to do this, moreover, with exceptional grace and exceptional versatility ... You should fix your eyes every day on the greatness of Athens and you should fall in love with her.'

Beautiful as he considered Athens to be, Pericles was determined to make the city more lovely than ever. After their destruction by the Persians, the sacred buildings on the Acropolis had not immediately been rebuilt in compliance with an oath that their ruins should serve as memorials to the barbarians' impiety. But the military defeat at the Pass of Thermopylae and the subsequent sack of Athens had been followed by a resounding victory over the Persian fleet off Salamis and the withdrawal of King Xerxes to Asia. In 499 BC peace with Persia was finally ratified; the oath was annulled; and rebuilding on the Acropolis began.

In the intervening years the fortifications of the city had been repaired. The city wall had been rebuilt and enlarged; and the four-mile route between Athens and its port of Piraeus had been protected by the Long Wall, sometimes called the

Legs – two parallel rows of massive stonework 550 feet apart with a road between them – which had been begun in 493 BC and completed in 431. A few secular buildings had also been erected in the Agora, among them the Tholos, the circular building that was used for meetings of the Council, and the Stoa Poikile, the Painted Colonnade, which was decorated with paintings by Micon and Polygnotos of Thasos showing the Battle of Marathon, the decisive victory of the Greeks over the Persians in 490 BC when messengers had run with news of the triumph to Athens.

Plans for the sacred buildings on the Acropolis were so ambitious that many of the more cautious

The caryatids on the north porch of the Erechtheum of the Acropolis.

members of the Council doubted that they could ever be completed. But, in fact, large sums were available, both from the silver mines which were worked by slaves in the Lavrion Hills and from donations which had been made by Athens' allies for the prosecution of the long war against the Persians and which, although the war was now over, were still being made and, in defiance of all protests, were appropriated by Pericles for his great design.

Tiered seats in the Theatre of Dionysus.

The grandest monument in this design was the temple of the goddess Athena, the Parthenon. The largest and loftiest building on the Acropolis, it was built of white marble from the quarries of Mount Pentelikon between 447 and 438 BC, work continuing on the pedimented sculptures until 432. It measured 228 feet by 101 feet on the top step and had seventeen columns on the side and eight, instead of the usual six, at the front and back. The smallest, western room served as a treasury; the largest eastern room contained the cult statue of the goddess who was attended by invisible virgins – Parthenos means 'maiden'. The statue was made of wood and covered with ivory for the body of the goddess and with gold for her raiment. It was the work of the Athenian sculptor, Phidias.

Painter, engraver, skilled craftsman in metal-work, as well as a sculptor of genius, Phidias was responsible for the general plan of the Acropolis and for the siting of the Parthenon on its highest part. The architect who worked under his direction was Ictinus who was assisted by Callicrates. The frieze and the sculptures of the temple were probably made in the workshop of Phidias.

While work on the Parthenon was being completed, the monumental roofed gateway known as the Propylaea was started on the west side of the Acropolis to the designs of Mnesicles. This was also of white Pentelic marble with details of black Eleusis stone. It had a central hall measuring seventy-eight feet by sixty feet, with porticoes to east and west as well as a vestibule, and would have been even larger and embellished with a colonnade had not the original plan encroached upon sanctuaries whose sacred sites were jealously guarded by their priests. In front of it stood the thirty-foot-high statue of Athena Promachos, the crest of whose helmet could be seen by sailors coming from Sounion as they rounded Cape Zoster. Completed in 458 BC, the goddess was represented standing with her right arm leaning on a spear and holding in her left a shield. Probably the work of Phidias, and one of the finest memorials of the Persian War, it was removed to Constantinople at an unknown date and there destroyed in a riot in 1203.

South of the Propylaea, standing on a platform twenty-six feet high on an outcrop of the Acropolis, stood the small Temple of Athena Nike which, designed by Callicrates, was planned in 449 BC but not finished until after Pericles's death. It was intended to commemorate a victory over the Persians in 479; and, as Professor Bury, the historian of ancient Greece, wrote almost a hundred years ago, the Athenian citizen could stand on the steps of this temple and see Salamis and Aegina below him. 'His eye ranged along the Argolic coast, to the distant citadel of Corinth and the mountains of the Megarid; under the shadow of Victory he could lose himself in reveries of memory and dreams of hope. The motive of the temple, as a memorial of the Persian War, was written clear in the frieze. Whereas the sculptures of other temples of this period only alluded indirectly to that great struggle, by the representation of mythical wars – such as the War of Greeks and Amazons, or of Lapiths and Centaurs, or of gods and giants; on the frieze of Athena Nike a battle between the Greeks and Persians is

ABOVE *Wrestlers : bas-relief decorating the base of a kouros.*

RIGHT *A chariot race in a hippodrome : fragment of an Athenian cauldron, signed by the vase-painter, Sophilos.*

portrayed. It is the battle of Plataea.' Destroyed by the Turks in 1686, the Temple was reconstructed in 1836–42 to be once more dismantled and rebuilt in 1936–40.

Soon after this Temple was completed, work on another of the great monuments of the Acropolis began. This was the Erechtheum. Built, like the Propylaea, of marble from Mount Pentelikon and of black Eleusis stone, it was remarkable not only for its complicated form – which was dictated by the number of ancient shrines and precious cult objects it had to unite and accommodate – but also for the beauty and elaboration of its decorative detail. The north porch in particular is remarkable for the six marble caryatids, female figures in flowing robes supporting the entablature. These figures may represent the women who took part in the solemn procession that made its way across the Agora and up to the Parthenon to present a new robe to the goddess Athena during the celebrations of the Panathenaic Festival.

The Agora, too, was embellished in the time of Pericles. Overlooking it, crowning the hill of Kolonos Agoraios, was the Temple of Hephaistos, god of fire and smiths and, by extension, of other craftsmen who practised their skills below. Built almost entirely in marble, the main structure in Pentelic, the sculptured members in Parian, the temple, which is surrounded by a peristyle of thirty-four columns, is the most complete example of a Doric hexastyle temple which has survived.

Beneath it, east of the Theatre of Dionysus on the south slope of the Acropolis – where the plays of Aeschylus, Sophocles, Aristophanes and Euripides had all been performed – stood the concert-hall known as the Odeion. A large rectangular building constructed before 446 BC with interior columns in nine rows of ten, it was here that rehearsals were held for the tragedies performed in the nearby theatre during the Dionysiac Festival and that the musical contests of the Panathenaic Festival took place.

Before the stadium was built outside the city walls, all the athletic contests of that Festival seem to have been conducted in the Agora which was, indeed, not only the civic and commercial centre of Athens but also its principle meeting-place. It was always crowded. Particularly so were the three stoai or porticoes – the Stoa Poikile, where the philosopher Zeno, and his successors used to teach; the Stoa of Zeus, later to be decorated with three fine paintings by Euphranor; and the Stoa of Herms (columns surmounted by busts and with genitals half-way down their length) where Socrates could have been seen talking to his young pupils and cross-examining them. There were crowds, too, on the west side of the Agora, by the Temple of the Mother of Gods and outside the Council House where the Assembly was convened and matters concerning ostracism were discussed.

One of the ways in which Athenian democracy was expressed, ostracism involved banishing for ten years any prominent citizen who had become unpopular. On a day appointed for the vote, the Agora was enclosed by a fence and all those citizens who wanted to take part were admitted by one of ten entrances. They handed to an official a potsherd with the name of a man they wished to

A shoemaker's workshop : a black-figure pelike of c.490–470 BC.

see banished written on it. When all the potsherds had been collected, they were counted and, provided there were over six thousand of them, the man whose name appeared most was ostracized. He had to leave the city within ten days; but, after ten years of his exile were over, he could return without either disgrace or curtailment of his rights as a citizen. It was a method of government which Pericles himself found useful when a leading opponent of his building programme was ostracized in 443 BC, leaving him to pursue it unchallenged.

The Agora was crowded, too, with shoppers. Apart from the numerous potters in the area called *cerameicos*, there were all manner of craftsmen and shopkeepers making and displaying their wares. There were workers in bronze and iron, booksellers, dealers in wine and oil and food, barbers, cobblers, tailors and fishmongers. Some no doubt had shops but most appear to have traded from stalls and booths or from tables, as the bankers did. The whole place seemed like an unruly fair, yet all the traders were subject to rules imposed by officials who fixed measures, regulated prices and established standards of quality. There were officials, too, to control the unemployed men, who offered their services near the Hephaisteion, and the slaves who were gathered for hire near the shrine of the Dioscuri dedicated to the sons of Zeus, at the foot of the Acropolis.

Slaves – usually well treated and mostly foreign – were to be found both in the mines and in the workshops of craftsmen where they were paid wages with which they might one day buy their freedom. They also worked in many households as servants, flute-girls, harpists and tutors.

The houses in which they served were mostly built of mud bricks on stone bases and with roofs made of tiles, often beautifully shaped in potters' workshops. They were entered from the street through passages which led into courtyards from which the rooms were approached on every side. In some houses there were rooms on an upper floor, as traces of stairs and reference in literature indicate, although, as Professor Webster has noted, none of these upper storeys has survived. The larger houses had bathrooms with drains leading outside the building and with terracotta baths supplied with water from the well in the courtyard. Some houses also had kitchens; but cooking was often done in the courtyard on

portable hearths and in small clay ovens from which dishes were taken into the *andron*, the men's dining-room. Here the diners – wearing wreaths round their heads in traditional honour of Dionysus, god of wine – reclined on couches which had carved and painted frameworks and raised ends for cushions. The couches were covered with patterned blankets and rugs which were also hung on the walls but rarely, if ever, laid on the mosaic floors. The food, together with salt and vinegar, spices and seasoning, was placed on round or oblong tables beside the couches and, since, as in Jerusalem, there were apparently no spoons or forks, it was eaten with the fingers, the hands being washed in bowls of scented water. Apart from the tables and the couches, there was likely to be no other furniture in the room. Cupboards were unknown, though there might be a *kylikeion*, a sort of dresser for cups, jars and

Relief on the stela of Aeschylus showing a doctor treating his patients.

statuettes. Cups and jugs were also hung on the walls; so were wreaths, strands of vines and bunches of ivy.

Bread was usually baked at home and was eaten at every meal. Dishes of eggs, poultry and fish, all cooked in olive oil – and served perhaps on plates with depressions in the middle to hold sauces – were enjoyed in most households; but meat was eaten less often. On the festivals of gods an animal might be slaughtered as a sacrifice and then eaten by the worshippers; and at family celebrations such as weddings meat might also be served as well as game – hare, venison or wild boar – brought home from a hunting expedition. But even on the tables of the rich it was not a common sight, while the poor almost never tasted it unless at such an *eranos* as described by Homer in which each guest contributed to its cost.

Wine, much of it imported from Chios and stored in big, two-handled amphorae, was drunk, mixed with water, both during the meal and afterwards at the drinking party, the symposium, when songs and poems were sung, stories related, excerpts from plays recited, riddles asked and conversations conducted far into the night by the light of glazed clay lamps. Hired performers, jugglers, jesters, female acrobats and sword-dancers, entertained the guests at these symposia; and flute-girls, slaves of the household – and frequently the sons' mistresses – would sit on the men's couches and accompany them as they sang.

The principal room for the women of the household was the loom-room in which they worked and talked. As in the mens' dining-room, furniture was sparse and decorations few. There might be a few chairs or stools on which the women sat while working at the large wooden frame of the loom; but the walls and floor would probably be bare, only the houses of the well-to-do being painted and decorated with friezes of wreaths and ivy.

On rising in the morning both men and women, having washed themselves in the large basins supported on stands which most households possessed, would rub themselves with olive oil and sometimes with perfumed ointment. The men

would often then leave for one or other of the gymnasia outside the city walls. There were three of these, each sited in a sacred grove beside a stream and each associated with a hero or a god. The Academy gymnasium by the banks of the Eridanus was named after the hero, Academus; the Lyceum, beside the waters of the Cephisus, was associated with the god, Apollo, and the Kynosarges, by the Ilissus, with Heracles. All contained a wrestling school, and the Academy and Lyceum also provided riding lessons. There were running tracks and jumping pits, rooms for ball games, ranges for throwing the discus and the javelin, boxing rings and dressing-rooms, bathrooms and rooms where the young athletes powdered their bodies before taking part in the exercises. Older men came to watch them and talk to them, sitting on the benches in the dressing-rooms or walking up and down in the open air where the naked athletes raced past them. It was at the Academy that Plato later established his school of philosophy, and at the Lyceum that Aristotle founded his. The gymnasia, in fact, were kinds of university as well as sports centres – in Aristotle's day they had libraries and lecture-rooms – and in them were formed many of those passionate affections between men which, often consummated physically, played an important part in Athenian life. This homosexual love was generally accepted, but there were those who condemned it and, when disasters struck the city, proclaimed that their own disapproval was shared by the angry gods.

Scenes of the women's quarters decorating an epinetron *or* onos.

Disaster struck in 430 BC when the city was visited by a dreadful plague in which countless numbers of people died. 'The bodies of the dying were heaped one on top of the other,' wrote Thucydides who contracted the disease himself. 'Half-dead creatures could be seen staggering about in the streets or flocking around the fountains in their desire for water. The temples were full of the corpses of those who had died inside them. For the catastrophe was so overwhelming that men, not knowing what would happen next to them, became indifferent to every rule of religion or law ... And the most terrible thing of all was the despair into which people fell, when they realized that they had caught the plague; for they would immediately adopt an attitude of utter hopelessness, and by giving in in this way, would lose their powers of resistance.'

Pericles himself contracted the disease; and, although he recovered from it, he died within six months. The Peloponnesian War had already broken out; and it ended with the final defeat of Athens in 404 BC. Building, intermittently interrupted throughout hostilities, now came to an end. The city which Pericles had inspired, however, his proclaimed 'education for Greece', was already a worthy memorial to the civilization that had made its creation possible.

———————————————————————

As the long struggle known as the Peloponnesian War (431–404 BC) raged all over the Greek World, the Roman Empire was expanding its frontiers. From the city, traditionally founded by Romulus in 753 BC, armies were marching out to defeat rival peoples in central Italy, including the Etruscans, a mysterious race who seemed to have arrived on the peninsula either by sea from the Balkans or overland from the north and to have established themselves in the Po Valley and along the western coast of what was to become Tuscany. Some of the vanquished were granted full Roman citizenship, others lesser privileges; the unmanageable were kept in subjection until they too were considered worthy of joining the growing federation of states; thousands were brought to Rome as slaves and many later set free. By 265 BC Rome had become the supreme power in the Italian peninsula south of the Po; and little more than a century later, after the defeat of the north African maritime power, Carthage, it had also won control over Sicily, Sardinia and Corsica, and its dominion had spread not only across the Mediterranean into north Africa but across the Adriatic into Illyria, Spain and Syria; Macedonia had been taken over as a Roman province, a prelude to the incorporation of Greece itself as a Roman province. Vast amounts of plunder and wheat came to Rome, as well as slaves, so that after 167 BC there was no need for Roman citizens to pay taxes.

Rome was still nominally a republic; but the Senators chosen to fill the more important republican offices were assuming increasing powers. In the middle of the first century BC the three great men in Rome were Marcus Licinius Crassus, Gnaeus Pompeius, afterwards known as Pompey the Great, and Gaius Julius Caesar, all ambitious and gifted army commanders. Crassus and Pompey were both elected consuls in 70 BC; but Crassus's death in battle left Pompey as Caesar's only rival. In 49 BC Caesar, who was then, at the age of fifty-one, governor of Gaul, marched south with his troops across the Rubicon. Pompey retreated from Rome and, defeated in battle on the plain of Pharsalus, fled to Egypt where he was murdered by officers of the young Ptolemy XIII who offered his head to Caesar as a peace offering.

Having made Egypt a client state of Rome and having become the lover of Ptolemy's half-sister, Cleopatra, who became Queen upon Ptolemy's death, Caesar returned to Rome in triumph. His adopted son, Augustus, became the first of the Roman emperors; and it was he who claimed to have transformed the city from one of brick into one of marble. By the time of his successor, Trajan, Rome was universally recognised as caput mundi, *the capital of the world.*

4

Rome
in the Days of
the Emperor Trajan
AD 53–117

Embedded in the wall on the southern side of the Via dei Fori Imperiali in Rome, the wide thoroughfare that was opened up between the Colosseum and Piazza Venezia in the Fascist era, is a series of maps depicting the growth of the Roman Empire. At no time in its history was it more extensive than in the days of the Emperor Trajan who had been born in Seville in AD 53, the son of a Spanish mother and a father descended from Roman settlers. At the time that he erected the column which celebrates his successful military campaigns in what is now Romania, and which still stands to the north-west of the ruins of his market and forum, Trajan's empire stretched from the Scottish border to the deserts of North Africa, from the Iberian peninsula to the Euphrates, from the Caspian Sea to the lower Nile. It was an empire of numerous races and tongues in which all men might aspire to Roman citizenship, to have the right to proclaim 'Civis Romanus Sum', and to come to Rome, where as many as ninety per cent of the population may have been of foreign extraction, to share in the benefits which that citizenship conferred. Trajan's predecessor Augustus, the adopted son of Julius Caesar who had effectively brought the Roman Republic to an end, had styled himself First Citizen; and it was theoretically possible for any citizen of eligible age to be elected to the legislative body, the Senate, and to be chosen as Consul, one of two chief executives who were elected annually. In fact,

The Roman Forum at dawn, showing the Sacred Way, the Temple of Vesta, the Arch of Titus, the Temple of Castor and Pollux and the Colosseum.

however, it was the Emperor who controlled the state, who dictated the policies, who commanded its armed forces, who appointed the governors of its provinces, who ruled the lives of the people of its capital.

In Trajan's time the population of the capital was about a million, many of them foreign slaves. Few of these were slaves in the popular sense of the word. There were, of course, slaves in domestic service and employed in the most menial and degrading tasks that the life of the city demanded. But slaves were also secretaries and clerks, book-keepers, accountants and tutors, cashiers, the managers of counting-houses, foremen as well as labourers in workshops. They were allowed to save up any money that might come their way as gratuities and presents, and with their savings, their *peculium*, they could buy their liberty, become freedmen, and then perhaps make fortunes as did Petronius's Trimalchio, a former Greek slave, who invested in a cargo of wine, added 'bacon, beans, perfume and a load of slaves' and made 'a cool 10,000,000 on that one voyage'.

Indeed, many slaves lived in far greater comfort than free men whose poverty required them to live

LEFT *The Emperor Trajan (53–117).*

BELOW *Trajan's Market in Rome, which, under the directions of Apollodorus of Damascus, was built into the slopes of the Quirinal Hill to form a graceful part of Trajan's great new forum.*

in the tall apartment blocks, the *insulae*, which towered, as many as six storeys high, over the narrow lanes of the city. The buildings of the city covered an area of almost eight square miles; but since there were so many large public basilicas, temples, markets, circuses, baths, and theatres, so many acres of imperial gardens, and so much land that could not be developed for fear of offending the gods, those who could afford no better accommodation were obliged to live in a few cramped rooms in one of these crowded *insulae* which were at least within walking distance of their work in a city without public transport. The buildings looked pleasant enough from the outside, with balconies projecting from each storey, terracotta pots of flowers behind the railings, and façades decorated with tiles and mosaics. Yet many were so ill-constructed that parts of them frequently collapsed in clouds of swirling dust and a roar of tumbling brick, concrete and wood. 'Two of my properties have collapsed,' Cicero once resignedly told a friend. 'And the rest are developing cracks. Not only the tenants but even the mice have cleared out.' Inside these dilapidated structures above the ground floor, which was usually let as a single apartment, the rooms were dark and ill-ventilated, becoming increasingly less desirable on each successive floor. The top floors were stifling in summer and bitterly cold in winter when the moveable braziers were as likely to set the building alight as to warm the chilly air.

Augustus had supplied the city with both a fire service and a police force. The fire service consisted of seven thousand men recruited from free men and stationed in twenty-one barracks around the city. They were well trained and well equipped with pumps and buckets, long-handled axes, catapults for knocking down walls, blankets soaked in vinegar for smothering flames, and mattresses to break the fall of those who had to jump from upper windows. But the incidence of fires demonstrated how inadequate the fire-fighting methods were. There had not been an outbreak as calamitous as that of AD 64 when, in Nero's time, a fire had raged for six days and left most of Rome in smouldering ruins; yet there were so many minor conflagrations that Romans had constant cause to be grateful for the city's abundant water supply.

More than two hundred million gallons of water were brought into Rome every day by eight aqueducts. Streams cascaded into the public baths and gushed from six hundred public fountains. In the villas of the well-to-do, private bathrooms, kitchens and garden fountains were well supplied, usually after the appropriate official had been bribed to tap an aqueduct or an underground pipeline. The occupants of the *insulae*, however, had to fetch water in buckets from the fountains in the streets or pay notoriously grumpy and indolent water-carriers to bring it up for them. Moreover, while the drainage of the city had been regularly extended and improved since it was started seven centuries before when the *cloaca maxima*, the largest of the city's sewers, had been inaugurated in the days of the Etruscan kings of Rome, the upper floors of the *insulae* were not connected to it. Their occupants had to take their receptacles downstairs to empty them into a pit in the basement or into nearby cess trenches. Those who could not or would not do so hurled their contents, or even the brimming pots themselves, into the streets below.

'Think of the number of times cracked or broken pots fell out of windows,' wrote Juvenal. 'Anyone who goes out to dinner without making a will is a fool. You can suffer as many deaths as there are open windows to pass under. So offer up a prayer that people will be content with just emptying out their slop bowls!' Buckets of rubbish were thrown out, too; since, although an authority was entrusted with the task of sweeping, cleaning and repairing streets, its duties did not extend to the collection of refuse from houses and apartments. The problem was not, however, as severe as it might have been, for all rain water and waste water from the public baths was satisfactorily carried away into the underground drainage system; and in all the baths, and at several other places throughout the city, there were public latrines with marble seats, kept clean by attendants, warmed in winter, and flushed by fast-flowing streams of water.

As the rooms in which they slept were so uncomfortable, it was natural that many Romans preferred to spend their days in the street, joining the shopkeepers who displayed their wares there, the children repeating their lessons, the itinerant vendors shouting their wares, the butchers sharpening their knives, the jugglers, snake-charmers and acrobats, the craftsmen working at their various trades, the beggars thrusting forward their bowls and cans, the sausage sellers cooking their meat, the barbers cutting men's hair with iron scissors in an attempt to imitate the latest fashion, curling the locks of the young, dyeing those of the old, and, without benefit of soap, shaving chins with razors which were usually blunt despite frequent recourse to the whetstone, and, when their arms were jogged by the crowd, staunching the consequent flow of blood with spiders' webs soaked in oil and vinegar.

Despite the wholesale reconstruction of the city after the fire of 64, the streets were as narrow, dark and twisted as they had ever been, the sun being almost permanently excluded from some by the height of the buildings on either side. The widest streets were scarcely more than twenty feet across; in the centre of the city the Via Sacra and the Via Nova were not even as wide as this; many thoroughfares were less than fifteen feet, and some no more than six. By no means all were paved or had sidewalks, and vehicles were constantly getting bogged down in the mud as pedestrians pushed past them in their endeavour to find their way about a city in which many of the streets had no names and none of the buildings had numbers.

The passage of baggage animals and carts was forbidden in the streets in the hours of daylight, but there were numerous exemptions from the general regulation. Builders' carts were not subject to the ban; nor were horsemen; nor were slaves carrying litters and chairs; nor were chariots on their way to the amphitheatre when public games were held there; nor, on the days of

Roman weavers and cloth-sellers on Vecilio Verecondo's shop-sign from the Via dell'Abbondanza in Pompeii.

religious festivals, were the carriages of priests or of Vestal Virgins, priestesses of the goddess of the hearth and guardians of the sacred flame. In one of his satires, Juvenal described the difficulties of getting about in the narrow streets in which a passenger, pressed on all sides by a huge mob, was shoved in the hips, hit by poles and elbows, buffeted by beams and barrels, and his toes trodden on by a soldier's hobnailed boot and his newly-mended shirt torn once more. At night sleep was impossible for 'the movement of heavy wagons through constricted streets and the oaths of stalled cattle drovers would break the sleep of a deaf man or a lazy walrus ... Most sick men die here from insomnia.'

This was not true of the rich senator who woke, usually at dawn, in the relative quiet of his villa and – while slaves with brushes and buckets of sand and water set about their daily tasks, washing floors, cleaning oil lamps, emptying chamber pots and ashes from the charcoal braziers – rose from his bed and began to dress. The room in which he had slept, the *cubiculum*, was a small one in which there was little if any furniture other than the bed, a chest and a chair, washstand and table. The window was a mere aperture fitted with shutters. The other rooms in the house, which were also small and led one into the other around flower-filled courtyards, were almost equally sparsely furnished, though what pieces there were would be of the finest quality and made of a variety of beautifully fashioned materials, not only wood (often maple wood) but ivory and tortoiseshell, bronze and terebinth and porphyry with inlays of gold and silver. The walls might well be painted with such pictures of birds and flowers in a *trompe-l'oeil* manner as decorated the plaster of

the villa of Augustus's widow, Livia, at Porta Prima. The mosaic or marble, tiled or concrete floors were left uncovered. There were ornaments on shelves and window-sills, examples of Greek art, statues and busts and death-masks of distinguished forebears to remind the owner of the house and his guests of the part his family had played in the long history of Rome. On ceremonial occasions, and particularly at funerals, the busts were borne aloft by respectful servants and the death-masks worn by actors who also put on the robes and carried the insignia of high office, and orations were made in honour of the family's name.

It did not take long for the senator to dress, for

ABOVE *Three musicians, detail from a Roman mosaic in Pompeii.*

BELOW Trompe l'œil *wall decoration at the house of Lucrezio Frontone at Pompeii.*

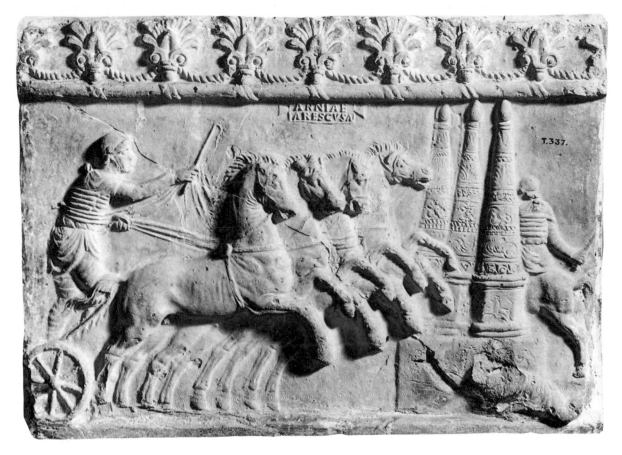

Bas-relief showing a chariot race in the Circus Maximus.

he slept in the undergarments he wore by day; and over his loincloth he pulled a woollen or linen knee-length tunic, buckled with a belt, and then put on the *synthesis*, a loose outer garment, less formal than the toga which was generally reserved for ceremonial occasions and for the clothing of a corpse at a funeral, a mark of the dignity of a Roman citizen and one that, in its variations, indicated his social rank. On his feet he slipped a pair of sandals, or, if he had far to walk, leather boots laced round the calves. A splash of water on his face was all that he would have by way of washing, for he would have a bath later; and a mouthful of bread and cheese and a glass of water flavoured with a little wine was all he would have for breakfast, since he was likely to eat well at dinner time.

His wife also slept in her underclothes, her brassière (*fascia* or *stropium*), loincloth and shift (*intusium*); and she was soon clothed in her ankle-length white *stola* and her *palla*, a shawl, usually gaily coloured, which could be wrapped round her head if it were cold or if she did not want to be recognized in the street. In earlier days she might have worn a toga, but this was now a female garment worn only by prostitutes and disgraced wives who had been discovered committing adultery. Prostitutes also revealed their trade by the startlingly bright colours of their clothes, traditionally shunned by the respectable, by the anklets they wore above their exposed feet and by the amount of the make-up on their faces.

The senator's wife, however, also used make-up, if more discreetly. The forehead was whitened, lips reddened, eyes outlined with antimony, eyebrows painted with dampened ash, hair reddened, dyed blonde or covered with a wig frequently made of fair hair, acquired no doubt from Nordic slaves. If she displayed her own hair, its arrangement occupied the careful attention of her *ornatrix* or *tonstrix*, that is to say her hairdresser, or a slave specially trained in the tonsorial art. Styles changed repeatedly. In earlier times the hair had been parted in the middle, drawn across the temples in waves, long curls falling over the ears, the rest tied at the back in a chignon; this had been followed by a more elaborate style incorporating two partings favoured by Augustus's sister, Octavia; and this, in turn, was succeeded by a style involving the high piling up of elaborate curls in the manner displayed by the female busts in the Palazzo Capitolino, examples of that portrait sculpture, executed in the Greek style, which was one of the highest achievements of Rome. Released from the hands of her *ornatrix*, sprayed with scent, jewels in her curls, glittering studs in her ears, a necklace round her throat, bracelets at her wrists, and rings on her fingers, the Roman lady was now ready to go abroad into the morning sun carrying perhaps a feathered fan and followed by a servant with a parasol.

She might return for a light midday meal; but the main meal of the day was eaten in the evening in the *triclinium* whose name was derived from the couches for three people – either fixed stone benches or moveable pieces of furniture – on which the bare-footed diners reclined on pillows, supporting themselves on their left elbows while carrying the food from the serving table to their mouths in spoons or in their fingers. Greasy hands were surreptitiously wiped on the edges of the cloth that, laid with knives and toothpicks as well as spoons, covered the serving table; but servants were in constant attendance with bowls of warm, scented water and napkins.

The meal was eaten at a leisurely pace, commonly taking up to three hours, sometimes six,

Relief depicting a scene from a Roman comedy.

and, in houses renowned for gluttony, as many as ten. There were rarely fewer than three or four courses and occasionally seven or more. The dishes for a banquet were filled with both the rich delicacies and the less exotic food that Romans relished: oysters, boiled eggs and truffles, snails, sea urchins, lobsters and goose liver, mullet, turbot, lamprey and capons, sucking pigs and roasted veal, pheasant, goose and peacock, asparagus, mushrooms, fruits and cakes. Wine, in labelled amphorae with wooden or cork stoppers, was decanted through strainers into mixing bowls where it was either mixed with warm water or cooled with snow before being poured into drinking-bowls. At a grand banquet the wine might be the Sicilian Mamertine or the Italian Falernian from the hills between Rome and Naples, an Alban or a Setian, or a Greek wine imported from Chios or Lesbos. But lesser wines were served to inferior guests who, reclining on remote couches in the *triclinium*, might, as Juvenal complained, be served a muddy eel or crab – not at all pleasing to Roman palates – while his host and more favoured guests were guzzling boar garnished with truffles and 'shrimp walled round with asparagus'.

Between courses guests, wearing their brightly coloured dining tunics, spitting on the floor and belching even in the better houses, were entertained by slaves reciting poetry, by storytellers or musicians or, in the less respectable houses, by obscene acrobats and naked Spanish dancing girls who pranced between the couches. Guests staggered out to be sick in the room specially assigned for this purpose or, like the vulgar host described by the poet Martial, summoned a slave with an amphora so that they could 'remeasure the wine [they] had drunk from it, relying on the slave to guide the stream'.

After the meal the guests sat down to talk, to play board-games or dice, to drink more wine as they listened to the jokes and anecdotes and riddles of jesters, or perhaps they went out to one of the city's numerous baths, where, if they did not have a bathroom in their own house, they would already have been washed and scraped and showered and massaged before dinner; for the baths given to the city by a succession of emperors did not merely offer the usual range of halls and chambers, the *apodyteria* for undressing, the *sudatoria* for sitting and sweating, the *calidaria*

where, in an atmosphere slightly less hot, they could splash themselves with water, and the *frigidaria* for diving into baths of cold water. Baths were places where men and women met for conversation and gossip, for playing games and wrestling. There were reading-rooms and libraries in them, exhibition halls and promenades lined with works of art; outside there were shops and cafés; inside the women's were beauty parlours. Most baths had separate women's apartments, or at least staggered opening hours, though some of the less decorous establishments permitted mixed bathing and a few were scarcely distinguishable from brothels.

In later Roman times there were forty-five brothels in Rome, open from three o'clock in the afternoon and supervised by the *aediles*, the Roman officials who were responsible for the streets, temples, sewers and market-places of the city, as well as for the organization of public displays, festivals and games. Their walls were no doubt decorated with erotic frescoes like those still to be seen at Pompeii. The prostitutes who were employed in them, and paid rent for the use of a room there, were mostly foreigners from the Near East. They sat outside the brothels on benches in their strikingly colourful clothes and ornaments. Other prostitutes, taxed by the authorities on the basis of the fees they charged their customers, were a common sight in the Subura, the noisy, crowded area of the city which Juvenal called 'the boiling Subura'. They also paraded about in large numbers on the Caelian hill, along the Sacra Via and in the Circus Maximus.

This Circus, the largest of several in Rome, had been in use perhaps since the time of the kings and had been improved and enlarged by Julius Caesar. Its immense arena, measuring 1,800 feet by 600 feet and capable of accommodating well over 150,000 spectators, was surrounded by shops and eating places, by taverns and the booths of fortune-tellers and prostitutes. It was celebrated as a place in which to pick up young girls.

'Many are the opportunities that await you in the Circus,' Ovid advised in his *Art of Love*. 'No one will prevent you sitting next to a girl. Get as close to her as you can. That's easy enough, for the seating is cramped anyway. Find an excuse to talk to her ... Ask her what horses are entering the ring and which one she fancies. Approve her choices ... If, as is likely, a speck of dust falls into

Men carrying Booty, Sacrificial Bulls and Trumpets, *from Andrea Mantegna's Triumph of Caesar, a series of panels depicting Caesar's triumphal return to Rome after his conquest of Egypt. This work was possibly inspired by the bas-reliefs decorating Trajan's Column.*

her lap, brush it gently away; and, even if no dust falls, pretend it has done and brush her lap just the same. If her cloak trails on the ground gather up the hem and lift it from the dirt. She will certainly let you have a glimpse of her legs ... The deft arrangement of a cushion has often helped a lover ... Such are the advantages which a circus offers to a man looking for an affair.'

After the signal had been given for the sport to begin by a state official who dropped a white napkin onto the sand-covered arena, there would be displays of equestrian skill followed by horse races, then by chariot races, as many as twelve chariots emerging from the stables at once. Drawn by two or four horses, occasionally by ten, the chariots hurtled round the track, bearing the colours, red, white, blue or green, of the *factiones* or stables from which they came, their highly skilled and highly rewarded drivers, heroes to the shouting crowd, leaning back against the reins, whips in their hands, clothed in tunics of their stables' colours, daggers sheathed by their side in case they had to cut themselves loose after one of the accidents that frequently occurred when a charioteer turned too close to the posts at the end of the track or brought his chariot into collision with another in the clouds of sand thrown up by the wheels and the thundering hooves.

While women and men were allowed to sit next to each other at the Circus, this was not permitted in the Colosseum, the vast amphitheatre with surrounding walls rising in four storeys to a height of 187 feet, that had been opened in the reign of the Emperor Titus on the site of the drained lake which had once stood in the grounds of Nero's vanished palace, the Domus Aurea. Women were relegated to the top storey, an enclosed colonnaded gallery which they shared with the poor; beneath them, also enclosed, sat slaves and foreigners; below them were tiers of marble seats, the upper reserved for the middle class, the lower for more distinguished citizens. The most distinguished of all, senators, magistrates, priests, Vestal Virgins and members of the Emperor's family, sat in boxes just above the level of the ringside from which they were separated by rotating cylinders which prevented enraged animals from getting into the stands should they manage to leap over the barriers. These privileged spectators were further protected from the rain or the rays of an unpleasantly hot sun by an awning which was pulled across the top of the amphitheatre by sailors on the roof of the topmost gallery.

The combats which were staged in the amphitheatre had been adopted by the Romans from the Etruscans who had sacrificed both men and animals to propitiate the unquiet spirits of the dead. They had, however, long since lost most of their religious sacrificial significance and had become part of that system by which the authorities placated the people of Rome, a large proportion of whom were always out of work, by providing them with regular entertainment as well as with free and regular distributions of food, the 'bread and circuses' of Juvenal's phrase. Great men vied with each other in the presentation of more and more thrilling spectacles, both for their own glory and to gain the gratitude of the people, while the imperial court valued the gatherings in the enormous amphitheatre as an opportunity of bringing the Emperor closer to the people.

The show was usually opened by a parade of gladiators, impressed criminals, prisoners of war and men who had chosen the precarious existence in the hope of achieving fame or the admiration of women. Wearing purple and gold cloaks, they drove around the arena in chariots, then, followed by slaves carrying their weapons, they marched towards the Emperor's box where with raised right arms, they cried, 'Hail, Emperor! We who are about to die salute thee!' They then withdrew and, as late arrivals hurried through one or other of the seventy-six entrances and pushed their way to the numbered seats, a comic interlude was provided by clowns and cripples, dwarfs and fat women who pretended to fight each other with wooden or floppy leather swords in parody of the deadly earnest combats which were to follow.

Some gladiators appeared in armour, others were almost naked, most had heavy swords and daggers, some had nets in which they hoped to entangle their opponents before killing them with a spear or a trident. The fate of a wounded gladiator who fell to the ground was decided by his antagonist if the Emperor were not present or, if the imperial box was occupied, by the Emperor himself who, raising his thumb as a sign of reprieve, turning it down as a verdict of death, made his decision known, as the spectators who had roared in wild excitement throughout the contest shouted their advice. After a sentence of death had been given, and the fatal blow struck, an attendant, usually dressed as Charon, ferryman of the Underworld, held a hot iron to the victim's cheek to ensure he was not shamming, then delivered a ceremonial *coup de grâce* to the head.

As well as gladiatorial combats there were wild-beast shows in which thousands of bellowing, howling animals, leopards and bears, tigers and lions, giraffes, camels and deer, bursting forth into the arena from the labyrinth of cells beneath, would be taunted and slashed to death by expert beast slayers who knew by constant practice how best to drive an animal to fury and to satisfy the blood lust of the crowd: in one *venatio* in the reign of Titus no less than five thousand animals, so it was calculated by Suetonius, were slaughtered in a single day. There were also displays in which the victims were members of that religious sect who, in Tacitus's words, were 'detested for their abominations and popularly known by the name of Christians after one Christus who was put to death in the reign of Tiberius by the Procurator, Pontius Pilate'. Regarding them as alien troublemakers and suspicious of their exclusiveness, their strange rites and their supposed 'abominations' which included cannibalism, the Roman people found the death of Christians in the arena one of the keenest, fiercest thrills that the shows could afford. They watched them being eaten by half-starved lions, burned alive before images of the sun-god, shot down by arrows, hacked apart with swords. In the reign of Diocletian alone there were probably as many as three thousand martyrs. Yet the Christian religion could not be suppressed; and its evident capacity to attract converts from all peoples and classes in the empire was one of the main reasons why it appealed to Diocletian's successor, Constantine.

In Rome, Constantine contrived to benefit the Christian community without giving too much offence to the rich and influential who were still mostly, and in many cases devoutly, pagan. Ensuring that the sites were well away from the centre of the city, he gave the Christians buildings in which they could meet and worship their God, bury their dead, and revere their saints and martyrs. The Emperor also provided Rome with many fine secular buildings, including the Basilica Nova, an immense structure, the last of ancient Rome's law courts and meeting places, three of whose huge coffered vaults still remain. Yet though Rome was still splendid in his day, the *caput mundi*, showplace of the civilized world, it was, he had to accept, endorsing Diocletian's view, too far removed from the threatened northern and eastern frontiers to remain the empire's capital. Constantine had also to recognize that he had failed to make Rome fully Christian, that the deep-rooted pagan beliefs of most families were as strong as ever. He began to look for a new capital. And after his death Rome's final decline began. In 408 the German people known as Visigoths invaded Italy; they marched south towards Rome, and in 410, for the first time in eight hundred years, a foreign force occupied the city. 'It is the end of the world,' lamented St Jerome, 'Words fail me . . . The city which took captive the whole world has itself been captured.' Other invaders followed the Visigoths; Vandals came in the wake of Huns, Lombards after Ostrogoths. By the end of the sixth century Rome's decay was pitiable. Eyewitnesses painted a desolate picture in which buildings were crumbling into ruins, aqueducts and public granaries collapsing, monuments and temples being dismembered, statues looted and violated. The Tiber carried along in its swollen, yellow waters dead cattle and snakes; people were dying of starvation in their hundreds; and the whole population went about in dread of infection. Those who could afford to do so had already forsaken the city for the comforts of Constantinople.

Trajan died in 117, his adopted son, Hadrian, in 138. For over twenty years thereafter Hadrian's heir, Antoninus Pius, ruled over a largely peaceful empire. But Antoninus's successor, the conscientious and idealistic Marcus Aurelius, had to spend most of his reign fighting the German tribes of the north; and when he, the last of the four good emperors of Rome's triumphant age, died in 182, the decline of the Empire, so vividly recorded by Edward Gibbon, began. Marcus Aurelius's successor, his cruel and arrogant son, Commodus, was possessed by so wildly consuming a passion for gladiatorial contests that he took part himself in almost a thousand combats before being strangled on the orders of a commander of the Praetorian Guard. This assassination inaugurated a period of intermittent civil war in which a succession of reigns was brought to a violent end. Emperor followed emperor with bewildering frequency, there being six different rulers in Rome in the one year 238. As the fourth century approached the Empire was in financial chaos; and, although Diocletian, an exceptionally able administrator from Dalmatia, helped to save it for a time from disintegration, he was obliged to recognize that it could no longer be satisfactorily ruled from Rome which was too far from its northern and eastern frontiers. He removed his own capital to Izmir on the Sea of Marmara and created three other rulers whose capitals were established at Milan, Trier and Salonika. A few years after Diocletian's death in 316 the Emperor Constantine decided that the time had come to create a New Rome in the East.

PART II

THE DEVELOPING CITY

5

Constantinople
in the Days of Constantine and Justinian
330–565

In a characteristic passage of his *Decline and Fall of the Roman Empire*, Edward Gibbon described the morning upon which the Emperor Constantine, having slept within the walls of Byzantium, strode out to mark the boundaries of the city he had, by divine inspiration, conceived as the New Rome: 'On foot, with a lance in his hand, the Emperor himself led the solemn procession, and directed the line which was traced as the boundary of the destined capital, till the growing circumference was observed with astonishment by the assistants, who at length, ventured to observe that he had already exceeded the most ample measure of a great city. ''I shall advance,'' replied Constantine, ''till He, the invisible guide who marches before me, thinks proper to stop.'' '

Constantine had chosen well. The small town of Byzantium stood where Europe and Asia meet at the confluence of the waters of a sixteen-mile-long strait, the Bosphorus, leading from the Sea of Marmara into the dark waters of the Black Sea. On the north side of the town an estuary reached five miles into the Thracian Hills. This was known to the Byzantines as the Golden Horn in allusion to the curve which it describes like the horn of a stag, and the riches 'which every wind wafted from the most distant countries into the secure and capacious port'. It was, indeed, one of the finest natural harbours in the world, commanding the land route from Europe to Asia and the waterways that led to the numerous ports on the shores of the Black Sea and, through the Dardanelles, to the Aegean and the Mediterranean.

The Haghia Sophia.

Head of Constantine on the obverse of a silver medallion.
The Emperor has a chi-rho *badge on his helmet.*

The importance of its site had been recognized in the seventh century BC by a party of Greek emigrants from Megara led by a man named Byzas. Before leaving their homeland they had sought the advice of an oracle who had cryptically instructed them, 'Go, settle opposite the city of the blind.' Several of their countrymen, and emigrants from other city states of Greece, had founded independent colonies along the shores of the Black Sea and the Sea of Marmara. The Megarans sailed for one of these Greek colonies which had been established on the Asiatic coast of the Sea of Marmara by the southern entrance to the Bosphorus; and as they looked northwards they saw a triangular promontory on the European shore that seemed to them a far more promising site than the one developed by their hosts who were, surely, the blind men of the oracle's pronouncement. The Megarans, therefore, sailed into the strait and established the town which they called Byzantium after their leader.

Although it had been destroyed by Septimius Severus as a punishment for supporting a rival and then rebuilt on a site almost twice as large, it was still a small town in Constantine's day; and he determined to transform it into a capital worthy of his empire, a city built like Rome on seven hills, a Christian city dedicated to the Trinity and the Blessed Virgin. Work on the New Rome, or

Constantinople as it soon came to be called, began in 324 and continued unremittingly for six years. Sea walls were built along the Marmara shore as well as land walls that stretched from a port on the Golden Horn to a point on the coast nearly two miles west of the old fortifications. And within these walls a forum, a palace, a hippodrome, baths and a church all began to take shape. The forum, approached by way of triumphal arches at either end, was enclosed on every side by porticoes filled with statues; in its centre stood a lofty column on whose summit, over 120 feet above the ground, rose a colossal statue of Apollo, supposed to be the work of Phidias, the Athenian sculptor. The Hippodrome or Circus was described by Gibbon as 'a stately building about four hundred paces in length, and one hundred in breadth . . . filled with statues and obelisks . . . From the throne, whence the Emperor viewed the games, a winding staircase descended to the palace, a magnificent palace which scarcely yielded to the residence of Rome itself, and which, together with the dependent courts, gardens and porticoes, covered a considerable extent of ground.'

Work on the city was sufficiently far advanced for Constantinople to be proclaimed the capital of

The Emperor Theodosius receiving tribute at the
Hippodrome : detail of reliefs on the base of the fourth-
century obelisk erected at the Hippodrome in
Constantinople to record events and ceremonies there.

the new empire in 330. Constantine died seven years later. Yet, while Rome declined and decayed, his new city grew and became ever more splendid under his successors. In the days of the Emperor Theodosius II, who was born in Constantinople in 401, there were, according to an official list, no less than 52 porticoes in the city, 8 public and 153 private baths, most embellished with marble and bronze statues, 14 churches, 14 palaces, 5 granaries, 8 aqueducts, a capitol, a circus, 2 theatres, 4 large halls for meetings of the Senate and of the Law courts, and 4,388 houses, 'which, for their size or beauty, deserved to be distinguished from the multitude of plebian habitations'. Also, the walls of the city had been so strengthened and enlarged that for more than a thousand years, until the Turks captured the city in 1453, they withstood all attempts at invasion. A terrible earthquake badly damaged them in 447; but, under threat of an attack by Attila and his Huns, the citizens worked so effectively to repair them that in two months they had been completely restored and supplied with an outer screen, an intervening moat, and 96 towers, some of them 60 feet high, at intervals of less than 70 yards. In the reign of Anastasius II the defences were further strengthened and an outer wall was constructed; and in that of Justinian they were perfected, by then enclosing a city whose population had risen to about three-quarters of a million people.

Justinian, a Latin-speaking Illyrian, was born in 483 in what is now Yugoslavia, the nephew of the Emperor Justin I, a former swineherd who rose to be Commander of the Imperial Guard. As a young man Justinian came to join his uncle in Constantinople where he received a good education, although he never learned to speak Greek well. He was adopted by Justin and in 525, having proved an invaluable aide to his illiterate uncle, he was appointed co-Emperor. A handsome, gifted and industrious man of commanding presence, Justinian set about reconstructing the Empire immediately upon his accession. With the help of his general, Belisarius, he recovered North Africa from the Vandals; his eunuch commander, Narses, defeated the Ostrogoths in Italy, allowing Justinian to re-establish an imperial administration there; while repeated attacks by the Persians on the Empire's eastern frontiers were successfully fought off. At the same time Justinian

The triple walls of Theodosius II, still standing in Old Constantinople.

undertook a wholesale consolidation of Roman law in two great works, the *Code* of 529 and the *Digest* of 533; and he pushed through numerous administrative and financial reforms in a campaign against corruption and vested interests which provoked such widespread discontent that the rival factions in Constantinople united in opposing him.

For generations the people of the city had given their allegiance to one or other of four factions which seem to have derived their support firstly from regional and then from social, religious and political distinctions. They were known as the Reds, Whites, Greens and Blues from the colours of the flashes worn on the shoulder, and the banners which they waved in the circus in support of their favoured teams of charioteers. After a time the Whites were amalgamated with the Blues, and the Reds with the Greens. The Greens drew much of their most influential support from businessmen, merchants, civil servants and members of the lower classes, whereas the Blues' supporters included many land-owning families and young aristocrats. The more flamboyant of them wore the most outlandish clothes, 'far too showy for their various stations in life', according to the historian Procopius. Their hose and tunics were as tight as possible, so were the sleeves of their shirts at the wrist, 'but from there to the shoulders they expanded to an enormous breadth; and as often as they waved their hands in the

Justinian surrounded by priests and soldiers : detail from a sixth-century mosaic in the church of San Vitale in Ravenna.

theatres and hippodromes while shouting and cheering in their usual way, this part literally rose up on high ... They adopted a new and strange way of wearing their hair. They shaved the front as far as the temples, but let the back hair grow full length in an absurd way like the Huns ... The moustache and beard they did not touch, but always let them grow to the greatest possible length like the Persians.'

They often came to blows with their rivals at the circus and afterwards called up large street mobs eager for a fight and for acts of hooliganism and vandalism. 'They formed organized bands which after nightfall robbed respectable people both in the market and in side streets, taking their victims' clothes and girdles and brooches of gold

and anything else they had on them,' Procopius added. 'Sometimes they dared to follow up robbery with murder to prevent these victims reporting what had happened to them.'

When the Blues and Greens united in opposition to Justinian, therefore, he faced formidable enemies. They proclaimed their alliance at a vast meeting in the Hippodrome where shouts of support for both factions and loud cries of 'Nika! Nika! Victory! Victory!' filled the air. From the Hippodrome they poured out into the streets, gathering supporters at every step. They broke into the gaols of the city, released the prisoners, slaughtered the guards and set the buildings on fire; they stormed the palace and the Senate, and burst into the cathedral which was soon also in flames. A military force set out to help the civil magistrate who was stoned by women from roofs and windows and overpowered by the mob. Flames spread across the city, destroying many houses, several churches and a large hospital with all its patients. Those who could do so escaped across the Bosphorus to the Asiatic shore, abandoning Constantinople to the fire and to the mob.

In the beleaguered palace Justinian heard that the rioters were demanding the heads of his two chief ministers. 'Wishing to win over the people', in the words of Procopius, he dismissed both from office. But the factions were not appeased; the riot continued unabated; and on the fifth day, Hypatius, a nephew of the late Emperor, Anastasius, was thrust upon the imperial throne in Justinian's place. Justinian and his advisers considered flight. But the resourceful Empress Theodora, a beautiful and vindictive woman of strong personality who had once been an actress, dissuaded them in a stirring appeal reported by Procopius. 'When a man has once been born into the light,' she declared, 'it is inevitable that he should also meet death. But for an emperor to become a fugitive is a disgrace not to be endured . . . If you wish to flee to safety, Emperor, it can easily be done. We have money in abundance. Yonder is the sea. Here are the ships. Yet reflect whether, when you have reached safety, you may not prefer death to security . . . As for me, may I never exist without this purple robe and may I never live to see the day upon which those who meet me shall not address me as Queen.'

Heartened by those defiant words, the Emperor and his household determined to stay and resist the rebels. Belisarius and his retainers marched out of the palace to confront the mob, accompanied by another general in command of a force of Herule barbarians. The rioters were driven back and overwhelmed. Thirty thousand men are said to have been slain in the ensuing massacre; and the bodies of Hypatius and his brother were thrown into the sea.

Once more in firm control of the city, Justinian was able to return to his plans for its restoration and embellishment. Much of Constantine's great Palace of Byzantium had been destroyed in the Nika Riots, as they came to be called; and this was now reconstructed on an even grander scale with a vast underground water cistern. It was, indeed, not so much a palace as an imperial city of numerous buildings and containing as many as twenty thousand servants, attendants, guards and officials. It was approached by way of the Chalke, a magnificent gatehouse containing a domed

Mosaic pavement from the Basilica of Theodosius showing Jonah delivered from the whale.

chamber with marble walls and a ceiling of glass mosaics. Another gateway, which led to the Emperor's box in the Hippodrome, was an equally splendid structure faced with ivory panels. Within the enclosure between them were several separate palaces, the Sacred Palace of Daphne, the Purple Palace, the seaside Palace of the Bucoleon, the Pearl Palace, in whose cool halls the imperial family spent the summer, the Magnaura Palace, which contained the bathroom where the Empress, in accordance with ancient rites, was washed on the three days following her wedding. The enclosure also contained numerous churches, oratories and chapels; storehouses; counting-houses; the celebrated lighthouse, the Pharos, standing on a promontory near the Palace of the Bucoleon; and the workshops of goldsmiths and silversmiths, mosaicists and ivory carvers, jewellers, weavers of brocade, workers in enamel and inlay and all those other craftsmen skilled in the manufacture of the precious objects which adorned the rooms of the palaces and of those silken raiments in which the members of the imperial household were attired. There were stables for the Emperor's horses and polo ponies, kennels for his dogs and the cheetahs used in bear-hunts across the strait, cages for his falcons, an aviary, and a menagerie filled with strange and exotic beasts. There were armouries and libraries, a mint and a treasury. Approached from the Hall of Tribunals were several dining- and banqueting-halls in one

A sixth-century Justinian tapestry depicting stylized horsemen.

of which a table, large enough to accommodate thirty-six couches, was made of solid gold. Works of art could be seen on every side. Beside a magnificent pair of bronze gates stood the celebrated bronze horses which were said to have been brought from Ephesus.

Apart from the horses, which are now in Venice, little of all this survives other than such fragments as a marble mosaic of trees and flowers in a rural setting that testifies to the Byzantines' appreciation of nature. But elsewhere in modern Istanbul are churches or parts of churches which date from the time of Justinian, who was credited by Procopius with having dedicated as many as twenty-five churches in the city or its suburbs, many of them afterwards ruined by fires or earthquakes, some converted into mosques by the city's Muslim conquerors. Notable among those are the Churches of SS. Sergius and Bacchus, of S. Irene, and the Church of the Holy Apostles. SS. Sergius and Bacchus, dedicated to the two Christian soldiers martyred during the reign of the Emperor Maximian, was built on the south slope of the peninsula overlooking the Sea of Marmara. Assigned to the papal legate in Constantinople, it was a church of great beauty and originality, roofed by a large flat dome and bearing a strong resemblance to another masterpiece of Byzantine art, S. Vitale in Ravenna. It served as a Christian sanctuary for almost a thousand years until converted into a mosque at

the beginning of the sixteenth century. Now nothing remains of its once sumptuous interior of which Procopius wrote, 'The sheen of its marbles was more resplendent than the sun, and everywhere it was filled with a profusion of gold.'

The Church of S. Irene, one of the oldest foundations in Constantinople which was burned to the ground in the Nika Riots, was rebuilt by Justinian as the largest church in the city after the Cathedral and one of the most lovely Byzantine churches ever created. Damaged by fire in 564, it was almost destroyed in 740 by an earthquake which caused havoc in Constantinople. After the Turkish conquest it was enclosed within the precincts of the seraglio and used as an armoury, probably by the janissaries who had quarters nearby. It later became a museum of arms.

The Church of the Holy Apostles was designed as a repository for the remains of the emperors and patriarchs. One of the few churches in the city to be built on a cruciform plan, it had a large dome on the crossing and four others on the arms of the cross. Like SS. Sergius and Bacchus, it was turned into a mosque after the Turkish conquest.

Yet, fine as these and the other churches of Constantinople were, none could be compared with the Haghia Sophia, the Holy Wisdom, that supreme masterpiece of Byzantine architecture, a fusion of techniques of the Greek, Roman and Eastern artistic traditions tempered by the directing influence of the Christian faith. Professor David Talbot Rice, the historian of Byzantine art, has contrasted the Haghia Sophia with the Parthenon. The Athenian Temple, he suggests, represents the apex of finite perfection; Constantinople's Cathedral seeks the infinite. The Haghia Sophia 'is still not only the greatest monument of Byzantine art, but perhaps also the greatest monument of Christian art. Justinian, when he entered it, on its completion, exclaimed in awe, "Glory be to God who has found me worthy to finish so great a work, and to excel thee, O Solomon." Solomon's temple has not survived. But no other faith, no other benefactor, has ever been responsible for a structure that can in beauty, in spatial conception, or in its religious atmosphere surpass the Church of the Holy Wisdom at Constantinople.'

Work began in 532, little more than a month after the earlier Cathedral had been burned down on the first day of the Nika Riots, under the direction of two architects from Asia Minor, Anthemius of Tralles in southern Lydia and Isidorus of Miletus on the Carian coast. Anthemius was a skilled mathematician as well as an engineer; and his talents were put to good use in the creation of one of the most daring, imaginative and original buildings in the history of architecture. Faced with the problem of combining the basilica type of church, essentially a rectangle containing a nave and aisles, with a large superimposed dome, the architects erected exterior walls of brick encasing a nave, flanked by two aisles and separated from them by a row of marble columns in the line of which stand four massive piers supporting an enormous, shallow and slightly eliptical dome. Additional support for the dome – which measures approximately thirty-six yards across and is approximately sixty-one yards above the floor at its highest point – was given by pendentives to direct the thrust of the dome's weight on to the piers rather than on to the arches between them. Yet the whole concept was designed so inconspicuously that, as a contemporary writer observed, the dome 'appears to be supported on chains from heaven'.

The interior of the great edifice, lighted by

The Interior of the Haghia Sophia.

windows all around the back of the dome, was a gorgeous blend of colours. The walls were covered with polychrome marble from all parts of the Empire; there were porphyry columns from the Temple of the Sun in Rome and eight columns of green marble presented by the magistrates of Ephesus; spacious galleries above the aisles provided accommodation for the women worshippers who were segregated from the men; and around them all were mosaics covering four acres of wall and consisting mostly of floral and geometrical designs on a glittering gold background. These have disappeared, the figurative mosaics now to be seen dating from after 843 when the ravages of the iconoclasts ended. Also no longer to be seen is the gigantic bronze equestrian statue of Justinian which was erected on a brass column standing upon a stone pedestal in the great square laid out by Constantine in front of the cathedral and which was melted down for cannon by the Turks in the sixteenth century. Yet, despite fire and earthquake, restoration, rebuilding and some additions made by the Turks, who erected four minarets, the cathedral of Haghia Sophia stands today little changed from the day that Justinian entered it on its completion in 537.

To the west of the cathedral and the palace, the city had been laid out in a rectilinear plan so far as the triangular shape of the peninsula would allow. Most houses were of brick, though some were of stucco-covered stone. Roofs were tiled, except those of the mansions of the rich, which usually had flat roofs used as terraces. Windows at ground-floor level facing the street were uncommon; but in the upper floors there were glass bow windows with balconies. The entrance door, often of iron studded with nails, led into a courtyard with a well, cistern or fountain in the middle. Overlooking the courtyard were galleries approached from the rooms of the upper floors, the women and children and slaves usually occupying the highest storey, leaving the one below for men. In the coldest days of the city's often bitter winters families who did not enjoy the luxury of central heating on the Roman hypocaust system gathered round a charcoal brazier in a hot room. There were braziers or charcoal stoves also in the kitchens as well as wood fires. Here excellent meals were cooked, breakfast as well as a midday meal and supper, the main meals usually comprising three courses in the houses of the well-to-do. At these meals, so Tamara Talbot Rice tells us, hors-d'œuvres were served first, then a fish or meat course, poultry or game, then some kind of pudding or sweet dish. 'Soups, many of them elaborate and requiring long hours of cooking, were customary; tripe and stews were often on the menu, and so were salads of many sorts. Cheese was much liked and so was fruit, whether fresh or stewed ... Oil was used for cooking and much wine – mostly from Chios – was drunk ... A meal represented on a mosaic discovered at Antioch is seen to have included artichokes, a white sauce, grilled pig's trotters, fish, ham, duck, biscuits, fruit and wine, as well as hard-boiled eggs served in blue enamel egg cups with small long-handled spoons to eat them with. Gourmets were numerous and took delight in serving regional specialities such as Vlach cheese.'

The fish was particularly excellent, for, as Gibbon said, the Sea of Marmara 'has ever been renowned for an inexhaustible store of the most exquisite fish, that are taken in their stated seasons, without skill, and almost without labour'.

Meals were served in as attractive a manner as possible, and eaten with a delicacy at that time most unusual in western Europe. Although food was often lifted to the mouth with the fingers,

Sixth-century Byzantine weights used in trade.

knives and spoons were generally laid on the clean, embroidered table-cloth as well as napkins and bowls of water. And forks, which were still unusual in Italy at the beginning of the sixteenth century and virtually unknown at that time in France and England, were commonly seen in Constantinople from the fourth century onwards.

Standards of personal hygiene were also much higher than they were in the West. The slums in the poorer quarters were abominable, while the clothes of those numberless and homeless unemployed who slept under rags between the columns of the porticoes were crawling with vermin. But most houses had lavatories, with drains emptying into the sea, and bath houses leading off the courtyard or the garden.

After his bath the rich merchant would clothe himself in a long tunic, extravagantly trimmed with embroidery and gold thread. Over this, in cold weather, he would wear a long coat or cloak, also embroidered, and possibly lined with fur imported from Russia. Ladies also wore tunics, closer fitting than their husbands' and often made of silk or some diaphanous material. Over this they placed an embroidered dalmatic and a pallium whose long train was carried over the arm. Also, like the men, they wore cloaks; and some walked abroad in veils. Others proudly revealed eyes whose pupils were made more alluring by belladonna and whose brows were plucked into narrow painted lines. Lips were reddened with rouge; ears pierced for rings; wrists adorned with bracelets, and throats with necklaces; great care was taken with the braiding and coiling of the hair which was decorated with jewels and slides and combs of tortoiseshell, ivory and gold filigree.

When they stepped out of their houses they found the streets as crowded and noisy as they had once been in Rome. In some of them there were shops on both sides for the entire length, the book shops being congregated near the Augustaion, the city's most favoured meeting place. There were also several markets and hundreds of street sellers peddling all manner of wares from rich embroideries to dates and nuts. Making their way through the throng, ladies on foot were guided by eunuchs, who pushed aside the passers-by to clear a path, or they were carried in elaborately decorated sedan chairs, or rode in brightly painted carriages some of which had solid gold wheels and were pulled by mules harnessed in gilt leather trappings. Quiet could be found in the public gardens and in some of the public baths, but elsewhere the clamour was continuous and deafening, particularly on days when there were public executions, popular religious festivals or processions or chariot races in the Hippodrome whose serpent column, brought from Delphi, and Egyptian obelisk still survive, but whose vast arena with its tiers of marble seats has long since been buried beneath the streets and gardens of the modern city.

In the theatre the noise was almost as deafening before the performance began as it was in the Circus when the chariots raced round the course beneath the eyes of forty thousand spectators. Theatrical performances in Justinian's time were still highly indecent, the actresses often playing their parts almost completely naked as Theodora had once done. Procopius, who both feared and strongly disapproved of her, described Theodora, the daughter of a bear-keeper, as a wild and wanton actress who, while 'still too under-developed to be capable of having intercourse, acted as a sort of male prostitute to satisfy customers of the lowest type, and slaves at that who, when accompanying their owners to the theatre, seized their opportunity to divert themselves in this revolting fashion ... She was not a flautist or a harpist, she was not even qualified to join the corps of dancers; she merely sold her attractions to anyone who came along, putting her whole body at his disposal. Later she joined the actors in all the business of the theatre, making herself the butt of their ribald buffoonery. She was extremely clever and had a biting wit and soon became popular ... She would throw off her clothes and exhibit herself naked both in front and behind ... Often she would go to a party with ten young men or more ... and would lie with all her fellow-diners in turn the whole night long; and when she had reduced them all to a state of exhaustion, she would go to their servants, as many as thirty on occasions, and copulate with every one of them, but even so she could not satisfy her lust. And although she brought three bodily apertures into service, she often grumbled that Nature had not made the openings in her nipples wider so that she could devise another method of intercourse'.

This may well have been malicious gossip. Yet Procopius's strictures do provide a realistic impression of what the theatre in Constantinople was like: 'Often in the theatre in full view of all the people, Theodora would stand naked in their midst, having only a girdle about her private parts – not, however, because she was ashamed to expose these also to the public, but because no one is allowed to appear there completely naked: a girdle round the loins is compulsory. With this minimum covering she would spread herself out and lie face upwards on the floor. Servants would sprinkle barley on her private parts and geese trained for the purpose used to pick them off one by one with their bills and swallow them.'

On 28 June 548, when she was about forty-eight, Theodora died in Constantinople of cancer. Her devoted husband, to whom she had been a loyal wife, however lascivious she may have been in her youth, was heartbroken. He had her buried with the most reverent ceremony in the still unfinished Church of the Holy Apostles whose construction he had begun over ten years before. He himself lived on for a further seventeen years. And when he died in 565, so a modern historian, P.N. Ure, has written, 'nothing probably gave him such satisfaction as the fact that he was leaving the empire with something like the frontiers that it had boasted in the days of its greatest power and glory ... The light that came into the world with Solon and Cleisthenes and Pericles and the heroes and statesmen of the young republic of Rome had illumined only a small corner of the world. The books that had recorded the new age and the two languages in which that record had been written might easily have disappeared altogether if the empire had not spread and preserved them ... That is the great debt that we owe the Byzantines ... and the richly documented age of Justinian in particular ... They have passed on to us a great inheritance which they did their utmost to preserve.'

In the end, of course, the Byzantine Empire could not be preserved; and Justinian's reign might be seen as marking the end of an age rather than the opening of the new era he had intended. Yet, if he failed in that ultimate endeavour, if he is remembered for what he preserved rather than for what he created, his architects were truly creative. The great days of Byzantium were numbered; but in Constantinople the tangible remains of that greatness beneath the dome of Haghia Sophia have endured throughout the passing centuries.

After the appearance of the Sumerian civilization along the Euphrates in about 3500 BC, that of Egypt soon afterwards, and the civilizations of Crete and India between 2500 and 2000 BC, men living beside the banks of the Hwang-Ho or Yellow River in China in about 1500 BC had built themselves walled cities, had learned how to cast bronze, to carve jade and marble, to make beautiful objects in gold and porcelain, to grow silk and to write, having a written language of no less than 2,500 characters. They may have learned some of their skills from others, but their country was for the most part isolated from the outside world and their civilization developed in a peculiarly Chinese way. The first Chinese state was ruled by a dynasty of warriors known as the Shang; this was displaced in about 1050 BC by the Chou who called themselves 'Sons of Heaven'.

The Chou presided over a society at once highly organized, highly religious and highly cultured. Most people lived on the land, often in pits underground. But in the cities, at court, and in the houses of the rich, the handicrafts and metal implements were as sophisticated as they were beautiful. The Chou kings reigned for more than eight hundred years, gradually increasing their domains and believing that all those who lived beyond the boundaries of the Middle Kingdom were barbarians. But, weakened by prolonged military campaigns in the eighth century BC, the Chou empire eventually disintegrated into numerous, small, belligerent states until, some time after 250 BC in the western state of Ch'in, there came to power a young king who was to become the first emperor of a united China. The Han dynasty, which came into being after his death, lasted for four hundred years until AD 220, a mighty counterpart of the Roman Empire in the West; and after its collapse the four hundred years of constant warfare and unrest, of droughts, pestilence and famine, the so-called Period of Disunion, was an age comparable to the one in Europe after the fall of Rome. Hordes of nomadic horsemen constantly rode down from the steppes beyond the Great Wall, which had been completed in the time of the Ch'in, in search of plunder and women, massacring tens of thousands of people and eventually occupying immense tracts of land. But these fierce invaders were at length obliged to seek the help of the old and experienced Chinese ruling caste in the territories they overran. Many of their leaders married daughters of Chinese aristocrats, and from one such marriage came Yang Chien who was to establish a new dynasty, the Sui (582–618). This dynasty imposed order upon the devastated country and united north and south. And just as the Ch'in had prepared the way for the Han, so the Sui laid the foundations of that great dynasty, the T'ang (618–907), rulers for almost three hundred years of an empire of nearly fifty-three million people. Visitors to this empire returned to their own countries with marvellous reports of the wonders of its cities, of the efficiency of its government, of the extraordinary inventiveness of its people. They had invented gunpowder – not for warfare but for fireworks – they had invented block printing and the wheelbarrow; they had long since been users of coal; they were expert in the manufacture of paper and ceramics; they were as skilful at cartography as at calligraphy. By the end of the tenth century, however, the great days of the T'ang came to an end; the last of the T'ang emperors were debauchees and wastrels, governed by the women and eunuchs of the palace; and another cycle in the imperial history of China was closed.

Yet, as at other times when the Chinese Empire was on the verge of collapse, a strong man came to power. This was Chao K'uang-yin, also known as T'ai-tsu, a soldier and a scholar, who founded the Sung dynasty (960–1127) in whose time the Empire was to be divided.

The Hangzhou Bore in moonlight : painting on silk by Li Sung.

6

Hangzhou

in the Days of
the Sung Emperors
1138–1279

Describing the adventurous journey he made from Peking to Amoy in the late thirteenth century, the Venetian traveller, Marco Polo, wrote that for three days from Ch'ang-an the road passed through a 'fine country full of thriving towns and villages' whose inhabitants were 'amply provided with all the means of life'. After making his way through this countryside, rich in rice and productive of the best green tea and silk, the wayfarer reached the splendid city of Kinsai (Hangzhou) whose name means 'City of Heaven'. This place, 62 miles from the East China Sea and 120 miles south-west of Shanghai, well merited a description, Marco Polo said, for it was 'without doubt the finest and most splendid city in the world'.

'The lay-out', he continued, 'is as follows. On one side is a lake of fresh water, very clear. On the other is a huge river, which entering the city by many channels carries away all its refuse and then flows into the lake from which it runs out towards the ocean. This makes the air very wholesome. And through every part of the city it is possible to travel either by land or by these streams. The streets and the watercourses alike are very wide, so that carts and boats can readily pass along them to carry provisions for the inhabitants. There are said to be twelve thousand bridges, mostly of stone, though some are of wood. Those over the main channels and chief thoroughfares are built with such lofty arches and so well designed that big ships can pass under them without a mast, and yet over them pass carts and horses, so well are the street levels adjusted to the height. Under the other bridges smaller craft can pass. No one need be surprised that there are so many bridges. For the whole city lies in water and is surrounded by water like Venice, so that many bridges are needed to let people go all over the town.'

This beautiful city, so well served as a centre of communications by the rivers of South China and the nearby coast, had been established as his capital by the Emperor Kao-tsung of the Sung dynasty in 1138. Previous emperors of this dynasty had been forced into costly wars with both the Khitan tartars and the fierce nomadic Jurchen-Chin tartars, former vassals of the Khitans, who had become masters of north-east Asia. In 1126 a large force of Jurchen-Chin warriors had ridden into the great Sung city of Kaifeng in the Yellow River valley, and had taken three thousand men into captivity, including the Emperor Hui-tsung himself who had been forced to appear before the Tartar leaders in the blue robes commonly worn by servants. His captors had addressed him sardonically as the Duke of Confused Virtues and had sent him away beyond the Great Wall, where he died. The Tartars had then advanced south and had come so close to capturing the Sung city of Hangzhou (Hangchow) that the Emperor's successor, Kao-tsung, had made an alliance with them. The pact left the Jurchen-Chin to control the north on condition that the Sung were left in peace in the rice-growing valleys of the south and in Hangzhou, their new capital.

At its height, Hangzhou, whose population of over a million was then the largest in the world, covered eight square miles, the city proper being circumscribed by crenellated walls of white-washed earth and stone, thirty feet in height and pierced at intervals by gates surmounted by towers and, on the eastern side where an enemy attack was most likely, fortified by outer defence works. A straight, wide thoroughfare known as the Imperial Way ran north to south; the main canals ran parallel to it; other canals and thoroughfares crossed it east to west. All the main streets were paved with stones and bricks, well gravelled in the middle, drained by conduits that carried off the rainwater into the canals, and regularly swept. The numerous bridges, as Marco Polo observed, were each guarded by ten men, five by day and five by night. 'These are,' he wrote, 'to protect the city from malefactors and check any attempt at rebellion. In every guardhouse there is a big wooden drum with a big gong and a clock by which they tell the hours of the night and also of the day. At the beginning of the night, when the first hour has passed, one of the guards strikes a single blow on the drum and the gong, so that the whole neighbourhood knows [the time]. At the second hour they strike two blows; and so on, hour by hour, increasing the number of strokes. They never sleep but are always on the alert ... A detachment of them patrols the district [and if] they find anyone abroad at night after the approved hours they arrest him. Again if they come across some poor man who is unable to work on account of illness, they have him taken to one of the hospitals of which there are great numbers throughout the city. When they find a house with a light or fire burning beyond the authorized hours they put a mark on the door and in the morning the owner is summoned to appear before the magistrates.'

At dawn the bells of the Buddhist and Taoist monasteries began to ring and monks walked through the streets beating strips of iron or pieces of wood shaped like fish to announce the break of day. And from then on throughout the hours of sunlight the streets and canals were scenes of constant activity. The streets were filled with porters carrying goods suspended in baskets or jars from long poles, or chairs with canopies and folding doors. They were thronged with carriages behind whose curtained windows the five or six passengers reclined on cushions, with men on horseback, and with donkeys and mules and pack-horses, some of which were less than three feet high. Boats propelled by pole or oar and laden

Marco Polo observing the points of a horse, from a painting on silk by Chao Meng-fu, 1254–1322.

with rice and wine, with bricks and firewood, sacks of salt and fresh vegetables, passed northward through the city and down to the river where innumerable barges, fishing boats and junks with sails of pleated matting or deep blue canvas, were anchored beneath the green mountains.

'Vegetables from the east,' so it was said, 'water from the west, wood from the south and rice from the north' came into the city in enormous quantities every day. Rice, of nine different kinds, was the staple diet of the people, and barges transporting it were being constantly unloaded at the Ricemarket Bridge and the Black Bridge whence they were carried away to shops and restaurants all over the town. Pork, too, arrived in the shops in immense loads; so did salt fish which was the only merchandise available in almost two hundred shops. Most other food shops sold a variety of goods from pork and rice to noodles and candles, vegetables and thread, soya sauce, fruit, oil and incense; and all those spices, peppers, gingers, pimentoes, salts and vinegars that made

ABOVE *A bridge at Kaifeng during the April Ching Ming Festival, by Chang Tse-tuan: twelfth-century painting on silk from the Ching Ming Scroll.*

OPPOSITE *Street scenes from the Ching Ming Scroll, showing the Ching Ming Festival.*

Hangzhou cooking so varied and excellent. There were also specialist markets for all kinds of produce, for flowers and books, cloth and precious stones, herbs, oranges and olives. Marco Polo counted ten principal markets but there were 'a vast number of others in different parts of the town'. 'In each of the squares,' he said, 'is held a market three days a week, frequented by 40,000 or 50,000 persons, who bring hither for sale every possible necessary of life, so that there is always an ample supply of every kind of meat and game, as of roebuck, red-deer, fallow-deer, hares, rabbits, partridges, pheasants, francolins, quails, fowls, capons, and of duck and geese an infinite quantity.' Indeed, every imaginable kind of foodstuff was available in the markets except beef – since the ox was an expensive animal regarded rather as a servant for the farmer than as material for the butcher – and milk and cheese – since the Chinese were not, and never had been, dairy farmers.

There were restaurants in every quarter, many of them renowned for their specialities or for their manner of cooking them, and most approached through flower-bedecked archways from which hung some symbol indicative of their business, a bowl of noodles, perhaps, or a leg of mutton. There were shellfish restaurants, and salt-fish restaurants, restaurants that specialized in the cooking of Szechwan or Shantung, restaurants that served dog meat and even those, according to one authority cited by Jacques Gérnet in his *La Vie quotidienne en Chine à la Veille de l'Invasion Mongole*, which served 'two legged mutton' that was to say human flesh which was offered as that of men, women, young girls and babies, each, evidently, having its own particular flavour. In most restaurants, it appears, the din was tremendous as customers called out their orders, and waiters repeated them in loud shouts to the kitchen staff. 'As soon as the customers have chosen where they will sit,' Gérnet quotes from a contemporary account, 'they are asked what they want to have. The people of Hangzhou are very difficult to please. Hundreds of orders are given on all sides: this person wants something hot, another something cold, a third something tepid, a fourth something chilled; one wants cooked food, another raw, another chooses roast, another grilled. The orders, given in a loud voice, are all different, sometimes three different ones at the same time. Having received the orders, the waiter goes to the kitchen and sings out a whole list of orders . . . Then he goes off to serve each customer with the dish ordered. He never mixes them up, and if by any unlucky chance he should make a mistake, the proprietor will launch into a volley of oaths addressed to the culprit, will straightaway forbid him to continue serving and may even dismiss him altogether.'

Those who ate at home had three meals a day, all eaten with spoons or chopsticks, breakfast at dawn when most people got up, a midday meal about noon and an evening meal at a time which varied from family to family. To improve their diet of rice, pork and vegetables, the poorer families ate a good deal of offal, particularly kidneys, liver and tripe. The rich, whose meals were brought into the room in porcelain dishes on lacquered trays and served on low tables, naturally enjoyed a more elaborate diet and seem to have been particularly fond of fish and game cooked with fruit, generally plums or apricots, lotus-seed soup, lobsters marinated in herbs and scented rice wine. All classes drank rice wine of which there were over fifty different kinds and of which even foreign travellers spoke very highly, some preferring it to the wine made of grapes they were accustomed to in the West. And all classes drank deeply, drunkenness being so common that

Whiling Away the Summer by Liu Kuan-tao : a silk handscroll painted in ink and light colour showing fashionable ladies of the late thirteenth century.

the canals had to be balustraded to prevent revellers falling in. The need for this precaution was never more evident than on the days of festivals when the taverns and tea-houses were full of customers all day and serving girls brought cup after silver cup of wine, all lukewarm and accompanied by nuts, by little glazed and salted biscuits and, if desired, by beancurd soup, oysters, silkworm pies or shrimp tarts. On the upper floors of several taverns and tea-houses were singing-girls and prostitutes. Indeed, the number of courtesans in Hangzhou was extraordinary. They could be encountered everywhere, not only in those inns where their presence was indicated by a bamboo shade over the porch light, not just in brothels, but in parks and in markets, on bridges and by the canals – in fact, as Marco Polo testified, 'all over the city': 'There is so great a multitude of them that I do not venture to state the number. They all serve men for money, and they all find a living . . . They exhibit themselves magnificently attired and heavily perfumed with trains of handmaidens. These ladies are highly proficient and accomplished in the use of endearments and caresses, with words suited and adapted to every sort of person, so that foreigners who have once enjoyed them remain utterly beside themselves and so captivated by their sweetness and charm that they can never forget them. So it comes about that, when they return home, they say they have truly been in the City of Heaven, and can scarcely wait for the time when they go back there.'

Numbers of prostitutes, singing-girls with eyes 'brilliant and bewitching' and lips like cherries, as well as male prostitutes with painted faces, could be seen in the arcades of the bathhouses of which there were almost as many in the city as there were restaurants. They could accommodate a hundred bathers at a time, most of whom were washed by the attendants in cold water, 'which they say, is much to be recommended for health', and with many applications of herb-scented liquid soap.

The richer families had bathrooms of their own, and upon emerging from these the ladies of the household would, with the help of their servants, begin the long process of dressing and making-up, applying a rose-coloured powder to their cheeks, painting their nails, pencilling over the line of their plucked eyebrows, choosing their dresses and blouses, their jackets and skirts, and the gold and silver ornaments and combs with which they decorated their shining hair – brushed back and gathered into a chignon – taking out their white silk fans and the shoes into which they placed their tiny, misshapen feet, the result of foot-binding, a painful practice that had come to be a sign of wealth, since who but a rich man could afford to keep handicapped wives and daughters?

For both men and women, dress was an important indication of wealth and status. The rank of a mandarin was indicated by the colour of his robes and the style of his headgear; and on ceremonial occasions he wore a silken brocade robe embroidered with symbols, dragons or flowers, white cranes or quails, that informed the world of his grandeur. Attached to his satin shoes were pattens to lend him the dignity of height. His girdle had a buckle of jade or rhinoceros horn; his cap a button whose shade and style were further evidence of his importance.

Poor people always wore some form of headgear, usually a turban, a leather cap or a straw hat, and some kind of footwear, too, often rope or wooden sandals or clogs. The men wore trousers, a barbarian form of dress disdained by the rich, and a blouse that reached almost to the knees. Most of them were cleanshaven, a beard suggesting that a man had once been, or still was, a soldier, or wished to be taken for one.

The houses in which the poor lived were cramped constructions of wood and bamboo, some as many as five storeys high, the lower floor being used as a shop or workroom. Fires were common, but, owing to an efficient system of control, were generally kept in check before they had spread. Soldiers on constant duty in watchtowers were equipped with buckets, hatchets, ropes, grappling irons and waterproof clothing. By means of flags by day and lanterns by night, outbreaks of fire were immediately notified to troops trained in fire-fighting, so that while an occasional conflagration was catastrophic – in June 1132 thirteen thousand houses were destroyed – most were put out before too much damage had been done.

The wealthier people were not so much at risk because their houses, built of sturdier and less inflammable materials, with trellised windows of oiled paper, were spread over a wider area in the hilly regions. They consisted of several apartments and pavilions, dining-halls, music-rooms and sleeping chambers, generally on one floor only, arranged in extensive gardens in which rare and exotic flowers grew between mounds of veined and polished stones, in which walnuts, pears and apricots threw their shade on to the grassy slopes, gold and silver fish darted in the clear water of rock pools, porcelain lions stood on guard beside painted bridges, burning sticks of perfumed wood puffed small clouds of white smoke into the sky, and images of gods beside the screened gate kept evil spirits at bay. And whereas the roofs of the poorer dwellings were commonly thatched, those in the hills were coloured with yellow and green glazed tiles, their exposed beams carved and painted and often decorated with terracotta animals and dragons, adornments forbidden by decree to ordinary people.

Inside these houses the furniture was simple but decorative. There were small tables, circular stools, chairs with crossed legs known as 'barbarian chairs', armchairs, beds of black lacquer enclosed by screens – red lacquer being permitted only to the Emperor – with pillows of painted porcelain or lacquered wood and covers of silk. Floors were often of glazed bricks, walls hung with scrolls depicting country scenes or the activities of the family's ancestors.

The Emperor's palace was the most magnificent of all. Its pavilions were ornamented with gold, its walls painted with delicate representations of the triumphs of his dynasty. In its rolling gardens were artificial hills planted with pines and bamboos, waterfalls splashing their waters into lakes across lotuses and water lilies, enclosures where all manner of animals roamed and birds of the brightest plumage flew from tree to tree, courtyards in which orchids, jasmine and cinnamon blossomed in urns.

The Emperor himself and the princes of the imperial blood were waited upon by numerous attendants and servants, all divided into categories with carefully defined duties. As well as attendants with ceremonial duties and servants to care for the furniture, to purchase, prepare and serve food, to take charge of heating and decorating the rooms, of incense, medicines and flower arrangement, there were tutors and poets, painters and musicians, librarians and copyists, chess players, raconteurs, jewellers, sculptors, embroiderers, acrobats, actors, calligraphers, messengers and concubines.

*The Emperor Ming-huan watching a cock fight : a late
twelfth-century painting on silk by Li-Sung*

The rich had no need to stir from their estates to enjoy every pleasure that life could afford, while for the less well off Hangzhou itself was a pleasure ground. In the streets there were jugglers, puppeteers, singers and dancers, marionette performances and shadow plays, tightrope walkers, sword swallowers and fire-eaters, men with performing bears and performing ants and hypnotized fish, archers and boxers, wrestlers and snake-charmers, comedians and story-tellers and men who asked riddles standing on their heads. There were several parks and pleasure grounds and on the great West Lake there were hundreds of boats of all kinds and sizes, some of them floating tea-houses, others barges that were propelled around the shores by poles so that the passengers could, in one traveller's words, take in 'the whole prospect in its full beauty and grandeur, with its numberless palaces, temples and monasteries, its gardens full of lofty trees sloping to the water's edge', its Buddhist pavilions, the high pagoda on Thunder Rock, the woods of willows, haunts of golden orioles, and the Pao-chu Pagoda on Precious Stone Hill. Others were filled with singing-girls, and yet others with passengers playing darts or chess, dominoes, mahjong, or 'double six', a sort of backgammon.

The pleasure ground contained numerous clubs and training centres where poetry was read and plays rehearsed, drama, music and dancing taught, calligraphy and painting practised, and books read. For the Chinese set great store by education and nearly every *nouveau riche* merchant was anxious that his sons should acquire as much learning as would enable him to comment upon quotations from the prescribed classics, write essays in the traditional eight sections and sit for the civil service examination, and so become a scholar official, a member of a privileged élite, exempt from taxation, despite the difficulties that the existing mandarinate put in his way. Daughters were not considered suited to such education. It was expected that they should be able to read and write and, perhaps, use an abacus. They were taught music and singing if they were to be courtesans; but for most girls spinning and embroidery were considered more important than literature, and a good marriage more desirable than learning.

When a marriage had been decided upon, the father of the intended bride sent a card with her name and age upon it to the proposed bridegroom's father through a professional go-between, a woman whose clothes reflected the social standing of her employer, whose appearance in a veil and a purple robe, for instance, would indicate that she came on behalf of a most distinguished family but whose arrival with her hair in a yellow chignon-bag and carrying a green umbrella would arouse no false hopes in the young man's family. The card brought by the go-between was examined by a fortune-teller and, if a favourable view of the proposal was forthcoming, there was an exchange of further cards and of information relating to the bridegroom's family, ancestors, fortune and prospects and to the bride's antecedents and dowry. Once everything had been accepted and agreed, the go-between arranged a formal meeting of both families at which cups of rice wine were exchanged and, as a sign that the bridegroom was satisfactory to her, the bride stuck two pins in her chignon. If she was not pleased with him, his family were later sent two strips of coloured satin. A favourable response was followed by the bestowal of more gifts by both families including bracelets, chains and pendants of gold from those who could afford them and of gilded metal for those who could not.

The day before the wedding there was an

Scholars meeting in a garden to enjoy food and talk : detail from a painting attributed to the twelfth-century Emperor Hui-tsung.

Ladies spinning and sewing : painting on silk by Ma Ho-chih.

exhibition of items for the bride's dowry; and, on the wedding day itself – a day chosen by the fortune-teller – she was escorted to the house of the groom's family in a procession of singing-girls, one girl walking backwards in front of her, holding a mirror to her face, other girls carrying torches and candles in the shape of lotus flowers or throwing seeds and fruits to the watching crowds to ward off evil spirits. Once inside the house, before proceeding to a room specially hung with curtains for the reception, she had to sit astride a horse saddle and a pair of scales, a custom of presumably erotic significance whose origins are now unknown and were, perhaps, unknown even then.

She was now considered part of her husband's family, and thereafter made rare visits to her own. She was expected to be modest and unassuming, obedient to the wishes of her parents-in-law, tolerant of any concubines that her husband might wish to introduce into the house, while remaining faithful to him herself. Yet many wives did manage to escape from this constricting domesticity: 'complementary husbands' were a common accretion in Hangzhou marriages, Buddhist monks, so it was said, being particularly useful in this respect.

Condemning the moral laxity and sybaritic luxury of Hangzhou life, the poet, Su Tung-p'o, had already struck a warning note: 'When will the singing and dancing on West Lake cease?'

In the golden days of the Emperor Hui-tsung such warning seemed misplaced. The Sung Em-

pire appeared to be well run by the Son of Heaven aided by a Secretariat and Chancellery which dealt with civil administration, by a Privy State Council in charge of the armed forces, and by a Department of Financial and Economic Affairs, the officials who staffed these ministries having all passed competitive examinations. Hangzhou's trade flourished, and its production of works of art in poetry, painting and, above all, ceramics was unrivalled. Sung painters were producing those beautiful misty landscapes and delicate pictures of birds and flowers that are among the finest treasures of the Eastern world. The Emperor himself was a talented painter and discriminating patron. He established an imperial institute of calligraphy and painting and supervised the compilation of a catalogue of over 6,000 paintings by 231 artists. Skill in painting, like expert calligraphy and facility in the composition of verse, became increasingly important attributes in candidates for the civil service examinations. The Sung stoneware and porcelain produced

A Sung stoneware vase with floral design painted in brown slip under a white glaze.

in the city's two factories – one within the precincts of the imperial palace, the other at the south end of Imperial Way by the altar for the sacrifices to Heaven and Earth – are among the most beautiful ever seen, more highly prized in China than the later blue and white Ming porcelain so treasured in Europe. Indeed, on every side there was evidence of a civilization far in advance of any in the West, of great advances in science and technology. On the rivers locks and bridges demonstrated the ingenuity of Chinese engineers, while off the coast there were ships with multiple masts and treadmill-operated paddles. Water-mills ground corn by intricate systems of interlocking cogs; workshops used water power for spinning hemp. The magnetic compass had been devised; so had the astronomical clock. In mathematics and algebra, medicine and zoology, history and geography, additions were constantly being made to the stock of knowledge. Following the invention of movable type, publishing centres were flourishing.

Yet the direst poverty existed beside the most ostentatious wealth, not only in the countryside but also in the towns to which want drove the destitute peasant who endeavoured to make a living beyond the protection of the guilds, undertaking any work that he could find as pedlar, porter, scavenger or water-carrier, and often turning to crime when there was no work to be had. As peasant discontent and economic problems grew towards the end of the thirteenth century, so did the threat from the Empire's foreign enemies. The Sung armies were celebrated for their skill and bravery, and for their expert use of gunpowder, explosive bombs, rockets, grenades, flame-throwers and poisonous smokes. But they were no match for the ruthless Mongol tribesmen who had poured over the Great Wall from the Steppes. In 1279 the last surviving Sung prince died and Kublai Khan, grandson of Genghis, who had already conquered most of the north, became Emperor of all China.

———————————————

Some seven centuries after the first civilization developed in China, another independent and isolated civilization began to emerge in Central America where maize and, further south, squashes, gourds, and root vegetables such as potatoes had been cultivated in about 5000 BC. By 2000 BC farmers were living in villages, wearing woven clothes and using pottery vessels and dishes; and by 1000 BC the Olmecs of eastern Mexico were carving monuments and figures of stone and jade, building huge earth pyramids, and temples in honour of gods who were to be worshipped for thousands of years, and beginning to develop the calendar.

They were descended from those migrant hunters who had arrived on the American continent in about 25000 BC by way of the bridge of land which is now submerged beneath the Bering Strait. These hunters had reached the Andes by about 9000 BC and had domesticated the llama by 3500 BC and the alpaca by 1500 BC. Some two thousand years after the domestication of the alpaca, a remarkable civilization reached its zenith in Guatemala, Honduras and Yucatan. This was the civilization of the Mayas who, though they did not discover the wheel or the arch and lived in small villages rather than towns, wrote books on bark paper, were masters of mathematics, and constructed buildings on a scale to rival those of Egypt.

After the decline of the Mayas, another somewhat similar civilization developed in Mexico. This was that of the Aztecs whose capital at Tenochtitlan built on islands in Lake Tetzcoco was by the middle of the fifteenth century a magnificent city of stone courts and stairways, temples and pyramids, marred by the ferociously cruel religious rites that took place there, involving human sacrifices, torture, flaying, and the tearing out of hearts from living bodies: as many as twenty thousand victims are believed to have been sacrificed to the insatiable gods when the largest of Tenochtitlan's temples was dedicated. Human sacrifices, though on a far less horrifying scale, also took place in the empire of America's other great civilization, that of the Incas.

7

Cuzco
in the Days of the Incas
1300–1533

Sailing down the Pacific coast of the Americas in 1526 a party of Spanish explorers caught sight of a large ship, the first of its kind they had come across in the whole of the new world. 'The keel and bottom were made of reed stems as thick as posts, lashed together with a fibre resembling hemp,' one of them reported. 'It has slender masts and yards of wood, well-cut cotton sails, of much the same design as those in our ships, excellent rigging and stone anchors.' The ship's cargo, however, was even more intriguing than its construction or the fine cloth, embroidered with birds, in which its crew were arrayed. Stowed on raised platforms were 'many personal ornaments of gold and silver, crowns, diadems, belts and bracelets; armour ... rubies in strings and clusters ... beaded bags of emeralds, chalcedonies, crystal and amber ... mounted mirrors, cups and other drinking vessels. There were quantities of woollen and cotton mantles ... and other garments lavishly embroidered with designs of animals, birds, trees and fish, in scarlet, purple, blue and yellow ... They had little weights for weighing gold ... The ship was loaded with these goods.'

The Spaniards took the ship, captured the crew of thirty men, put most of them ashore, detaining three to act as interpreters, and soon afterwards sailed down the uncharted coast to the Gulf of Guayaquil, stepping ashore at a neat and prosperous city known as Tumbes where they 'saw further wonders which persuaded them they had come upon the borders of a civilization of untold riches', the outskirts of the empire of the Incas.

The Inca fortress of Sacsahuaman, overlooking Cuzco.

The leader of the expedition was Francisco Pizarro, an able, tough, illiterate, vindictive and silent man who for several years had been mayor and magistrate of the newly-founded town of Panama. Born in Spain in about 1475, the illegitimate child of a girl from a poor family in Trujillo, he had been brought up by grandparents and seems as a boy to have worked as a swineherd. He had gone out to Hispaniola with the governor of the colony in 1502 and had subsequently taken part in various expeditions of discovery into the *terra incognita* of the South American continent.

Convinced by what he had already discovered that the land of the Incas in what he called Peru – presumably after a corruption of the name of a coastal river, the Viru – was more excitingly promising than any others he had seen, he sent to Panama for reinforcements. His request was refused; but, determined to continue with his explorations, he decided to approach the Emperor, Charles V, himself. He sailed from Panama in the spring of 1528 and reached Spain that summer.

Also at the Spanish court at this time was Hernán Cortés; and the Emperor, stirred by his stories of the conquest of Mexico, was eager for further triumphs. He listened to Pizarro's descriptions of prosperous townships and gold-filled temples, of a thriving culture and mineral wealth beneath the snow-capped peaks of the Andes and was convinced. He appointed Pizarro governor of the province of New Castile for a distance of two hundred leagues along the coast south of Panama and granted him the powers and authority of a viceroy with a *capitulación* empowering him to conquer 'Peru' for the Spanish crown. So, having filled three ships with stores, Pizarro sailed back across the Atlantic to the Americas with 180 men, including his cousin and three half-brothers.

It was a small enough force to conquer an empire, and it was smaller still by ten men when, in September 1532, it set out down the coast for Cajamarca to confront Atahualpa, the ruler of the Incas. But it was well equipped with splendid steel swords and lances, firearms and armour, and some sixty of the men had horses, animals which most Incas had never seen.

The small company moved slowly south, unopposed past silent Inca watchtowers until in the middle of November, Cajamarca was reached. It was a handsome town of grey stone houses, each 'with its fountain of water in an open court'. The Spaniards occupied several of the deserted buildings that surrounded the large central plaza and, while the rain poured on to the thatched roofs, waited for Atahualpa to come out to meet them. After a long delay the Inca appeared, 'a man of thirty years of age, good-looking, somewhat stout,' in the words of Pizarro's secretary, 'with a fine face, handsome and fierce, the eyes bloodshot. He spoke with much dignity, like a great lord. He talked with good arguments and reasoned well . . . He was cheerful; but when he spoke to his subjects, he was very haughty and showed no sign of pleasure.'

The supreme master of his people, Atahualpa was the last of a line of rulers that stretched back to the beginning of the thirteenth century. According to Inca legend, the founder of the empire was Manco Capac, a child of the sun, who had been set down with his sister on an island in Lake Titicaca. He had been given a rod of gold and been told to settle wherever the rod became embedded in the earth. He had journeyed into the broad, high valley of Cuzco; there the rod was pulled from his grasp; and there, accordingly, he built the city from which he was to rule as Inca, or Emperor, over a people know also as Incas, the dominant tribe of the region. Descended from those migrant hunters of mongoloid race who had arrived on the American continent in about 2500 BC, the hunters had reached the Andes by 9000 BC; and one of their tribes had settled in Peru where it had developed those institutions which distinguished the Incas from the other Indian tribes of America.

The Incas were an orderly people, subservient to their masters who frequently led armies to war upon neighbouring tribes, subjecting them to the same despotism to which the common people of Inca stock were reduced, imposing upon them Inca officialdom and taxation, making Quechua the common language, sun worship the common religion, and uprooting and resetting whole populations if they proved troublesome. By defeating the tribe of the Chancas, the ninth Inca, Pachacuti Inca Yupanqui, dramatically increased the Empire which, further extended by his successor, Topa Inca Yupanqui, eventually extended over the whole of Peru, parts of Bolivia and

The Inspector of Bridges from a series of sixteenth-century drawings of Inca life by Felipe Guáman de Poma.

Quipu-Man, the Grand Treasurer, Keeper of Accounts by Felipe Guamán de Poma. He carries a quipa *made from knotted string, which was used for counting.*

Ecuador, and most of Chile, an area of nearly four hundred thousand square miles.

The authority of the Inca was maintained over these vast dominions by a supremely efficient system of communications. The roads that extended all over the Empire were equipped with markers at distances of four and a half miles from each other, with rest houses or relay posts at every twelve miles or so, and with houses for the runners who, covering 150 miles a day, carried both verbal messages and, since the Incas had no written language, despatches contained in a complicated code of knots in coloured cords. Over mountainous country special stairways were constructed for the Incas' pack-animals, the llamas; and over gorges and rivers bridges were built with tree trunks and rope cables which were renewed every year. 'From one side of the river to the other there are cables made of reeds but as thick as a man's thigh,' wrote a notary in Pizarro's expedi-

tion. 'Smaller cords are interwoven between the cables, and great stones are fastened beneath to steady them. By one of the bridges the common people cross over and a porter is there to receive payment for transit. By another beside it, lords and captains cross; but this is always closed except for them.'

Throughout the Empire such class distinctions were rigidly observed. At the head of the pyramidal social hierarchy was the Inca himself who exercised absolute jurisdiction over all his people. Following the example of Manco Capac, offspring of the sun, Incas married their own sisters and had children by them. They also maintained a large harem which, according to the Spanish soldier and historian Cieza de León, who lived in Peru for fifteen years in the middle of the sixteenth century, numbered at least seven hundred concubines. They were known as the Virgins of the

Sun and were selected for service at puberty from among the most beautiful of the daughters of aristocratic families. Attended by other virgins, they lived in a convent near the Temple of the Sun and were served their food on dishes of gold or silver. 'They also had the privileges of a garden of precious metals,' wrote another sixteenth-century Spanish chronicler, Garcilaso de la Vega, whose mother was an Inca princess. 'But if one of the virgins transgressed her vow of chastity she was buried alive and her accomplice hanged, together with his wife, children and servants.'

The virgins spent much of their time spinning and weaving clothes for the Inca, for his sister and queen, the Coya, and for use in sacrifices at the Temple of the Sun. 'When the Inca wished to possess one of these women,' Garcilaso continued, 'she was brought to wherever he happened to be. Those who had once had relations with the sun could not go back into the convent. They were brought to the royal palace, where they served as royal attendants or ladies in waiting to the Coya, until the day they were sent home to their provinces, richly endowed with land and other benefits.'

Spanish soldiers with pipe and drum decorating an Inca-style lacquered kero *or jar of the colonial period.*

Their male children, on growing up, would take part in the government of the Empire, assisted by the chief men of conquered tribes who had shown themselves worthy of honour. A Supreme Council of these men, consisting of the governors and prefects (*apus*) of the four areas into which the Empire was divided, was presided over by the Inca whose decision was law. Below the *apus* in rank came the *curacas*, native rulers in the provinces, then the *camayocs* or leaders of local districts. And at the bottom of the pyramid, toiling to support the weight of this officialdom, were the peasant householders whose life was severely regimented so that the requirements of the state were met. They had few possessions, were denied all those luxuries which were reserved for the members of the ruling caste, and permitted the one privilege of being provided for from the Inca's stores when they were too old or became too disabled to work. Theirs was a rich land with great resources of gold and silver, of copper and livestock, of abundant cereals, principally maize, and of at least 220 varieties of potato. But they enjoyed little profit from its riches.

They were organized into village groupings known as *ayllus* in which the land was taken over in the name of the people by the Inca who, having divided it into three, gave one part to the Sun so that priests and temples would be maintained and the victims of drought and pestilence provided for. The Inca kept a second part for himself so that he could maintain the court, government and army; while the third part was assigned to the *ayllu* whose people paid for it by farming the other two parts as well.

They worked in groups of ten, singing rhythmic songs in praise of the deity when farming the Sun's land, and songs of imperial praise when labouring on those of the Inca. Their own land was divided up into holdings whose size depended upon the number of mouths in the families to which they were allocated. On these holdings their primitive homes were built, adobe huts, usually of no more than one windowless room, covered with a thatched roof. Here they passed their simple lives, dressed in the cloth which the women wove, eating maize, potatoes and the dried meat of the llama, drinking *chica*, the fermented juice of maize, occasionally chewing coca leaves as a stimulant, obeying the laws and customs of the state and being punished if they transgressed them. Punishments seem to have been severe and summary. Prisons were rare, and were mainly used for executions and beatings; but they were extremely unpleasant, their dungeons being filled with snakes. Capital punishment, on the other hand, was common.

The children of the peasants were from birth taught to accept silently the rigours of their life. Washed in cold water, they were kept tightly bound in swaddling clothes until they were four months old. Their mothers leaned over them to feed them, dangling their breasts over their mouths, never holding them. When they were old enough to crawl they were placed in holes dug in the ground as deep as the child's chest and, at feeding time, they were lifted out to make their own way to the kneeling mother. The mothers themselves thought nothing of giving birth beside a river, washing themselves afterwards in the running water, then going back to work as though little out of the way had happened. They had to reconcile themselves to the knowledge that their child might one day be required for sacrifice.

Sacrificial offerings were usually llamas, white llamas for the Sun, brown for Virachoco, the Invisible God, and piebald for the God of Thunder. But occasionally a peasant family was called upon to supply young children for human sacrifices on special feast days or in the ceremonies attendant upon the enthronement of a new Inca when two hundred children were customarily sacrificed, among them girls from the convents where daughters of good families were educated to serve as assistants or concubines in the households of public officials. Occasionally children were buried alive with golden vessels, powdered sea shells and llamas; and, at the death of an Inca, when some of his favourite women and most trusted servants were expected to offer themselves for voluntary immolation – and were first made drunk and strangled – further sacrificial children were required.

Ceremonies formed an important part in the life of the Incas and were held to mark all manner of occasions from those connected with the growth of crops to the puberty rituals held for the sons of the nobility which included athletic competitions, singing, dancing, recitation and much drinking of *chica* as well as sacrifices. During the national festivities of the feast of Raymi, held at the period of the summer solstice, there was a general fast for three days before the appointed day when the Inca and his court, followed by the whole population of Cuzco, the capital city of the Incas, assembled at early dawn in the great square to greet the rising of the sun. 'They were dressed in their gayest apparel, and the Indian lords vied with each other in the display of costly ornaments and jewels on their persons,' wrote William H. Prescott in his classic *History of the Conquest of Peru*. 'Canopies of gaudy feather-work and richly-tinted stuffs, borne by the attendants over their heads, gave to the great square, and the streets that emptied into it, the appearance of being spread over with one vast and magnificent awning. Eagerly they watched the coming of their deity, and no sooner did his first yellow rays strike the turrets and loftiest buildings of the capital than a shout of gratulation broke forth from the assembled multitude, accompanied by songs of triumph and the wild melody of barbaric instruments, that swelled louder and louder as his bright orb, rising above the mountain-range to the east, shone in full splendour on his votaries . . .

'The sacrifice usually offered was that of the llama; and the priest, after opening the body of his victim, sought in the appearances which it exhibited to read the lesson of the mysterious future. If the auguries were unpropitious, a second victim was slaughtered. A fire was then kindled by means of a concave mirror of polished metal, which, collecting the rays of the sun into a focus upon a quantity of dried cotton, speedily set it on fire . . . The sacred flame was then entrusted to the Virgins of the Sun; and if, by any neglect, it was suffered to go out in the course of the year, the event was regarded as a calamity that boded some strange disaster to the monarchy . . . The sacrifice was but the prelude to the slaughter of a great number of llamas, part of the flocks of the Sun, which furnished a banquet not only for the Inca and his court, but for the people, who made amends at these festivals for the frugal fare to which they were usually condemned.'

As a direct descendant of the Sun, the Inca Atahualpa naturally did not welcome the words of the Spanish friar who thrust a Bible into his hand at Cajamarca with some words about the Christian faith, the one true God and his divine Son who had allowed himself to be sacrificed for the sins of the world. Atahualpa is said to have angrily thrown the Bible to the ground and, pointing to the Sun, to have declared, 'My God still lives!'

As though this were a sign for which they had been waiting, the Spanish soldiers now appeared from the houses around the square in which they had been concealed; and, without warning, both cavalry and infantry fell upon the Inca's retinue, firing their arquebuses and swinging their swords above their heads. They lashed out at the Indians, hacking at skulls and slicing through limbs. Chiefs and attendants alike were slaughtered. Some members of the Inca's unarmed bodyguard attempted to defend their master with their bare hands until they, too, were cut down, while the blood-splashed Inca himself was dragged from his golden litter and hurled to the ground. 'And when the Indians saw their lord lying on the ground a prisoner, and themselves attacked from so many sides and so furiously by the horses they so feared,' wrote Augustin de Zárate, who collected his information from the participants, 'they turned round and began to flee in panic ... running away so fast that they bowled one another over ... The Spanish horsemen continued to chase them till night turned them back ... and the morning after Atahualpa's capture they went to pillage his camp, and were amazed at so many fine gold and silver vessels.'

Atahualpa, evidently surprised that he himself had not been massacred, offered for his release as much gold as would fill a room and more silver than they could carry away. This vast ransom was accordingly collected, the gold plating of the Temple of the Sun being dismantled to make up the amount. The precious objects were melted down and distributed; and Pizarro's men, each of them now as rich as the most prosperous merchants of Seville or Toledo, waited for reinforcements before marching further south. When the newcomers arrived, jealous of the others' riches – and resentful that, having taken no part in the slaughter, they could not share in its consequences – they pressed for the Inca's death. So Pizarro, whose captive was now an encumbrance, ordered his execution without the trial which, described by Prescott, was a subsequent invention. Offered the choice of being burned as a heretic or strangled as a baptized Christian, he chose baptism and was garrotted. His leading general, Chalcuchima, who had brought some of the ransom gold, refused to be baptized and was burned alive, showing 'in the midst of his tortures the characteristic courage of the American Indian and dying with his last breath invoking the name of Virachoco, the Supreme Being of the Incas'.

The Spaniards watched the execution, then marched on towards Cuzco; and, on 15 November 1533, they at last reached the walls of the great capital which stood, 'surrounded by high and snowy mountains', at a height of over eleven thousand feet on one of the six great upland basins of the Empire.

It seemed to the conquistadors that the city was so large and beautiful that 'it would be remarkable even in Spain'. 'It is full of palaces,' wrote one of them. 'No poor people live here ... Most of the buildings are of stone, or else faced with stone, but there are also many adobe houses, very well built, arranged in straight streets crossing each other at right angles. All the streets are paved, and each has running water in a stone-lined gutter down the middle.'

The city had been entirely replanned in the 1440s by the ninth Inca, Pachacuti Inca Yupanqui, whose architects, drawn from the ranks of the nobility, had the services of twenty thousand labourers to call upon. The Inca had had the central area of the city laid out in the shape of a puma with the great stone fortress of Sacsahuaman in the north, representing the animal's head, and the area in the south, where the botanical gardens lay, forming its tail. The body of the puma was the huge central plaza, the Huacapata, the Holy Place, where the Empire's most important ceremonies and sacrifices were held and where every day before sunrise a fire was lit and food thrown into it for the Sun's sustenance and appeasement.

Out of the Huacapata plaza four roads led diagonally to the four quarters into which the city, like the Empire, was divided. And adjoining the plaza was another ceremonial square, the Cusipata, the Place of Joy, reached by steps and paved by pebbles, in which social gatherings took place. In every quarter there were fine palaces of dressed and painted stone, the monolithic polygonal

Atahualpa in his litter meets Pizarro and the Spanish priest Valnerde at Cajamarca, from Francisco Xeres's Narration of the Conquest of Peru, *1534.*

⁖ Verdadera relacion de la conquista del Peru

y prouincia del Cuzco llamada la nueua Castilla: Conquistada por el magnifico
y esforçado cauallero Francisco piçarro hijo del capitan Gonçalo piçarro caua
llero de la ciudad de Trugillo: como capitan general de la cesarea y catholica
magestad ol emperador y rey nro señor: Embiada a su magestad por Francisco
de Xerez natural de la muy noble y muy leal ciudad de Seuilla secretario del
sobredicho señor en todas las puincias y conquista de la nueua Castilla y vno
de los primeros conquistadores della. ⁖ ⁖ ⁖ ⁖ ⁖ ⁖ ⁖ ⁖ ⁖
C Fue vista y examinada esta obra por mandado de los señores inquisidores
del arçobispado de Seuilla: z impressa en casa de Bartholome perez en el mes
de Julio. Año del parto virginal mil z quinientos y treynta y quatro. ⁖ ⁖

✠   ✠   ✠

ABOVE Inca Life: *modern mural by the Peruvian artist Salamon at Cuzco University. The Inca, with fringed headdress and golden earrings, holds out his hands to his people in a protective embrace.*

OPPOSITE ABOVE *Pisac ruins above the Vilcanota river. The road to Cuzco is in the background.*

OPPOSITE BELOW *The fortress of Sacsahuaman, with its massive walls, trapezoidal openings and stone steps.*

blocks being precisely shaped with stone hammers and having as many as thirty-two angles. Some palaces had been built for noble families, others for the Inca and his numerous attendants; many were up to forty feet high. By the principal doorway of the Inca Atahualpa's palace two thousand soldiers stood on guard, while beside an inner door were 'a hundred captains, well experienced in battle'. A courtyard beyond this led to the Inca's private apartments. 'This was full of delights: there were many kinds of trees and gardens, and the dwellings were very spacious and worked and adorned with much gold and carved engravings of the figures and exploits of the Inca's ancestors ... At intervals there were niches and windows worked with silver and inset with precious stones.'

As well as private reception rooms ornamented with gold and silver, this and the other imperial palaces had reception halls which could hold as many as three thousand people, bathing-rooms with immense gold or silver basins, and fountains from which water flowed into stone channels. Beyond the bathing rooms were gardens; and here, so Garcilaso said, 'were planted the finest trees and most beautiful flowers and sweet smelling herbs, while quantities of others were reproduced in gold and silver ... There were also all kinds of gold and silver animals in these gardens, rabbits, mice, lizards, snakes, butterflies, foxes and wild cats. There were birds set in the trees and others bent over the flowers, breathing in their nectar. There were golden deer, pumas and jaguars and all animals in creation, each placed just where it should be'.

Within the palaces, as in the lesser houses, there was little furniture, a few stools, a chest or two perhaps, but not much more. There were stone pegs for hanging clothes and niches in the walls to serve as cupboards; piles of blankets were placed on the floor to serve as seats and beds. A new palace was built for each new Inca and furnished with objects specially made for him. In his presence-chamber visitors granted the honour of an audience approached with lowered eyes the screen behind which he sat, the sandals removed from their feet. They stood with their backs to him, bowing before speaking. Atahualpa himself had spoken to no one directly, addressing remarks to his visitors through his brother.

When his business was done, the Inca was served with food by his concubines who placed

Silver figure of an Inca orejon. *His enormously stretched ear-lobes are a sign of his rank.*

the gold dishes before him on rush matting. When Atahualpa had indicated the dish of his choice, one of the women would hold it up for him and he would dip into it with his fingers. If he hawked a woman held out her hand and he would spit into it. If a hair fell from his head, a woman would pick it up and eat it so that it did not fall into the hands of an enemy who might bewitch him with it.

The Inca was distinguished from the other great men at his court by the designs on his clothes, the multi-coloured braid which was wound round his head, and the *borla*, the royal fringe of red vicuña wool tassels which, issuing from small gold tubes, fell across his forehead. His ears were pierced, and in the holes of the stretched lobes were fitted gold plugs of the largest possible size. These were also worn by the officials of the blood royal at his court, the *orejones*, 'the big-eared ones', 'Incas by privilege'.

North of the royal palace, looming over the lower town, was the magnificent fortress of Sac-sahuaman whose immense, perfectly fitting monolithic blocks, some of them weighing nearly three hundred tons, centuries of earthquakes have not managed to dislodge. 'It has big embrasures looking over the city which makes its appearance more impressive still,' wrote Pizarro's secretary. 'And there are so many towers and other buildings that one could not inspect them all in a day . . . The stones are expertly cut, as smooth as planed boards, and so well fitted together that the joints can hardly be seen . . . Many Spaniards who have travelled in Lombardy and other foreign countries say that they have seen no building equal to this fortress, and no stronger castle. It could hold a garrison of five thousand . . . and could neither be breached by gunfire, nor sapped from below, because it is built on solid rock.'

Here amid these massive ruins can still be seen the throne upon which the Inca sat while reviewing his troops, broad steps leading up to it from either side, and the deep grooves carved in the rock down which at the time of festivals flowed the *chica*, made by the Virgins of the Sun who chewed its ingredients to a pulp which they spat out into jugs of warm water.

The Temple of the Sun, the Coricancha, was, before its spoliation by the *conquistadors*, decorated inside and out with plates of gold and silver. At the eastern end was a huge golden plate representing the sun 'and ranged beneath it in royal robes and seated in golden chairs, the dessicated – some say embalmed – bodies of the Inca rulers; the body of Huayna Capac, as the greatest of the line, being alone honoured with a place in front of the symbol'. Around the principal shrine were smaller sanctuaries dedicated to lesser deities, and nearby were the Intipampa, the Field of the Sun, an enclosure for sacrificial animals, and the Garden of the Sun, in which not only were cobs of maize represented in gold and their leaves in silver, but lumps of gold were scattered about like pebbles and twenty life-sized golden llamas were tended by a golden shepherd.

Fragments of the Temple of the Sun are still to be seen in Cuzco; and in almost every street in the middle of the city there remain parts of Inca walls, doorways, and protruding corbels, mementoes of a civilization that never recovered from the shock of the Spanish conquest.

Having entered Cuzco and accumulated further stores of gold and silver on the way, Pizarro's troops had a nephew of Atahualpa, named Manco, crowned with the *borla* as a puppet emperor, and declared the Inca capital to be a Spanish settlement. But their wayward and often savage rule, their profligate appropriation of Inca stocks and treasures, aroused the hatred of the Indians. Manco left the city to join the insurgents; and for six months the Spanish garrison in Cuzco was

A sixteenth-century drawing by Felipe Guamán de Poma, showing Cuzco framed by an Inca and a Spaniard.

besieged and would have been overwhelmed had it not been for the impregnable fortress of Sacsahuaman. But at length the revolt petered out; Manco was stabbed in the back by a treacherous Spaniard; and in time Cuzco became a characteristic Spanish colonial town. The walls of the Temple of the Sun now support the church and convent of Santo Domingo.

While the Incas held sway over 400,000 square miles in America, the 131,000 square miles of what is now Italy was a collection of states, usually in rivalry and often at war with each other. The word Italy itself, so Metternich was to say in 1849, was 'ein geographischer Begriff', a mere geographical expression. Since the beginning of the fourteenth century Milan had been ruled by the Visconti, who had made themselves supreme lords of the city, and subsequently by Francesco Sforza, a ruthless general who had married the illegitimate daugher of a Visconti. The Papal States, an assortment of petty tyrannies sprawling across the peninsula from Rome to the Adriatic, were nominally in the hands of the Church but actually in a condition indistinguishable from anarchy. The Este family ruled in Modena as well as in Ferrara, the Montefeltro in Urbino. The large kingdom of Naples and Sicily was claimed by both the Houses of Anjou and Aragon. Sienna was entering a period of economic stagnation. In Genoa, Simone Boccanegra had become the first doge in 1339, but his successors had been unable to bring order to the city, and since then it had been forced to submit to foreign rule either by the Milanese or the French. Venice was an independent republic where nobles, many of them effete, played a part in public life which would have been quite unacceptable in Florence. Indeed, the Florentines, who also lived in a republic, prided themselves on having a constitution and a government wholly superior to any other to be found in the peninsula.

8

Florence
in the Days of
the Medici
1389–1492

In his moving memoir of his friend, Michelangelo, Giorgio Vasari, the architect and art
historian, wrote that when 'the benign ruler of
heaven graciously looked down to earth' and 'saw
the worthlessness of what was being done,' He
'resolved to save us from our errors and send into
the world an artist who would be skilled in each
and every craft ... God also saw that in the
practice of painting, sculpture and architecture,
the Tuscan genius had always been pre-eminent,
for the Tuscans have devoted to all the various
branches of art more labour and study than all the
other Italian peoples. And therefore He chose to
have Michelangelo born a Florentine, so that one
of her own citizens might bring to absolute
perfection the achievements for which Florence
was already justly celebrated.'

Certainly, at the time of Michelangelo's birth in
1475 the Florentine artistic tradition was renowned throughout the civilized world, and his
own art was to prove its culmination. Already
Dante, Petrarch and Boccaccio had combined to
ensure that Tuscan had been accepted as the
literary language of Italy. Cimabue, whom Dante
considered the greatest of Italian painters, had
spent much of his working life in Florence.
Giotto, who may have been Cimabue's pupil, had
died there in 1337, having provided the city's
churches with exquisite frescoes and, as
capomaestro or surveyor to the Cathedral of Santa
Maria del Fiore, begun the lovely campanile
which still stands beside it. Brunelleschi, who also
died in Florence in 1446, had given it several of its

The Cathedral of Santa Maria del Fiore, Florence.

View of Florence : engraving of 1470.

finest buildings and had performed what had been considered the impossible task of designing the Cathedral's dome. Donatello, the greatest sculptor of the fifteenth century, was the son of a Florentine wool carder. Masaccio, who had come to Florence in 1417, had worked with Masolino in Santa Maria del Carmine and had created there those supreme masterpieces of Renaissance art, the frescoes in the Brancacci chapel, which were completed by Filippino Lippi, yet another Florentine.

While these and other great artists of the Quattrocento were at work in Florence, bringing the Renaissance into flower, Rome, long since fallen from its former splendour, was little more than a provincial town. The popes had deserted it in 1308 for Avignon, and after Gregory XI's return some seventy years later, visitors and pilgrims described a city which was 'a mere shadow of its former self,' a 'rubbish heap of history'. Its population had shrunk to less than forty thousand, no more than a twentieth of its size in the time of Nero, while the population of Florence, a far more prosperous and powerful city, had grown to almost fifty thousand, though it was impossible to be sure of the exact number, births being recorded by the haphazard method of dropping beans into a box, a black bean for a boy, a white one for a girl.

Florence was not the biggest city in Italy – Venice, Milan and Naples were all larger – but its population was greater than that of most other European towns, with the notable exception of Paris, and richer perhaps than all. Entering it through one of its eleven gates, the visitor was immediately struck by its air of prosperity, the sense, as one traveller put it, 'of a city in which much money was to be made and many were making it'. It was a city of busy, narrow, twisting streets, of squares and towers, of fortress-like palaces with massive stone walls and overhanging balconies, of churches whose façades were covered with geometrical patterns in black and white and green and pink, of abbeys and convents, nunneries and crowded tenements, all enclosed by a high brick and stone crenellated wall beyond which the countryside stretched to the green surrounding hills. Riding down towards the Porta di Fiesole or the Porta San Giorgio, the traveller would see rising above the tiled roofs, a cluster of splended campanili. Among these bell towers were those of the Dominican church and monastery of Santa Maria Novella, of the Palazzo della Signoria, seat of the city's government, and of the Bargello, then known as the Palazzo del Podestà which, as well as being a prison, was the headquarters of the foreigner, usually of noble birth, who served the city as a kind of Lord Chief Justice.

Inside the city four fine stone bridges crossed the Arno. These were the Ponte alla Carraia, named after one of the city's ancient gates; the Rubaconte, which had been built in 1237 by a Milanese *Podestà* or municipal magistrate, and was later to be known as the Ponte alle Grazie; the

Ponte Santa Trinità, which was of the twelfth century and on which stood a small hospice for monks; and the Ponte Vecchio, rebuilt in 1345, wider than the others, and covered with shops and houses from bank to bank. The Via Calimala which led to the Ponte Vecchio was, like the other main streets in Florence, paved with flagstones and flanked by footpaths and gutters which carried rainwater down to the river. The streets were therefore clean and dry, so the city's early-sixteenth-century historian, Benedetto Varchi, proudly claimed, quite free from the mud and slime to be encountered elsewhere in Italy in the winter. On the other hand, as Varchi reluctantly admitted, in the summer the flagstones sometimes became so hot that it was uncomfortable to stand on them and it was possible to keep cool in the afternoons only by staying indoors.

The city was divided into four *quartieri*, those of Santo Spirito, Santa Croce, Santa Maria Novella and San Giovanni; and each of these was divided into four wards which were known and distinguished by the emblems emblazoned on their banners, such as the Dragon, the Golden Lion, the Unicorn and the Viper. In a majority of these wards the most commonly encountered workshops were those in which undressed cloth imported from England, France and Flanders was fulled, pressed, smoothed, cut and dyed, in which Spanish, Portuguese and English wool was combed, carded and spun, native silk manufactured, tapestries woven and furs dressed and stitched. Examples of the products of these workshops could be seen in the Mercato Vecchio, the busiest place in Florence, its site now covered by the Piazza della Republica. In this large square, one of the fifty or so within the walls, were the shops of the drapers and clothes dealers, the houses of the stationers and feather merchants and the premises of the candle-makers where, in rooms smoky with incense to smother the smell of wax, prostitutes entertained their customers. The stalls of butchers and fishmongers, of poulterers and greengrocers were placed here too; here also, out in the open, barbers shaved beards and clipped hair; tailors stitched cloth in shaded doorways; and bakers pushed platters of dough into the communal oven. Children played dice on the flagstones and animals roamed everywhere: dogs wearing silver collars; geese and pigs rooting about in doorways; occasionally even a deer or a chamois would come down from the hills and clatter through the square.

On holidays there were dances in the Mercato Vecchio, mock battles in the Piazza Santa Croce, water displays beneath the Ponte Vecchio, while the Piazza della Signoria would be turned into a hunting field with wild animals running from side to side, boars goaded by lances, and the Commune's lions, brought out of their cage behind the Palazzo and incited – with rare success – to set upon dogs.

Thanks to the statutes of the various trade guilds there were no more than about 275 working days a year, so that the people had plenty of opportunity to enjoy themselves. They did so never more happily than on the festival of *Calendimaggio*, May Day – when the young men hung flowering shrubs on the doors of their sweethearts' houses, while girls danced to the music of flutes in the Piazza Santa Trinità – and on the festival of St John the Baptist, patron of the city, when the shops were decorated with streamers and banners, when riderless horses with spiked iron balls hanging at their sides to act as spurs raced wildly from Porta al Prato to Porta alla Croce, when processions of priests, choristers and citizens escorted the Cathedral's holy relics from church to church, when the Piazza del Duomo was covered with blue canopies, decorated with silver stars, and when gilded models of castles, symbolizing the towns that were subject to Florence, were paraded on wagons from house to house.

In Dante's time, the interiors of most houses in Florence, even of the rich, had been remarkably unassuming. Whitewashed walls were often quite bare, being decorated with tapestries only on special occasions; floors were also bare, their polished stone surfaces rarely covered with any material other than reed matting; the window apertures were generally fitted with shutters and covered with oiled cotton or paper; there were few fireplaces, families keeping out the cold on winter nights with warming pans and those earthenware jars of hot charcoal known as *scaldini* which were passed from hand to hand. There was little furniture other than plain wooden tables, benches, stools, chests, the most uninviting beds and the sideboards in which the family silver was kept. By the time of Michelangelo's birth, however, the Florentines had become noticeably more

The Ponte Vecchio as it is today.

self-indulgent. Their rooms were now likely to be carpeted, their windows glazed and curtained, their walls hung with tapestries, religious pictures and looking-glasses, their furniture painted and decorated with marquetry, their beds canopied, surrounded by footboards and large enough for four people or even more to sleep in them side by side, lying naked between linen sheets.

The clothes they wore in the daytime were also far less simple than they had been in the early fourteenth century. Over their trunk hose and jacket, merchants and craftsmen still wore the *lucco*, the long, ankle-length gown of dark-coloured cloth with long, wide sleeves, a hood attached to the neck and buttons down the front like a cassock. But, despite sumptuary laws, young men now appeared in far brighter colours, in satin and velvet, with white stockings shot with silver lace, in pink and red velvet caps with feathers stuck through the brim, wearing golden rings and necklaces, scented gloves, jewelled daggers and damascened swords. Wealthy Florentine women, renowned for their elegance, wore equally sumptuous clothes, their silk and velvet dresses sparkling with jewels and silver buttons, their winter suits heavy with damask and thick fur. Since a white complexion and fair hair were so much admired, they bleached and powdered skins which were unfashionably swarthy, dyed dark hair or covered it with wigs of white or yellow silk. They washed their hands in milk and kept them soft and smooth by leaving their housework to slaves, Greek and Russian girls, Turks, Circassians or Tartars, bought quite cheaply in the markets of Venice and Genoa.

The sumptuary laws which applied to food were as flagrantly disregarded as those intended to check flamboyance in dress. The dinner guests of a rich merchant might first be offered melon, then some kind of pasta, ravioli perhaps or lasagne, then a piece of the rich cake known as *berlingozzo*, then a few slices of roast chicken, capon or guinea fowl, followed by spiced veal, thrushes, trout, pigeon, partridge, turtle-dove or peacock. All kinds of fresh vegetables were served with these dishes; then came dishes of rice cooked in sugar of almonds and served with honey, jellies and sweetmeats and *pinocchiato*, a pudding made out of pine kernels. As elsewhere in Europe most dishes were highly flavoured or hotly spiced. Cloves and nutmeg, saffron and cinnamon, ginger, garlic, pepper and lemon juice were all used liberally in cooking, and the red sauce known as *savore sanguino* contained not only raisins, cinnamon and sandal, as well as meat and red wine, but also sumac which is now used only for tanning.

In less affluent households fish and joints of meat were not so often seen; but there was always plenty of garlic-flavoured pasta, liver sausage and black pudding, goat's milk, cheese and fruit; while the poor, though reduced in hard times to a diet of dried figs or bread made from oak bark, very rarely went hungry.

They had done so, however, in 1378 when the lowest class of woollen workers in the city, the *ciompi*, who took their name from the clogs they wore in the wash-houses, rose in revolt, protesting that their wages were scarcely sufficient to keep their families from starvation. Shouting, 'Down with the traitors who allow us to starve!' and demanding the right to form their own trade guilds, a privilege hitherto denied them, they sacked their masters' houses and forced the city's elected officials to flee for their lives. Their demands were met; but the power and money of their employers, combined with the jealousy of their fellow-workers in other trades, soon put an end to their short-lived guilds, and by 1382 the original guilds were once more in undisputed control of the city's government.

There were twenty-one of these guilds, or *arti*, seven major ones and fourteen minor. The most privileged and respected was that of the lawyers, the *Arte dei Giudici e Notai*; next in importance were the three guilds to which the wool, silk, and cloth merchants belonged. The fifth of the major guilds was that of the bankers who were becoming increasingly influential, despite the condemnation of the Church which looked down upon them as usurers. Next came the guild of the doctors, apothecaries and shopkeepers who dealt in medicines, spices and dyes, and of certain artists and craftsmen who bought their colours and their materials from members of the guild and were consequently admitted to its membership. Last of the major guilds was that of the *Arte dei Vaccai e Pelliciai* which cared for the interests of dealers and craftsmen in animal skins and furs.

The fourteen minor *arti* were those of tradesmen who were considered less worthy of esteem, such as masons and joiners, vintners and innkeepers, butchers, bakers and cooks, smiths, armourers and tailors. And below these in the hierarchy of the city were the ordinary workers in the textile and dyeing trades, as well as the carters, porters, boatmen and pedlars who belonged to no guild, were not permitted to form one and, though constituting over three quarters of the population of Florence, had no say in its government.

The marriage of Boccaccio Adimari and Lisa Ricaseli by an unknown fifteenth-century Florentine artist.

Those who did have a say in its government were inordinately proud of the city's constitution, comparing it most favourably with that of other Italian states and claiming that its administration, unlike theirs, was commendably stable, independent and democratic. Power rested with a body known as the *Signoria* whose members, *Priori*, wore fine crimson coats lined with ermine and with ermine collars and cuffs. One of their number was chosen as *Gonfaloniere*, standard bearer of the republic and custodian of the city's banner, a red lily on a white field, an appropriate emblem for Florence whose name was supposed to have been derived from the flowers that grew so plentifully by the banks of the Arno. The *Gonfaloniere* was distinguished from the other *Priori* by the gold stars embroidered on his coat. All of them were elected and obliged to relinquish office after two months when the ceremony of election was repeated, the leather bags containing the names of all those eligible for office being taken from the sacristy of the Church of Santa Croce where they were kept and the required number of names, nine in all, being drawn out of the bags at random. After election the members of the *Signoria* were required to leave home to take up residence in the Palazzo della Signoria where they received only the most modest of salaries but enjoyed the services of a large staff of green-liveried servants, splendid meals provided by excellent cooks, the entertainments provided by a *buffone* who told them funny stories and sang them songs, and the advice not only of elected councils to help them enact legislation and formulate foreign policy but also of permanent officials.

This then seemed an extremely satisfactory form of democratic government; but, in fact, it was highly exclusive. For no names were to be found in the bags other than those of men, aged thirty or over, who were members of one of the city's guilds; and even then these candidates were limited to supporters of one or other of the city's rich merchant families who, by one means or another, contrived to ensure that all potentially troublesome men were denied representation in the councils of the republic as were both the ordinary workers, the *Minuto Popolo*, and the nobles, the *Grandi*.

To the Florentines, noblemen were not considered worthy of high regard. 'One is not born noble,' said Petrarch, 'one becomes noble.' And his fellow-Florentine, Matteo Palmieri, the philospher, wrote, 'The man who seeks glory by reference to his ancestors' virtue exempts himself from personal merit. To give a good example by one's own efforts, not by one's family's, is to merit honour.' Palmieri came from old merchant stock, and for him, as for most other Florentines like him, to be a rich merchant in 'a comely and grand' way of business was the highest honour to which a man could aspire, bringing credit not only upon his family but also upon the republic itself. 'A Florentine who is not a merchant [and who has not acquired] some wealth,' remarked Gregorio Dati, himself one of the city's leading silk merchants, 'is a man who enjoys no esteem whatever.' Others went even further than this: it was the decided opinion of that characteristic Renaissance man, Leon Battista Alberti – philosopher, horse-tamer, fencer, athlete, linguist, mathematician, painter, musician, engineer, cartographer, cryptographer and architect, a member of one of Florence's oldest families of merchant bankers – that no one who was poor would ever 'find it easy to acquire honour and fame', for poverty 'threw virtue into the shadows' and subjected it to a 'hidden and obscure misery'. Riches, however, carried with them obligations. There was first of all, the obligation of service to the state: no one could aspire to high social rank unless he had held honourable public office, unless the name of his family appeared on one of the parchment lists of former *Priori* which had been scrupulously maintained since 1282. Indeed, the immensely rich Niccolò da Uzzano, one of the most respected statesmen in Florence, kept a copy of the lists hanging on the wall of his study so that when he was asked to lend his influence to a man whose name was unfamiliar to him, he could satisfy himself that the man was not a parvenu. The rich merchant also had an obligation not to conceal his wealth nor guard it like a miser. He was expected to possess a fine palazzo in the city and a villa outside it; he must also contribute to the cost of the public buildings of the city; he must be generous with his family and be ready to provide his daughters with handsome dowries; he must be generous, too, with his gifts to charity, his embellishment of the family chapel in his church, his commissions to the artists and benefactions to the scholars who contributed so much to the renown of the city. He should be able to echo when he died the words of Giovanni Rucellai, head of the family whose name was derived from the red dye, the *oricello*, upon which their fortune was based, that he had done himself much more honour 'by having spent money well than by having earned it'.

Such a man was Cosimo de' Medici. He came from a family long resident in the city, several of whose members had been appointed *Gonfaloniere*. The fortunes of the family had been eclipsed when one of Cosimo's forebears had associated himself too closely with the ambitions of the more militant of the *Minuto Popolo* and had been ruined in the reaction that followed upon the riots of the *ciompi*. Cosimo's father, however, the owner of two wool workshops in Florence and a successful banker, had restored the reputation of the family. He had been *Gonfaloniere* in 1421 but was cautious enough not to arouse ancient antagonisms by taking more than the customary interest in political life expected of all men of his rank, being content to remain in the shadows of his counting-house, to enjoy his riches which had been much increased by his wife's dowry and by the exceptionally profitable relationship his bank enjoyed with the Papal Chamber by which the *Curia's* revenues were collected and disbursed. While donating generous sums to public funds and private charities, he had been happy to allow the Albizzi family to exercise control of the government through their friends and nominees in the *Signoria*.

Cosimo himself was of far more ambitious stamp. In obedience to his father's advice and example, however, he never appeared to be so. He walked about the city in sombre clothes, attended by a single servant, politely giving the wall to his elders, showing marked respect towards the city's elected officials. In his early twenties he married the daughter of one of his father's partners, and moved with his wife into her family palace which had formed part of her dowry. And, while his wife bore him children and her palace was gradually decorated with his own family's insignia – the red balls on a field of gold, representing perhaps the pills of the doctors from whom the Medici, as their name implied, were believed to be descended – Cosimo worked conscientiously and with flair in helping his father turn the bank into one of the most profitable family businesses in Europe.

Portrait of Cosimo de' Medici by Jacopo Pontormo.

For a time Cosimo's success aroused little jealously in Florence. But the Albizzi and their friends deeply distrusted him and began to spread rumours to his discredit: it was said that his polite and accommodating manner disguised a determination to usurp the constitutional government of the city, that the numerous benefactions of the Medici were fraudulent, that they were intent merely upon the glorification of their family: when Cosimo endowed a monastery, did he not emblazon 'even the monk's privies with his balls?' Eventually with the help of a *Gonfaloniere* whose debts he paid, the haughty and envious head of the Albizzi family, Rinaldo di Messer Maso, arranged for Cosimo's arrest and imprisonment in a cramped cell in the belltower of the Palazzo della Signoria.

Rinaldo would have had his rival executed; but Cosimo had many friends and supporters. The Marquis of Ferrara, a customer of the Medici bank, intervened on his behalf. So did the Venetian Republic which was also financially indebted to him. So, too, did the Vicar-General of the Camaldolite Order, the representative of an even more influential customer, the Pope. Cosimo could also call on the support of the *Minuto Popolo* – who were grateful to his house for past favours – and upon several powerful families in Florence with whom the Medici were associated in business undertakings or who were indebted to them for loans or gifts or linked by marriage. Moreover, Cosimo was a cultured man with a humanist's respect for classical learning and ideals and a wide knowledge of classical manuscripts of which he was an avid collector: consequently he had many close friends among the distinguished humanists

Brunelleschi and Ghiberti presenting a model of the Church of San Lorenzo to Cosimo de' Medici, by Giorgio Vasari.

in the city whom the reactionary and priggish Rinaldo degli Albizzi condemned as enemies of the Christian faith. Above all, Cosimo had unlimited supplies of money for the payment of bribes. He bribed his guards; he bribed wavering families; passed a thousand florins to the impecunious *Gonfaloniere*, a silly fellow, Cosimo later commented, for he could have had ten thousand if he had asked for them. Thus it was that by the time Rinaldo heard that a large force of mercenaries under the *condottiere*, their captain Niccolò da Tolentinò, had been raised by Medici adherents, he felt unable to deal with Cosimo as effectively as he had once intended. He had to content himself with having the Medici declared *Grandi*, and thus for ever excluded from the

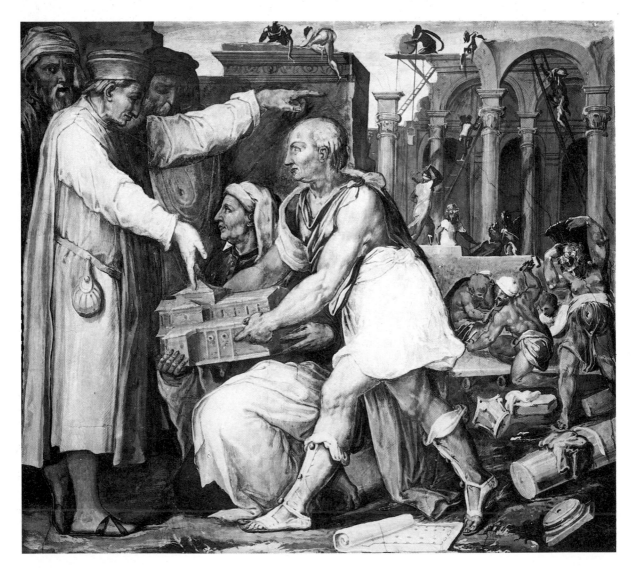

public life of Florence, and with sentencing Cosimo to ten years' exile in Padua. Thankful to escape from his uncomfortable cell, Cosimo rode by night under escort through the Porta San Gallo and made his way to Padua by way of Ferrara in 1433.

He did not remain in exile for long. His money, his friends, and the Pope proved too powerful a combination for the Albizzi to resist: and in October 1434 Cosimo returned to the city from which his enemies themselves were now banished. Thereafter by degrees, stealthily and unobtrusively, Cosimo became, in fact if not in name, the ruler of Florence. Taking care not to offend the susceptibilities of the guilds, avoiding all ostentation, riding a mule instead of a horse, repeatedly reminding his family that 'envy is a weed that should not be watered', and, as his friend Vespasiano da Bisticci said, persuading others to take the initiative 'whenever he wished to achieve something', he gradually gained for himself such a position of authority that he was recognized as the undisputed patriarch of Florence, *Pater Patriae*, 'master of the state'. 'Political questions are settled at his house,' wrote his fellow-humanist, Enea Silvio, known as Aeneas Silvius Piccolomini, who became Pope Pius II in 1458. 'The man he chooses holds office . . . He it is who decides peace and war and controls the laws . . . He is king in everything but name.'

He was the most lavish and discriminating patron that Florence had ever had. He paid a large share of the cost of a Statue of St Andrew for the Orsanmichele, Florence's communal granary, which was commissioned from Lorenzo Ghiberti whose bronze doors for the Baptistry were to be described by Michelangelo as 'fit to be the gates of Paradise'. Inside the Baptistry, Cosimo and his father arranged for another great work, the tomb of the Antipope, John XXIII, to be designed by Donatello. He contributed generously to the expense of that masterpiece of the early Renaissance, the Church of San Lorenzo, the family church of the Medici, which was begun in 1421 by Brunelleschi who had also designed the Ospedale degli Innocenti, a hospital for the foundlings of Florence, endowed by Giovanni di Bicci de' Medici. In addition, Cosimo helped to pay for the novices' chapel at Santa Croce, which was created by Michelozzo, as well as the choir of Santissima Annunziata which, begun by Michelozzo, was

Donatello, David, c.*1433.*

completed by Alberti. He contributed large sums towards the cost of the library of the now demolished Church of San Bartolomeo, the Church of San Girolamo del Monte at Fiesole, and the Badia Fiesolana at San Domenico di Fiesole. The year after Brunelleschi had completed the cathedral dome, as much an extraordinary feat of engineering as of architecture, Cosimo provided funds for Michelozzo's reconstruction of the monastery of San Marco whose exacting and ascetic Prior, Antonio Pierozzi, later to become Archbishop of Florence and a saint, was one of his closest friends. And from Michelozzo also, Cosimo commissioned a country villa at Cafaggiolo and a new family palace to be built on the corner of the Via

Botticelli, The Adoration of the Magi *(1482), with portraits of several members of the Medici family. The man on the extreme right is usually taken to be Botticelli himself.*

Larga (now the Via Cavour) and the Via de' Gori. He had originally asked Brunelleschi to provide plans for this building but when he saw them, and the wooden model that came with them, he thought them altogether too splendid and ornate. He liked his buildings to be as quiet, restrained, composed and unemphatic as his way of life; and he turned instead to the younger architect, a decision which so enraged the touchy and cantankerous Brunelleschi that he smashed his model 'into a thousand pieces'. But Cosimo's faith in Michelozzo was well justified. The Medici Palace was a fine building, the first in Florence to combine the delicacy of early Italian Gothic with the calm, considered stateliness of classic taste.

Inside its courtyard were placed two masterpieces of sculpture, *Judith Slaying Holofernes,* which now stands in front of the Palazzo della Signoria, and the astonishingly beautiful *David,*

the first free-standing figure cast in bronze since classical times, now in the Bargello. Both these were commissioned from Donatello, an unworldly, dishevelled artist for whom Cosimo assumed a kind of paternal responsibility. Cosimo was also more than a patron to both the saintly Giovanni da Fiesole, known as Fra Angelico – whom he evidently commissioned to paint the lovely frescoes in the chapter-house, cloisters and corridors of San Marco – and to Fra Filippo Lippi, a Florentine butcher's son, whose superiors had been profoundly relieved when he had abandoned his vows and left the community of Carmelite friars of Santa Maria del Carmine to whose care he had been entrusted as an orphaned boy. He was a liar, a fraud, a drunkard, and so compulsive a lecher that Cosimo had him locked up in a room at the Medici Palace to prevent him abandoning his work when seized by one of his periodic bouts of unassuageable lust. Lippi escaped, however, by cutting up the coverings of a bed and using them as a rope to climb out of the window. Having found him and persuaded him to come back, Cosimo was so thankful that 'he resolved in future to keep a hold on him by affection and kindness and to allow him to come and go as he pleased'. And it was while Lippi was living at the Medici Palace that several of his greatest works were produced, including the *Coronation of the Virgin*, now in the Museo dell' Accademia.

After Cosimo's death in 1464, his son Piero became head of the family. Piero was a methodical and considerate man whose chronic ill health had prevented him taking as active a part as he would have liked in either the business of the bank or the affairs of Florence. It was not expected that he would be capable of assuming his father's responsibilities, and there were families enough in the city prepared to ensure that he was not given the opportunity of doing so, among them those of the gifted orator, Niccolò Soderini, and of Luca Pitti whose palace on the high ground of the Oltrarno beyond the Ponte Vecchio was then nearing completion. But helped by his brave and talented elder son, Lorenzo, Piero nipped the rebellion of his rivals in the bud. He was soon firmly in control of the government, and ready to continue the family tradition of munificence. He paid for splendid tabernacles for the churches of San Miniato al Monte and Santissima Annunziata; he added numerous ancient coins to his father's precious collection; he bought quantities of rare manuscript books for the already famous Medici Library; he gave his patronage to four of the greatest artists of his day, all Florentines, Luca della Robbia, who had finished the beautiful Singing Gallery in the Cathedral in 1428; Antonio di Jacobo Benci, known as Pollaiuolo because his father was a poulterer; Paolo di Dono, whose passion for birds earned him the nickname of Uccello; and Alessandro di Mariano dei Filipepi, known as Botticelli ('little barrel'), who lived at the Medici Palace as one of the family. Piero's study was decorated with della Robbia's reliefs on the walls and his tiles on the floor, 'a new thing and most excellent for summer'. In his bedroom hung three Uccellos; one of them, a picture in three panels of the *Rout of San Romano*, was later divided, one panel going to the Uffizi, another to the Louvre in Paris and the third to the National Gallery in London. Elsewhere in the palace there hung three Pollaiuolos, the two *Labours of Hercules* (now in the Uffizi) and the *Hercules and Antaeus* (in the Bargello).

To celebrate the hospitality of his patrons, Botticelli seems to have introduced likenesses or idealized portraits of the Medici family in several of the pictures which he painted at this time: in his *Madonna of the Magnificat*, for example, in which the two sons of the house appear to have been introduced as angels, and in the *Adoration of the Magi* in which several other members of the family appear. They appear again in the gorgeous frescoes which Benozzo Gozzoli, yet another Florentine, painted for the chapel on the first floor of the Palace, in which can be seen the young Lorenzo, magnificently attired and riding a splendidly caparisoned horse whose trappings are covered with the seven balls of the family's emblem.

Lorenzo, to be known as Il Magnifico, inherited his father's fortune and responsibilities at the age of twenty in 1469 when Piero was buried in the old sacristy of San Lorenzo beneath a porphyry sarcophagus ornamented with acanthus leaves designed by Donatello's most brilliant pupil, Andrea del Verrocchio. Lorenzo was then a tirelessly energetic young man, clever, versatile, strong, ungainly and strikingly ugly. He was vain and intensely competitive, but he was also responsive and affectionate and his companions found the zest which he brought to his every

A scene from a fresco in the Pitti Palace by Ottavio Vannini. Lorenzo de' Medici (centre) *admires a bust of a faun by Michelangelo.*

activity marvellously infectious. He was considered by his family's rivals far too young and inexperienced to be entrusted with much authority in Florence; and once he had offended the Pope, the gruff and intimidating Sixtus IV, by declining to advance money to a grasping papal nephew for the purchase of the strategically placed town of Imola, some of these rivals felt that the time had come to destroy the power of the Medici once and for all. A group of conspirators, including Francesco de' Pazzi, whose bank was the leading rival of the Medici's, met in Rome at the beginning of 1477. It was decided that Lorenzo and his younger brother, Giuliano, should be murdered during Mass one Sunday in the Cathedral of Santa Maria del Fiore. On the appointed day, in a horrifying scene of slaughter,

Giuliano was stabbed to death, but Lorenzo escaped wounded. Francesco de' Pazzi and four of his accomplices were captured and hanged; their bodies were left dangling from the machicolations of the campanile of the Palazzo della Signoria above the heads of the surging mob.

A year later, in 1479, Lorenzo de' Medici was firmly in control of Florence. Although it suited him on occasion to protest that he was 'not *Signore* of Florence but merely a citizen' who had 'to conform to the will of the majority', his wishes were generally carried out when he made known to a council or an official what he wanted done. And when Pope Sixtus IV died in 1484 to be succeeded by the genial Innocent VIII – one of whose several sons was married to Lorenzo's daughter – the influence of Lorenzo and of Lorenzo's Florence in Italian affairs became decisive. Lorenzo, it was said, was 'the needle of the Italian compass'; and, although it is now admitted that his reputation as a master of diplomacy was largely undeserved, and that Italy was not plunged into war rather by good luck than by good management, his standing as a statesman during his lifetime was rarely questioned.

He was not, though, a successful banker. With little taste for business, he gave far too much scope to his branch managers. Excessive loans and general mismanagement led to the closing of one branch after another, until the fortunes of the Medici bank collapsed in the virtual eclipse of Florentine banking, and Lorenzo was reduced to helping himself to money from the public treasury.

With less money to spend than his father and grandfather, Lorenzo did not commission nearly as many sculptures or paintings as they had done. Several of those for which he was responsible have since been destroyed and others, such as Botticelli's two most famous works, *Primavera* and the *Birth of Venus*, until recently supposed to have been commissioned by him, are now known to have been painted for his rich namesake and cousin, Lorenzo di Pierfrancesco de' Medici. But Lorenzo Il Magnifico did open a school in a garden between the family palace and San Marco and it was here that the young, precociously gifted Michelangelo made his first works, 'showing the results of his labours to Lorenzo every day'. Lorenzo also went out of his way to ensure that, if he could not afford to employ them, Florentine artists were never short of other patrons. He found Botticelli, Filippo Lippi and Ghirlandaio work in Rome, sent Antonio Pollaiuolo to Milan, recommended Giuliano da Maiano to the Duke of Calabria, and obtained work for Verrocchio all over Tuscany. He also took a deep interest in an illegitimate twelve-year-old boy who came to work in Verrocchio's workshop from the Tuscan

Lorenzo de' Medici : a polychrome portrait bust in the style of Verrochio.

village of Vinci. Leonardo da Vinci may, indeed, have lived in Lorenzo's household for a time. Certainly when Leonardo decided to spread the wings of his astonishing versatility in Milan, where Duke Lodovico Sforza was looking for an artist to make an equestrian statue of his father, Lorenzo recommended him to the Duke by sending to Milan an example of Leonardo's work, a silver lyre in the shape of a horse's head.

Ten years after Leonardo had arrived in Milan in 1482, Lorenzo died at his villa at Careggi. When he heard the news, his friend Pope Innocent sadly observed, 'The peace of Italy is at an end.' The words proved to be true. The great days of Medicean Florence were also over.

A few years after Lorenzo the Magnificent's death, the future Emperor Charles V was born at Ghent. As a son of Philip I, founder of the Habsburg dynasty in Spain, and as a grandson of Maximilian I, the German King and Holy Roman Emperor, of Mary of Burgundy, and of Isabella I of Castile and Ferdinand II of Aragon, Charles also inherited other huge domains in Europe. Having been proclaimed sovereign of Spain and having assumed rule over the Netherlands at the age of fifteen, he was crowned Holy Roman Emperor in 1519 and King of Germany in 1520. King of Naples as well, and ruler of Spanish America, he became master of Italy by the Peace of Cambrai of 1529. For several years he ruled this vast empire from Spain whose capital then was Toledo.

9

Toledo
in the Days of Philip II and El Greco
1556–1598

From its source in the Sierra de Albarracín the
second longest river of the Iberian peninsula, the
Tagus, flows through the arid region of New
Castile, carving deep gorges in the rocky soil,
before it reaches Portugal to debouch into the
Atlantic Ocean at Lisbon. One of these gorges
almost encircles the city of Toledo which is set
high on a hill of granite, forty-seven miles south of
Madrid. For many centuries this city was supreme in the spiritual and secular life of Spain, one
of the most important historical, strategic and
cultural centres of the peninsula. Both Garcilaso
de la Vega, who was born here in 1503, and
Cervantes use the word *pesadumbre* to describe its
peculiarly solemn character. For Cervantes it was
'the sacred city . . . sorrowful and weighty as rock,
the glory of Spain' and the light of all cities; for
the poet Lope de Vega it was the Rome of the
Iberian peninsula; and for the historian, Gregorio
Marañón, it was a kind of synthesis of all Spain, a
bridge between East and West, a crossroad of
cultures, the sum of six layers of superimposed
civilizations.

The sixteenth-century traveller who approached the city from the south, taking the road
from Ciudad Real and Cordoba across the Montes
de Toledo, would pass by the country estates of
the richer citizens. Known as *cigarrales* after the
cicadas which chirrup on summer nights, these
estates were bounded by adobe walls, the cracks in
their surfaces partially concealed by prickly pear
and agave branches. Inside the walls were areas of

*The Alcantara Bridge with the Alcazar in the
background.*

Philip II in his St Quentin armour by Antonio Moro.

woodland, plantations of mulberry trees for the rearing of silk worms, orchards and gardens planted with almonds and apricots, oranges, lemons and fig trees, with lilies, geraniums, gilly-flowers and the most lovely roses, among the finest grown in Spain. The apricot was grafted on almond stock, a practice introduced by the Moors of Damascus, the resulting fruit, celebrated for its sweet flesh and bitter core – supposed to resemble in this the nature of Toledan women – being known as the Damascus apricot. In the shade of black poplars were deep wells from which water was drawn up in buckets: the value of the *cigarrala* depended almost as much upon the depth of water in its wells as upon the beauty of its views.

The houses were of one or two floors and,

taking advantage of the uneven ground, were built on different levels. Surrounding their snow-white walls were terraces and patios paved in the Moorish style from which their owners could contemplate the magnificent vista beyond the deep gorge through which the Tagus winds its way to the sea. Along the escarpment the city walls with their numerous towers and occasional forts and gatehouses stretched out of sight to east and west. Behind the walls were clusters of houses, most of them of brick with heavy, brown terra-cotta tiles on the slightly sloping roofs. In places a larger building, a palace or a convent, stood out from its neighbours; the towers and spires of many churches broke the skyline of the land through which the Rio Guadarrama flowed past Madrid; in the centre of the city the huge mass of the Gothic cathedral soared above the surrounding roof-tops; and beyond it to the right, on the highest of the seven summits of the Toledan hills, was the vast fortress of the Alcazar whose history is as old as the history of the city itself.

The Romans had taken advantage of the dominant position of the Toledan hills, which were easily defended and capable of controlling the main trade routes across the peninsula, to establish a fortified municipium here in 193 BC. Six hundred years later the Visigoths had occupied the fort, and their king Athanagild, had transferred his capital to the city where, in 589, one of his successors, King Recarred, announced his conversion to Christianity. Following the decline of the power of the Visigoths towards the beginning of the eighth century, Toledo was occupied by the Moors and, as Tulaytulah, it became renowned for its silk and woollen industries, a major centre of both Arab and Jewish studies, and the home of a large Mozarab community of Arabic-speaking Christians and of *muwallads*, Spaniards who had been converted to Islam. Already, however, the movement known as the *reconquista*, the reconquest of Spain by the Christians, had begun; and in 1085, after a long siege, Toledo was taken by King Alfonso VI of Castile, a descendant of the royal house of Navarre and husband of Constance of Burgundy. Under his powerful authority French influence at court became paramount, the Romanesque style in art was introduced into Spain, Visigothic script was replaced by Carolingian, and a French Cistercian was appointed the first of a remarkable line of

Archbishops of Toledo, primates of the Spanish Church. But Alfonso exacted such heavy tribute from his Muslim vassals that they turned for help to the Berber Emir of North Africa whose Saharan tribesmen landed at Algeciras in July 1086 and subsequently inflicted defeat after defeat upon him; and it was not for many years that the long delayed reconquest of Spain was virtually completed under Ferdinand III, King of Castile from 1217 and of Léon from 1230 until his death. Nor was it until the time of *Los Reyes Catolicos*, Ferdinand of Aragon and Isabella of Castile, who were married in 1469 and were joint sovereigns from 1479 to 1504, that a unified Spain began to emerge as the most powerful nation in Europe, a nation from which the Jews were expelled in 1492, and the Moors in 1501.

In the intervening period, Toledo had remained famous throughout Europe as a source and centre of Moorish science, art, philosophy and scholarship, the scene of a unique fusion of Arab, Jewish and Christian cultures whose buildings reflected a harmonious synthesis of civilizations. During the reign of Ferdinand and Isabella, Toledo remained the capital of Spain, as it continued to be in the reign of the supremely powerful Charles V and of his son, Philip II, who at the age of eight and seated on a donkey was led by his governor through the streets of Toledo, much to the amusement of the good-natured crowds.

It was not a frolic which would have appealed to Philip in later life; for he maintained in public a demeanour of solemn, even haughty dignity. Born at Valladolid on 21 May 1527, he had never been strong. The smooth skin of his face under his yellow hair was of an unhealthy pallor: he looked ill and often was ill. Increasingly as he grew older he suffered from gallstones and piles, malaria and asthma, constipation, toothache and indigestion, complaints which the medicaments prescribed by his doctors tended to exacerbate rather than relieve and which his monotonous diet also aggravated. He ate a great deal of meat and poultry, usually fried or roast, and served with rich oleaginous sauces, much white bread and very few vegetables. His doctors had frequent recourse to enemas, purges and emetics, blood-letting, and doses of turpentine, rhinoceros horn, coral, balsam and powdered coconut, Yet when he was well, Philip was active enough. He revelled in hunting and was never happier than when out in the country, riding and shooting. Although small in height, he carried himself well. 'His pace is princely,' a foreign observer wrote of him when he was twenty-seven, 'and his gait so straight and upright as he loseth no inch of height.' His over-full lips and prominent Habsburg jaw were partially concealed by his fair beard so that he was deemed quite handsome. As he grew older and his health deteriorated, as his hair turned grey and he suffered ever severer attacks of gout, nephritis and migraine, he appeared in his black and sombre clothes 'so withered and feeble that it was almost impossible to suppose that a human being in such a state could live for long'. But when young his clothes were colourful and fashionable; and, while never animated or sparkling in conversation or manner, he was capable of exercising a quiet charm. He listened carefully to what was said to him, without that wavering of eye which betrayed so many monarchs' lack of concentration, and occasionally his features would be lit by an appealing, if remote, shy smile. He was not unattractive to women, though he does not seem to have been particularly interested in them sexually, despite the stories circulated by foreign ambassadors. Certainly before he contracted his first marriage to his cousin, Maria Manuela of Portugal, his father urged him to remember that he was marrying her as the potential mother of his children and not for the sensual satisfaction she might afford him. 'When you are with your wife ... be careful and do not overstrain yourself,' his father wrote. 'Keep away from her as much as you can ... As soon as you have consummated the marriage, you should leave her on some pretext, and do not go back to her too quickly or too often; and when you go back let it be only for a short time ... You have not, I am sure, had relations with any women ... Do not commit any other wickedness after your marriage.' This advice appears to have been followed throughout the marriage until Maria Manuela died giving birth to their only child, Don Carlos, in 1545.

Indeed, Prince Philip's own inclinations drew him to the hunting field, to his library, chapel and study rather than to the bedroom. He had numerous consuming interests: he was fond of music, needlework and tapestry-weaving; he was an avid book collector and delighted in adding to his remarkable store of out-of-the-way knowledge; he was deeply interested in gardening and loved

Portrait of Elisabeth of Valois by Claudio Coello.

flowers; he enjoyed fishing as much as shooting with the crossbow; he spent much of his time in prayer; and after his father died in 1558, gripping a crucifix in one hand and a scourge in the other, he devoted himself to the cares of the greatest empire that Europe had known since the days of the Romans with an assiduity that was no less remarkable for being predictable. He became known as the King of Paper and confessed that he was so burdened with such heaps of documents that he felt like a pack animal. Whether at Toledo or in those other places to which the court was constantly on the move – Toledo itself was described by a contemporary French writer as a '*capitale théorique d'une monarchie nomade*' – Philip II commonly spent eight or nine hours at his desk, making his working day even longer than it need be because of his reluctance to place too much trust in any of his advisers and of the difficulty he experienced in making up his mind: he held on to important papers so long that, in the words of the court secretary, Cabrera de Córdoba, they wilted in his hand. Upon waking at about eight o'clock he would spend an hour or so reading documents in bed, before his attendants came in to shave and dress him. He then went to Mass in his private chapel, then granted a series of audiences until he had his midday meal. The afternoon and evening were spent at his desk which he did not usually leave until it was time for dinner at about nine. Before going to bed he would call dutifully upon his wife.

After the death of his first wife, Philip did not marry again for nine years until in 1554 he sailed to England to become the husband of Mary Tudor who had set her heart upon a match which might entail a Catholic heir, reunion with Rome and with her martyred mother's Spanish dynasty. But eleven years older than Philip, Mary died childless in 1558; and the next year Philip married Elizabeth of Valois, daughter of Henry II of France, holding a splendid wedding celebration in the grand courtyard of the Alcazar in Toledo.

The Alcazar had originally been built on the site of a much older fortress by Alfonso VI in the late eleventh and early twelfth centuries. Enlarged by his successors, its complete reconstruction had been taken in hand by Charles V and Philip to the designs of their architects, Alonso de Cavarrubias and Juan de Herrera. And when Philip brought Elizabeth of Valois there for her honeymoon, the castle had been provided with a grand new façade, a superb courtyard with arcades and an interior of solemn grandeur.

Elizabeth was almost twenty years younger than her husband and had been brought to Spain when she was a child. They were married by proxy and met for the first time at Guadalajara in January 1560 when she was fourteen and he thirty-two. Soon afterwards, following a wedding ceremony, at which both bride and groom appeared in person, they came to Toledo; and there began the happiest period in Philip's life. During these months the Queen's lady-in-waiting, Madame de Clermont, kept a diary whose pages are filled with descriptions of life at court. It was a court ruled by strict etiquette; but, although the

King was often constrained to dine in public in solitary splendour and preferred, when state occasions did not demand a formal display, to dine alone in private, he sometimes joined his wife, to her obvious pleasure. He took her, too, to bull-fights and to meals al fresco, eaten in the shade of poplars. In the evening, wearing gorgeous clothes adorned with pearls and jewels, her hair drawn up in an elaborate coiffure in the Spanish style, she danced with her ladies. One evening at the Alcazar, she was suddenly taken ill and had to be put to bed. She was seriously ill for a time with what was supposed to be smallpox. Her husband came to see her often, sitting beside her as she turned feverishly in the sheets, ignoring warnings of contagion, demonstrating an affection of which many had supposed him incapable. She recovered from this illness, and upon her husband's return from a visit to his possessions in Aragon they enjoyed a second honeymoon during which, so the Queen informed the French ambassador, she had no time to write to her family: she spent most of her days and nights with the King whose love filled her with happiness. She became pregnant but once more fell ill; and the officious ministrations of her court physicians brought on a miscarriage after which they gave her up for dead. Her life was saved, however, by an Italian doctor, and in August 1566 she gave birth to a daughter and to a second girl the following year. Her happiness in her marriage was much increased by her fondness for her stepson, Don Carlos, who was about the same age as herself.

Don Carlos came to Toledo to be sworn in as heir to the throne in the Cathedral and was afterwards installed in apartments in the Alcazar after receiving the oath of allegiance from the Cortes of Castile. He had been a backward child; and, while Gonzalo Pérez, Secretary to the Council of State, propounded the hopeful view that, since all Habsburg children were late developers, there was no cause for particular concern in his case, there were others less disposed to regard the boy's future with such sanguine complacency. And after he had fallen down a flight of stone stairs when he was seventeen and suffered such severe head injuries that a trepanning operation was necessary to save his life, his behaviour began to arouse increasing concern. His temper became uncontrollable, his violence notorious: he threw a sulky page out of a window, assaulted his father's

Portrait of Don Carlos by Claudio Coello.

ministers with a dagger, forced a shoemaker to eat a pair of ill-fitting boots. 'He is usually so mad and furious,' the French ambassador reported, 'that everyone here pities the lot of the woman who will have to live with him.' He seemed to have no interests in life other than making love, riding the horses which he lamed by his cruel treatment of them, eating and drinking. Yet in his calmer moments he was amusing, charming, even endearing; and the young Queen so much enjoyed

his company that it was whispered that she was having an illicit affair with him, difficult though such an intrigue would have been to conduct at a court in which secret meetings were virtually impossible to arrange. For long the King was tolerant; but when he learned that Don Carlos was threatening to flee to the Netherlands, where he might cause unimaginable trouble, he felt obliged to have him confined. He forbade the grandees of Spain to mention his name, and ordered the Queen not to weep for him. But she could not help weeping; he was such a pitiable creature, thin and wild, refusing to eat food, yet swallowing any object, including a diamond ring, upon which he could lay his hands. Although attempts were made to force soup down his throat, he died of starvation on 24 July 1568. 'His removal to heaven was a great boon to all of Christendom,' the Duke of Alva's agent considered, 'because certainly, had he lived, he would have destroyed Christendom. His mental state

ABOVE *View of Toledo with the sixteenth-century Alcazar in the centre.*

OPPOSITE ABOVE *Painting of the Escorial by an unknown sixteenth-century artist: the main façade from the west.*

OPPOSITE BELOW *Philip II's bedroom and private room in the Escorial.*

and his habits were entirely disordered. He is very well up there. All of us who knew him thank God for his death.' All, that was, except the Queen. Despite the King's orders she wept for two days. But she was young, resilient, and she was pregnant again; the rest of that summer passed happily enough. In the autumn she fell ill once more, and under the ministrations of the court physicians grew progressively weaker. She gave birth to another daughter on 3 October and died a few hours later.

Her husband, who had sat silent and alone in his room towards the end of his son's imprisonment, appeared now to be overwhelmed by grief.

And as though to overcome his desolation in the cares of state and of the court, he turned to his study, to his paperwork and to his building programmes with a zeal which surprised even those ministers who had grown accustomed to his industry.

He had already decided that the capital of Spain should be transferred from Toledo to Madrid; and work on the Escorial, the vast monastery palace to the north-west of Madrid, had begun in 1563 to the designs of Juan Bautista de Toledo who had been succeeded after his death by Juan de Herrera. But work in Toledo was not abandoned, and the Alcazar was still unfinished at the time of Philip II's death. In its later history it became a prison and a cavalry barracks. Burned down by British, German and Portuguese troops during the War of the Spanish Succession in 1710, it was further damaged in a fierce storm in 1731. In 1774 the Cardinal Archbishop Lorenzana y Butrón decided to utilize the enormous assets of his see to restore the building as a hospice for the indigent who were employed there in the manufacture of silk, linen and woollen textiles until they were dispersed in the Napoleonic Wars by Marshal Soult's troops. After the withdrawal of the French, it was burned down once more in 1810, just a century after the first great fire. By 1866 it had been completely restored as a military academy, and, although burned down yet again the following year, it was quickly reconstructed and soon resumed its career as a military academy. It was the scene of a brave episode during the Spanish Civil War in 1936 when its garrison endured a siege by overwhelmingly superior numbers of government troops.

While work continued on the Alcazar during the sixteenth century, so it did also on the Cathedral, on the church and Convent of San Juan de Los Reyes, which had been begun by Ferdinand and Isabella to commemorate the Spanish victory over the Moors in 1476 and was not completed until 1618, and on several other churches in the city. Two of these, San Benito and Santa Maria la Blanca, had originally been built in the fourteenth century as synagogues by the Toledan Jews.

Several of these churches now reflect a combination of Moorish, Jewish and Gothic styles; but the Cathedral is distinctly Gothic and was clearly inspired by the Gothic cathedrals of northern France. The earliest cathedral in the city, of which no trace remains, was converted into a mosque after the Moorish conquest of 712. The present grand building was started in 1227 – perhaps under the direction of a French architect, as the nineteenth-century English architect, G.E. Street, who had studied it closely, was convinced – and work continued until the end of the seventeenth century when, with its broad nave and four aisles, the Cathedral was wider, as it still is, than any other European church except the cathedrals of Seville and Milan. Spanish architects designed the tower and cloisters; Dutch and Flemish craftsmen contributed the magnificent stained-glass windows; while the superbly carved choir stalls are the work of medieval and Renaissance sculptors, pre-eminently of one of Spain's greatest artists, Alonso de Berruguete. Among the twenty-two chapels, all richly adorned, is one where the Mozarabic Rite, used throughout Spain until its replacement by the Roman Rite in the eleventh century, continues to be performed.

Even after the removal of the capital of Spain to Madrid, Toledo continued to be the principal ecclesiastical centre of the country as well as a busy commercial centre with a population of some two hundred thousand, about ten times as large as it is today. The silk industry was in decline by the middle of the century and other industries were to receive a severe setback with the expulsion from Spain of the *moriscos*, the Christianized Moors, in 1609. But there were still in the 1560s four thousand textile workers in full employment in the city and, although the introduction of firearms had diminished the demand for swords, Toledan blades were still prized above all others. The narrow, tortuous streets were filled with the bustle of church dignitaries and teachers, soldiers and archers, commercial travellers, artisans, peasants with their donkeys bringing provisions to the market in the Zocodover – the only open space in the city which can be dignified with the name of 'Square' – and a ceaseless procession of water-carriers coming up from the river, more and more of them appearing after 1568 when the great water-wheel constructed by the Moors broke down, and the Italian engineer who had kept it going for a time died and the mastery of its mechanism was lost with him.

The houses which provided a background for this restless human flow seem today to have been

preserved as carefully as though in a museum. 'Here,' wrote Richard Ford, author of *A Handbook for Travellers in Spain*, in the middle of the last century, 'everything is solid, venerable and antique ... Here the voice of the Goth echoes amid Roman ruins, and the step of the Christian treads on the heel of the Moor.' The characteristic house is set in a street so narrow that it would

El Greco, View of Toledo, c.*1600*.

almost be possible to shake hands across it from one window to another. But there are few if any windows facing the street and those that exist are set high up and barred by heavy grilles. Behind a solid door, with huge studs and a heavy knocker, a dark entrance corridor leads to a patio surrounded

The Convent of San Juan de los Reyes.

by two galleries, the upper supported by granite pillars. A staircase leads from one corner of the patio to the upper floor where the bedrooms, of which the woodwork is usually moulded and carved, give on to a verandah. In the courtyard below are wells into which the rainwater falls from the brown tiled roof. There are also tubs of water to which the housewives have constant recourse, scrubbing their brick floors as often, so it is said, as they wash their dishes.'

In one such house lived Doménikos Theotokópoulos who became identified with Toledo where, ignored by Philip II and rejected by Madrid, he came to live. He had been born in Crete in 1541 and came to Spain via Venice and Rome, arriving in 1576 at Toledo where he remained for the rest of his life and where his characteristic strange style was matured. From 1585 until 1600 and from 1604 until his death in 1614, El Greco, as he had come to be known, lived in an apartment in the large medieval palace of the Marques de Villena and here he painted the masterpieces for which he is principally remembered, several of which are still to be seen in Toledo. He painted numerous brilliant portraits; he executed landscapes such as the *View of Toledo* (p. 113) now in the Metropolitan Museum, New York, and the *View and Plan of Toledo* now in the Casa y Museo del Greco, the reconstruction of his rooms near the site of the demolished Villena palace. But, for the most part, he concentrated upon religious subjects, beginning with the *Assumption of the Virgin* which he painted in Toledo in 1577. This was followed by works for Toledo Cathedral, for the Chapel of San José, for the hospital of San Juan Bautista, for several other Toledan patrons, and in 1586 by his supreme masterpiece, *The Burial of the Count Orgaz* in the Church of Santo Tomé, Toledo, a work which expresses with profound insight both the sorrows and the consolations of death, and seems to incorporate within it the very essence of the sombrely beautiful city in which he himself had come to live and in which he was to die and be buried.

From the small study of his palace in Spain, Philip II had endeavoured to govern his immense empire single-handed, personally controlling all official appointments and laboriously dealing with endless streams of documents, reports and memoranda. After 1559 he never left the Iberian Peninsula and as his system of government ground almost to a halt under the strains imposed upon it by his conscientiousness and indecision, his subjects beyond the Pyrenees grew restless and rebellious. None were more resentful of the rule of this devout champion of the Roman Catholic Counter-Reformation than the Protestant peoples of the Netherlands.

In the Dutch United Provinces there was no such central government as that imposed by Philip II. Each province was ruled by a group of rich citizens and was as often as not in rivalry or competition with its neighbours. Yet, although jealousy of a rival province's commercial success made it difficult for the Dutch to join forces when a national crisis threatened, they did contrive to maintain a confederation, to enjoy far more personal freedom than the people who lived under the sway of absolutist monarchs, and to become the most successful overseas traders in Europe.

In earlier centuries the great European trading cities had been in Italy, while German towns on the Baltic coast had traded with Russia and Scandinavia. Later Antwerp took over much of the Baltic trade and became the principal port through which English wool and grain were imported to the Continent. Then, as Antwerp declined and as it became increasingly cheaper to transport goods by sea rather than in wagons or by packhorse overland, the cities of the Dutch United Provinces began to take full advantage of the skills acquired by the seamen of their North Sea fishing vessels and of the 'flute', a capacious cargo boat sailed by a small crew, which they had invented. Of all the cities of the Dutch – whose merchant fleet was by 1670 to exceed in tonnage that of France and England, Spain, Portugal and Germany combined – the most prosperous, the most fully dedicated to money-making commerce, was Amsterdam, capital of the province of Holland.

10

Amsterdam
in the Days of
Rembrandt
1606–1669

In the summer of 1631 Rembrandt Harmenszoon van Rijn, the twenty-five-year-old son of a miller from Leiden, already a successful painter, came to live in Amsterdam because, as the mayor of his home town recorded, 'his portraits and other pictures pleased the citizens of Amsterdam who paid him well for them'. They could certainly afford to do so. Amsterdam was then one of the richest cities in the western world; and not only wealthy merchants, but even their clerks and the book-keepers in their counting-houses bought pictures to display in the rooms of their clean, neat houses.

The city had developed from a little fishing village on the south side of an inlet of the Zuider Zee where the river Amstel runs out into the sea. Its early inhabitants were said to have floated down the Rhine in hollowed tree trunks in search of better land and on reaching the estuary had raised mounds upon which they built their huts above the marshy flats. Following Julius Caesar's conquest of the region, a period of Roman government had ensued; but then other Germanic tribes, Franks and Saxons among them, had invaded the area to which feudal government was subsequently introduced by Charlemagne. After the collapse of Charlemagne's empire a dam was built across the mouth of the Amstel to protect the settlement from high tides; and by 1275 Amstelredamme, as it was then known, was sufficiently important for its inhabitants to be granted freedom for the payment of tolls by the Count of Holland. In the next century it became a place of pilgrimage after a piece of communion bread, which a sick man had failed to swallow, proved miraculously resistant to the flames of a kitchen fire. Thereafter year by year its population increased; and so did its commercial activity. Ships without number sailed into its harbour. They came from France and England and from the Baltic, and they sailed down river from the towns of the Rhineland. By the beginning of the sixteenth century Amsterdam, largely constructed in brick after most of its wooden buildings had been destroyed by fire in 1452, had a population of some fifteen thousand. This grew to forty-five thousand in the middle of the century, partly due to the influx of Protestant refugees from Antwerp and Brabant during the religious wars then raging in northern Europe.

To the swiftly developing merchant class of Amsterdam, Protestantism was particularly attractive as a focus of opposition to the policies of Philip II of Spain, whose vast Habsburg domains included the Netherlands. And although Amsterdam was one of the last of the northern cities to join the revolt against Spain, it did so in time to become a party to the treaty by which the seven provinces of the north became a united republic. By the Treaty of Westphalia, signed at the end of the Thirty Years War in 1648, the southern provinces of the Catholic Netherlands remained under Spanish domination, but the independence of the northern United Provinces was assured.

By then the prosperity of Amsterdam had been much increased by the establishment of the East India Company, the Vereenigde Oostindische Compagnie. This had been founded in the city in 1602, following the opening of new trade routes to the East. At the peak of its operations later in the century over 150 merchant vessels, mostly of 600 tons, protected by 40 fighting ships and 10,000 soldiers, were regularly employed by the Company in overseas trade and were sailing not only to the East Indies but to India, Ceylon and the islands of the South Pacific, to the Caribbean, the

OPPOSITE *Jan Vermeer*, Lady writing a Letter with her Maid, c.*1667*.

BELOW *Rembrandt*, Self-Portrait Aged Thirty-Four, *1640*.

Gerrit Adrienz Berckheijde, A Gentleman's Hotel: *Old Amsterdam in the mid-seventeenth century.*

Baltic and South Africa. It was an English employee of the company, Henry Hudson, who discovered Manhattan Island on which the Dutch settlement, New Amsterdam, the precursor of New York was built; and it was another employee of the company, the Dutchman Abel Tasman, who explored Australasia, and discovered New Zealand, Tasmania, Tonga and the Fiji Islands.

As the greatest port in the world, controlling at least half of the entire trade of the United Provinces, Amsterdam now further increased its population and its wealth. By the time Rembrandt had settled here the number of its inhabitants had reached two hundred thousand and its boundaries had been extended far beyond the medieval core

Jacob von der Ulft, The Old Town Hall, *burned down in 1651.*

on either side of the Amstel river. There were hundreds of new buildings around the dam and inside the curved moat known as the Singel, today a canal running along the old fortifications. Beyond the Singel were three other wide semi-circular canals all built in the seventeenth century, the Herengracht, the Keizersgracht and the Prinsengracht, which are still among the main thoroughfares of the city. Four canals, running at right angles to these, intersected them, giving the expanding city the appearance of a fan made from a spider's web. In all, the canals had a combined length of about fifty miles. Crossed by hundreds of bridges, some arcaded, others constructed so that they could be raised to let barges pass through, they were bordered by elm and lime trees and by the long rows of tall, elegant, narrow-fronted, gabled red-brick houses, built on stout beams driven into the soggy soil. Most of the richer merchants lived in four-, five- or even seven-story houses along the Herengracht; the less wealthy had narrower, lower houses on the other canals. Houses tended to be narrow because tax was paid according to the width of the frontage to the canals. They also tended to be plain, there being so little room for decoration except at the top where the building was usually terminated by an ornamental gable. Most had courtyards or small gardens at the back.

The streets which ran in front of the houses were exceptionally clean, being not only regularly washed but also frequently sprinkled with sand. But their narrowness made them so difficult for carriages to negotiate that a system of one-way streets for all commercial traffic had to be imposed, and this was soon followed by a prohibition against all private vehicles within the city walls. This prohibition so inconvenienced the merchants, however, that the law was amended to allow them to drive to their front doors, provided they took the shortest route, and consequently the streets were soon as crowded with carriages as ever. After the 1660s they were also crowded with vehicles known as slide-carriages, kinds of sledges which had been devised to overcome the difficulty that wheeled carriages experienced in crossing the steep, hump-back bridges. The drivers of these sledges ran along beside their horses, sometimes darting forward to sprinkle the road with water scooped up from the canal in a perforated barrel and to stuff greased rags beneath the slides to ease the vehicle's passage, or to slow it down with bundles of straw. Slide-carriages were equipped to carry passengers as well as goods. Many families had their own. There were others for hire in ranks in the Dam, the square on the site of the original dam, where stables were built and drinking-troughs set up. Here pedestrians could summon carriages by ringing a bell; and when a number of carriages appeared, the drivers threw dice to determine who should secure the fare.

Perilous as they were made by these fast-moving carriages – which never stopped, unless forced to do so by some obstacle, until the journey was over – the streets of Amsterdam were even more dangerous at night, for the carriages had no lamps and, until the 1670s, there was no effective street lighting in the city. Towards the middle of the sixteenth century an occasional oil lamp could have been seen throwing an uncertain light over the street at the corner of a public building or at the approach to a bridge; in 1579 it had been ordained that innkeepers must hang a lamp over their doors after ten o'clock at night; and after 1595 one house in every twelve had to be equipped with a wall bracket to which a lantern with a candle could be fixed. But these measures were futile since, although a body of men was engaged to supervise their lighting and maintenance, the lanterns were as often as not unlit, and even when lit, most of their panes were so dirty that the light did not penetrate the horn. At length, in 1669, an Inspector of Public Lamps was appointed to direct the activities of the lamp-lighters and to ensure that the citizens observed the regulations. And by 1689 there were almost 2,500 oil lamps in the city which was by then acknowledged to be one of the best lit in Europe.

Behind the brick façades of the terraces the larger houses were furnished, decorated and ornamented far more profusely than would have been considered tasteful by fashionable people in France or England. The heavy, clumsy oak and walnut furniture of the beginning of the century was slowly being replaced by more elegant pieces; but most rich merchants and their wives chose to fill their rooms with so many objects, both as a display of their wealth and as a means of investment, that they often resembled rooms in a museum rather than in a private house. Apart from the tables, the chairs with their high backs and leather-covered seats, and the inlaid linen and china cupboards, there were dressers and display cabinets with glazed doors, chests carved in Holland and chests brought from the East. Cushions were heaped on chairs, and damask or serge cloths spread upon tables. In the bedrooms huge beds with thick damask curtains falling from the tester occupied a quarter of the floor space. A finely embroidered top sheet was folded back over the damask bedspread. 'This would be considered a modern bed for the period, when the "sleeping cupboard" was just beginning to lose favour in the towns,' wrote Professor Zumthor in his *La Vie Quotidienne en Hollande au Temps de Rembrandt*. 'But it still retained many features of the old-style bed, especially in the homes of the petty bourgeoisie; it was so high that a set of steps was needed to climb into it and the children's sleeping compartments were arranged underneath – a custom which inspired a good deal of ribaldry among foreigners. In wealthy houses the bed was placed in the centre of the room, sometimes on a plinth, and the tester was decorated with garlands and festoons and had the owner's arms carved into its top. Sprays of feathers were attached to its four corners and the four posts supporting it and the curtains were carved in the shape of caryatids, satyrs and angels. It must be said that this decorative extravagance did not compensate for the unsatisfactory nature of the bed-clothes; one slept on a thick feather-bag, the bed-frame had no cross-bars, one's body was kept in a slightly raised position by piles of soft pillows and one was covered by a second feather-bag similar to the first one.'

On entering the house the visitor first came to the *voorhuis*, an entrance-hall which was also used as a reception room. From this room flights of steps ran down to the kitchen, scullery, pantry and cellars, while the upper floors were approached either by a spiral staircase or by a marble or wooden staircase with carved banisters. In most houses all the rooms were on different levels and in some the partition wall divided the window into two so that the other half of it lit the adjoining room. The glass in the window was likely to be coloured, so that the interiors were often sombre, even gloomy, more so, of course, at night, even when the family could afford to have wax candles in their chandeliers rather than the usual dim oil-lamp. Floors were either tiled or of polished wood, ceilings of open beams or plastered and decorated with paintings; walls were also usually tiled or covered with gilt leather on which hung numerous pictures and looking-glasses in carved frames, though after the middle of the century mural paintings were more favoured than leather.

Servants slept in the attics beneath the immense black crossbeams of the roof and crept downstairs at dawn to their duties below stairs. The kitchen in nearly every house seemed as much designed to display the perfect cleanliness of shining pans and gleaming utensils as to serve the needs of a cook. The Dutch, indeed, would prefer to die of hunger surrounded by their glittering cauldrons and sparkling crockery, so the abbé Sartre considered, 'rather than prepare any dish which might conceivably disarrange this perfect symmetry. [One family] showed me proudly the cleanliness of their kitchen which was as cold two hours before dinner as it might have been after dinner.'

The whole house, in fact, was probably cold. It was also probably damp owing to its being continually cleaned with bucketfuls of water. The chimney was a prominent feature, large and ornate with a carved canopy and shelves containing rows of porcelain and other ornaments; but its peat fire gave out little heat, and in cold winters the ladies of the house sat sewing or reading encased in layers of bulky undergarments, with foot-warmers under their feet and thick shawls round their shoulders. Husbands were as well muffled as their wives. 'The true Dutchman cuts the strangest figure in the world,' wrote Oliver Goldsmith. 'He wears no coat but seven waistcoats and nine pairs of trousers, so that his haunches start somewhere under his armpits. The Dutchwoman wears as many petticoats as her husband does trousers.' They both wore the plainest clothes, another Englishman complained, with 'neither shape nor pleats; and their long pockets [were] set as high as their ribs'.

Warmth rather than fashion was a prime consideration. Indeed, fashions changed little and then slowly. Colours were generally drab. The woman's garment known as a *vlieger*, a kind of dressing-gown, was generally black. Men's breeches and trousers were also usually black as were their tall, wide-brimmed hats, Neither men nor women, even in the richest families, washed very often and they came to the table from the most menial tasks with dirty hands which they clasped in prayer both before and after meals, the children sitting apart from the adults, the servants at the bottom end, all facing an array of porcelain and glass and, above all, pewter.

They ate with gargantuan appetites, regularly consuming four meals a day, breakfast at five or six o'clock, the main meal, *de noen*, at midday, a snack of bread and cheese and dried fruit at about three, and an evening meal between eight and nine. It was generally considered that Dutch cheese was excellent and large quantities of it, as well as butter, were exported. But Dutch cooking was not admired by foreigners, who spoke almost with horror of the national dish, *hutsepot*, a stew of meat, vegetables and prunes, mixed with lemon juice and strong vinegar, and boiled at length in fat and ginger. Great amounts of this were prepared at one time, as in many families cooking was undertaken only about once a week, the same dishes constantly reappearing on the table, sometimes reheated, sometimes left cold and nearly always served with bread, butter, with the cheese that was produced at almost every meal, varieties of vegetables and fish, particularly herrings, platefuls of cakes, pastries, puddings and biscuits, gallons of beer and, towards the end of the century, tea and chocolate as well as wine.

The lack of interest in cooking was condemned by the abbé Sartre: 'Butter, cheese and salt meat are not foods which demand a great deal of attention ... Their meat-broth is nothing more than water full of salt or nutmeg, with sweetbreads and minced meat added, having not the slightest flavour of meat and showing quite clearly that it has not taken more than an hour to prepare.'

As well as eating enormous quantities of food, the people of Amsterdam, both men and women, drank prodigiously. They drank their own beer as well as beer imported from England and Germany; they drank wine from the Rhineland and from France; and they drank strong spirits. Sir William Temple, who was Ambassador at the Hague for several years, believed that every single Dutchman had been drunk at least once in his life. A French observer, however, gathered the impression that the Dutch were so inured to drinking heavily that they could drink pints of wine without getting noticeably intoxicated: at a banquet which lasted for five hours he reckoned that some of the guests got through as many as fifty large glasses each, yet at the end of the meal, while

there was a good deal of Rhenish slopped across the table and the pale faces of the drinkers had turned puce, none of them was actually drunk.

Tobacco rivalled drink as the Dutchman's greatest pleasure. Snuff-taking was almost universal; and pipe-smoking was indulged in by nearly the whole male population. 'People smoked everywhere,' Zumthor says, 'at home, at the office, in the shops and inns, in the stage-coaches and barges – even in church, sometimes.' The entire Netherlands stank of tobacco. Grosley related that on opening the door of a small coffee-house he was blinded by the thick clouds 'emanating from three hundred smokers seated inside'. Smoking was as popular among working-class women as it was with men, but ladies refrained from the habit and insisted that their husbands retire to a special room set aside for the unpleasant practice if they did not go out to a smoking-saloon to enjoy a communal pipe with their friends.

Ladies themselves hardly ever went out at all, except to shop accompanied by their daughters or a servant carrying a basket or wooden bucket. Most evenings were spent at home, either in summer sitting on the bench in front of their house with their daughters, or in winter wearing

Meyndert Hobbema, The Haarlem Lock, Amsterdam, c.*1662–8.*

their dressing-gowns indoors by the peat oven, busy with their needles as they listened to their husband reading aloud, usually from the Bible. On some evenings there would be musical parties, on others games or cards. Even if the family did go out together, possibly to the theatre – though this was open for only two days in the week for a few months in the year – they returned home early and were soon in bed.

Foreign visitors were rarely invited into a private house, but there were at least a hundred hostelries in Amsterdam to choose from. They were undeniably clean, the floors sanded and scoured, the linen fresh, the beds well aired, the food plentiful, if not to the foreigners' taste. It would, however, so they were advised, probably be unwise to make a fuss about the cooking, and certainly imprudent to question the bill. 'If you find fault with his bill,' wrote Sir Thomas Nugent of the Dutch innkeeper, '(tho' properly speaking they make no bills, but bring in the sum the reckoning amounts to by word of mouth) he will immediately raise it, and procure a magistrate to levy his demands by force, if they are not readily

Emanuel de Witte, Interior of the Oude Kerk, Amsterdam, During a Sermon, *1658–9*

speck of mud on his shoes was seized in a fireman's lift by a hefty maidservant who carted him to the foot of the stairs, unloaded him on a lower step and replaced the offending shoes with slippers before admitting him to her mistress's room.

Some visitors also complained of the complacent regularity of the houses, whose façades were repeatedly sprayed clean by jets of water, of the streets with their orderly little trees all trimmed to the same size, of the excessively neat, geometric gardens with their carefully arranged flower beds and immaculately clipped hedges, with their 'endless avenues and stiff parterres' which seemed to one English visitor 'like the embroidery of an old maid's work-bag'.

Yet the people of Amsterdam turned out to be far more lively and engaging that their reputation allowed. They were indisputably hardworking and conscientious; they held money in awesomely high esteem; but they did not let their industry dull their sense of pleasure. The city was as teeming with life as its harbour was teeming with ships. The streets were filled with sailors and porters, coachmen and rope-dancers, with women in wooden shoes washing the stones, with street vendors and money-changers, and young men and girls going to dance in the *Speelhuizen.*

It was generally agreed that, while the men of Amsterdam seemed more interested in money, drink and tobacco than in women, the women themselves, if not tied too closely to their families, were not averse to liaisons with foreigners. In France women who obviously enjoyed sex were said 'to make love like a Dutchwoman'. Family life in Amsterdam might appear to be eminently respectable; but there were numerous *cafés-chantants* frequented by girls who were only too willing to take men home with them. There were also certain streets near the docks where prostitutes congregated and paraded; there were lodging-houses in which rooms were let to girls whose idealized portraits were displayed outside the doors; and at the Spin-House, where 'incorrigible and lewd women' were incarcerated and made to spin for the benefit of the poor, the custodian for a fee allowed men access to their naughty charges.

For those of more sober tastes there was much sightseeing to do, trips to make in canal boats, in the 'sporting carts' – small wooden vehicles whose wheels rattled and bumped over the cobbles and

paid. For this reason I should generally prefer to be accommodated in an English house when travelling through Holland, because I have not only found it, by experience, to be every bit as cheap, if not cheaper; but moreover, you have the pleasure of having victuals dressed after the English way; as also of laying out your money with your own countrymen and of having to do with reasonable people.' There were English inns in nearly all the larger towns in the United Provinces, the English Bible and the Queen's Head in Warmoes Street, Amsterdam, being particularly recommended.

Apart from the innkeepers and the cooking, so the foreign visitor was warned, there was much else in Amsterdam that he would not like. And undoubtedly some visitors did find irritating the citizens' obsession with cleanliness and neatness, their continued washing and scrubbing of floors and benches rather than their own bodies, their habit of taking their shoes off before going upstairs, of offering guests mats to wipe their boots on and straw slippers to wear before stepping on to the spotless tiles of the *voorhuis.* Temple was told that a visitor who called at a house with a the planks of the bridges – and in the screeching slide-carriages. There were visits to make to the warehouses on the islands of Bikkers and Realen; to the Weigh House, the Waag, in the Nieuwmarkt Square, which had been built as one of the city gates in 1488; to the Exchange, modelled on that of Antwerp and finished in 1613; and to the immensely grandiose town hall, the Burgersaal, now the Royal Palace, constructed in 1648–56 of stone imported from Germany in contrast to the surrounding brick, its foundations resting on almost fourteen thousand stout piles hammered into the mud beneath the Dam.

There were also fine churches to see, among them the Oude Kerk, which was consecrated in 1300 and contains some fine stone carving and stained glass; the Nieuwe Kerk with its lovely Baroque woodcarving and sixteenth- and seventeenth-century organs; the Westerkerk which, begun in 1619, has Amsterdam's tallest tower; and the Zuiderkerk, finished in 1611, whose tower, so much admired by Christopher Wren, was said to have inspired some of his designs for his churches in the City of London and was painted more than once by Rembrandt who lived in a house opposite, now the Rembrandthuis.

Rembrandt had at first lived in the more modest house of the art dealer, Hendrick van Uylenburgh; but his immediate success as a portrait painter in Amsterdam, and his marriage in 1643 to Hendrick's wealthy cousin, Saskia van Uylenburgh, enabled him to rent a house in the smart Nieuwe Doelenstraat. A fashionably dressed young man by now, he became an art collector as well as a painter, bidding high prices at auctions for works that caught his fancy. In those days he had money enough to spare. More portrait commissions than he could undertake continued to come his way; his religious paintings were also eagerly sought; so were his scenes of Amsterdam life; so were the works of his pupils who paid high fees to be taught by him. His continuing success enabled him to pay a large sum for a big house in the Sint Anthonisbreestraat. But then Saskia died; their son's nurse, the widow of a ship's bugler, became his mistress until he fell in love with a younger servant. The nurse then left the house, sued Rembrandt for breach of contract; and thereafter his fortunes began to decline. He had trouble in meeting the payments due on his new house; other artists such as Bartholomeus van der Helst came into fashion; various commercial ventures in which he had invested failed; and Rembrandt was at length forced to buy a much smaller house and to sell many of his possessions at auction. He continued to paint and his paintings remained in demand. His declining years were not spent in the poverty and obscurity of popular legend. But the days of his greatest success were over, and it seemed to some observers that the most prosperous days of his adopted city were also drawing to a close. Certainly when Rembrandt died in 1669 there were already signs that Amsterdam would in the next century lose to London and Hamburg its reputation as the leading trading centre of the world.

Much as he loved Dutch tulips, Louis XIV, King of France, hated the Dutch. He hated their Protestantism; he hated their political pretensions; he hated them for giving asylum to French Calvinists and republicans, and for their commercial and financial success. Maintaining that their territories were the inheritance of his wife, Marie Thérèse, daughter of the King of Spain, he invaded the Netherlands in 1672 with the finest army in the world. He soon occupied Utrecht; and although, by piercing their walls and dykes, the Dutch flooded two hundred square miles around Amsterdam and thus held up the French advance, Louis went on to capture Maastricht. By 1678, despite the defection of their allies and the help afforded to the Dutch by those countries that entered the war on the side of the United Provinces, the French were able to dictate the terms of the Treaty of Nijmegen. Louis XIV was now the dominant figure in Europe. He set about establishing the supreme power of the monarchy, bringing the nobility to heel, extending the kingdom's frontiers, leading large armies upon expeditions of foreign conquest, curbing the privileges of the Huguenots and eventually revoking in 1685 the Edict of Nantes by which Henry IV had granted them a large measure of religious liberty. At the same time he began to make Paris a city worthy of his own greatness.

11
Paris
in the Days of Louis XIV
1651–1715

Having prudently avoided the Civil War in England by travelling on the Continent, John Evelyn, the diarist, came to Paris in 1651 and on 7 September called upon Thomas Hobbes whose masterpiece of political philosophy, *The Leviathan*, had just been published. And from an upper window of Hobbes's house the two Englishmen looked down upon 'the whole equipage and glorious cavalcade of the young French monarch Lewis XIV passing to Parliament'. Horsemen and trumpeters, foot guards and pages, heralds and marshals, grandees of the court, 'gallant Cavalieres habited in scarlet colour'd Sattin', 'Swiss in black velvet toques', 'Lieutenants generals of Provinces magnificently mounted', and 'members of the nobility exceeding splendid' all passed proudly by in the street below, followed by the King himself upon a splendidly caparisoned white horse. He was 'like a young Apollo' in a suit covered with rich embroidery, 'going almost the whole way with his hat in hand, saluting the Ladys and Acclamators who had fill'd the Windos with their beauty, and the aire with "Vive Le Roy". Indeede, he seem'd a Prince of a grave, yet sweete Countenance, now but in the 14th yeare of his Age'.

He had already been King for eight years but was still quite content to leave public affairs in the capable hands of his godfather, Cardinal Mazarin, and the supervision of his private conduct to his mother, Queen Anne, daughter of King Philip

The Louvre and the Seine: View from Pont Neuf *(detail), c.1655 by an anonymous seventeenth-century French artist.*

Nicolas de Largillière, Louis XIV and his Heirs, c.1709.

III of Spain. When Mazarin was dying in 1661, however, he had urgently enjoined the young man to take up the government himself, to rule personally. 'Govern,' the cardinal had said. 'Govern! Let the politicians be your servants, never your masters.' The King had cried bitterly when told that the Cardinal, whom both he and his mother loved, was dead; but he had quickly recovered himself and had informed the council in a firm voice, 'In future I shall be my own chief minister.' And this he became. Devoting himself to this task, he worked hard, supervising every aspect of government, considering himself by divine right an autocrat whom the nobility, summoned to his court, were obliged to revere.

It was not difficult to revere him. Even his enemies agreed that he was a most intelligent and attractive man. He had a finely proportioned face framed by flowing, curling, brown hair as beauti-

ful as any woman's. Tall and broad shouldered, he walked with exquisite grace. Women who looked at him often found it difficult to turn away until he disconcertingly returned their gaze through dark, mysterious, half-closed eyes.

He was married at the age of twenty-two to his first cousin, Marie Thérèse, daughter of Philip IV of Spain, whom he did not find in the least prepossessing though she seemed kind and good-tempered. She was distressingly stocky; her clothes and hairstyle were old-fashioned; she looked as if she might smell of mothballs. She spoke French haltingly with a heavy Spanish accent; she ate a great deal of garlic and chocolate flavoured with cloves, which made her teeth black; she had little conversation and no wit. But Louis was a polite young man, and he tried not to let her know that he found her so unappealing and boring. He dutifully made love to her every other week, and looked elsewhere for pleasure. He found it with his mistresses and at his country palaces.

He did not care for Paris. His childhood had been passed in the days of the Fronde, those uprisings of the nobles and the Parlement of Paris against the royal government; and at that time he had known poverty, adversity, humiliation, even cold and hunger. 'His sheets were so full of holes,' so one of his *valets de chambre* recorded, 'that I have found him several times with his legs sticking through them on the mattress.' He could never forgive the nobles and he could never forgive Paris or the Parisians. He was urged by his ministers to live in the Louvre, the rambling palace which had developed over the centuries on the right bank where a thirteenth-century king had built a square castle beside the medieval city wall. But Louis had no intention of living in Paris; he was instead to spend a fortune on converting the modest country house which his father had built as a *maison de plaisance* at Versailles-au-Val-de-Galie. Paris, though, would have to be made worthy of the great monarch he intended to be.

Fifteen centuries before, at the time of the Roman Conquest, the Île de la Cité, upon which the cathedral of Notre Dame now stands, had been a small settlement of a Celtic tribe known as the Parisii. The rough buildings of this riverside settlement had been burned to the ground by the tribesmen at the Romans' approach so that the conquerors could take possession of no more than smouldering ruins. Yet, by the time of Marcus Aurelius, a Roman town of eight thousand inhabitants had emerged on the banks of the river, complete with temples and theatres, aqueducts and baths, markets, monuments and arenas. Successive barbarian invasions in the third, fourth and fifth centuries had brought the further development of the city to an end; but after Clovis, the leader of the conquering Franks, had established his capital here in 508, Paris had begun to grow in size and reputation. As the Frankish domains became ever larger, however, the importance of Paris diminished; and under Charlemagne – whose vast territories spread across almost all of what is now France, Belgium and the Netherlands as well as parts of Germany and Switzerland – Aix-la-Chapelle became the capital and Rome the city from which Charlemagne dreamed of ruling an empire even greater than that of the Caesars. So Paris further declined. Repeatedly the Normans plundered it; its people,

ever shrinking in numbers, withdrew to the island in the Seine; and it was not until the reign of Philip II Augustus, the first of the great Capetian kings of France, that Paris – the city of Philip's birth in 1165 – became a capital worthy of his dynasty. He built a new defensive wall with sixty towers to withstand the assaults of the English; he built a new cathedral, a second castle, many churches and several monasteries; and he founded the university which was to be one of the glories of medieval learning. His successor, Louis IX, the pious monarch canonized at St Louis, continued his work, expanding the city by developments outside the walls, providing it with new religious foundations and hospices for the poor, as well as a college for poor scholars, the College of the Sorbonne, which was named after his chaplain. He also reconstructed the royal palace on the Île de la Cité, on the site of the present Palais de Justice, and built one of the finest of all examples of *rayonnant* Gothic architecture, the Sainte Chapelle, that lovely chapel in the courtyard of the palace which contained, beneath its vaulted ceilings, Christ's crown of thorns as well as nails and splinters of wood from the True Cross. A

Portrait of Madame de Montespan, mistress of Louis XIV, as Iris, messenger of the gods.

Le Pont de la Tournelle *(detail) by a seventeenth-century artist of the Dutch School.*

generation after Saint Louis's death the population of Paris had risen to about three hundred thousand.

The city grew larger and more prosperous still during the time of Charles V of the House of Valois in whose reign (1364–80), the city wall was much extended to incorporate the two fortresses of the Bastille and the Louvre, the latter being redecorated by Charles and given a magnificent library.

Following a period of trial and stagnation during the later stages of the Hundred Years War – and the occupation of the city by the English after their triumph at Agincourt in 1415 – Paris came into its own again with the accession of Francis I in 1515. The population increased; trade prospered; the rich bourgeoisie built grand houses to rival those of the nobility; new suburbs like the Faubourg Saint-Honoré to the north-west, spread over the surrounding fields; and lovely Renaissance buildings began to appear. The immense keep of the Louvre was demolished to make the apartments there less gloomy; and the Hôtel de Ville was reconstructed to the design of the Italian architect, Domenico da Cortona.

The Italianate influence upon Parisian architecture was continued under the Florentine Catherine de Médicis, regent during the minority of Charles IX, and under her kinswoman, Queen Marie, consort of Henry IV, who built the Luxembourg. It was Henry IV's father, Henry III, who built the Pont-Neuf to link the Louvre to

the Faubourg Saint-Germain which was thereafter to become a centre of aristocratic life. And it was Henry IV himself and his son, Louis XIII, who saw the centre of the city gradually begin to lose its predominantly medieval appearance as buildings rose in the classical – though recognizably French – style of so many of the new *hôtels*, the style of the façades in the Place Royale (now the Place des Vosges) which was inaugurated in 1612, and of the palace (later the Palais Royal) which Louis XIII's minister of state, Cardinal Richelieu, built north of the gardens of the Tuileries.

Yet, despite all that his predecessors had done, Louis XIV inherited a city still for the most part redolent of the Middle Ages: he instructed Jean Baptiste Colbert, his Superintendent of Finance and principal adviser, to make it a fit capital for the greatness of France.

Had he lived longer, Colbert would have demolished the remains of medieval Paris in their entirety and given the whole city the aspect presented by the Faubourg Saint-Honoré. Yet although his grand plans were never realized in full, a transformation in the appearance of the city came about under his energetic supervision, and the taste for order and magnificence which he shared with his royal master imposed upon it a discipline and grandeur quite at variance with the untidy Paris of the recent past. The girdle of bastions and bulwarks was swept away for wide avenues or boulevards, while the fine monuments which were erected were so sited as to afford

Louis XIV visiting the Gobelins carpet factory with Jean-Baptiste Colbert.

splendid vistas in the centre of the city. The workers, the poor and the sick were relegated to the outskirts, and workshops were kept well away from the *hôtels* and the centres of government and administration. A glass manufactory was built in the Faubourg Saint-Antoine, a carpet factory beyond the Cours de la Reine; and in 1662 Colbert took over, on behalf of the Crown, a tapestry factory which derived its name from the Gobelins who had established a scarlet-dyeing workshop on the outskirts of Paris in the fifteenth century.

An impressive number of new thoroughfares, monuments and bridges was contructed in these years, and existing buildings were enlarged and improved. Work on the Louvre continued under the direction of Claude Perrault and Le Vau. The first floor of the Petite Galerie was entirely reconstructed and the Cour Carrée completed. The Collège des Quatre Nations was begun in 1663 in accordance with a testamentary disposition by Cardinal Mazarin who had expressed the wish to provide accommodation for sixty gentlemen from the four provinces annexed by France in accordance with the Treaty of the Pyrenees of 1659. In 1667 plans were prepared by André Le Nôtre, Director Royal of Gardens under Louis

XIV, for the laying out of the Champs Elysées which was to open up a fine view from the Tuileries Palace to the Étoile where the Arc de Triomphe now stands. Along the left bank rose the immense complex of the hospital buildings of the Salpêtrière; while Claude Perrault's designs for the grandiose Observatoire were put into effect in 1667, the year in which the Church of the Invalides was also started under the direction of Jules Hardouin-Mansart.

The Invalides hospital itself, one of the most splendid monuments of the seventeenth century, was built in 1671–6 to the designs of Libéral Bruant; and the Pont Royal which gave access to it from the right bank was finished in 1689. While this bridge was being built – stimulating the construction of large houses in the Faubourg Saint-Germain – the Place des Victoires was also being erected and around this several rich merchants and financiers were building for themselves *hôtels* as imposing and sumptuous as the Hôtel Colbert. In 1699 work began on the lovely octagonal Place Vendôme.

The fish market at Les Halles : French seventeenth-century design for a fan.

Unlike the *hôtels* of Mazarin's day, which were built with wings of the same height as the central section of the mansion, it was now fashionable to keep the lateral wings low, to use them for kitchens, stables and servants' quarters, and to emphasize the importance of the main part of the house and of its porch. Access to the porch was gained from an oval or rectangular courtyard through the *porte-cochère* beside which liveried servants stood ready to receive the guests of their master whose name, proudly emblazoned on a marble plaque, was usually to be seen above the doorway. Inside these dressed stone mansions, which were much influenced by the décor of Versailles, the rooms were often oval, their white ceilings surrounded by friezes of sculpted and gilded plaster, their windows overlooking extensive gardens in which stone and bronze fountains threw their waters in high sprays above the gravelled paths.

Concerned not only with the splendour of the buildings of the new Paris, Colbert was also anxious that the city should be both more healthy and more secure. He paid close attention to its drainage system and its lighting by street lanterns; he improved its water supply by the installation of fifteen new fountains; he intro-

duced both a fire brigade and a postal service. Indeed, there could be no doubt that, when his master died, Paris could no longer be described in such disparaging terms as those employed by James Howell, author of *Instructions for Forreine Travel* (1642) – the earliest of continental handbooks printed in England – who, while admitting it was 'hudge', could not find much to say in its favour.

Even so, Paris did remain an extremely dirty city, and a very crowded one. In area it was still quite small, bounded on the north by the boulevards from Porte Saint-Antoine to Porte Saint-Honoré, the old line of Charles V's wall, and to the south by the present Boulevard Saint-Germain. Within this area, divided into sixteen *quartiers* – increased to twenty *quartiers* in 1702 – there were almost twenty-four thousand houses and a population of some five hundred thousand people which rose to seven hundred thousand by the time of the Revolution of 1789.

To many English travellers the city seemed even more crowded than London, and most of the streets appeared even narrower than they were at home. Apart from the Place Royale in the Marais quarter which had been built in the time of Henry IV, the Place Dauphine of 1607 – a triangular area in the Île de la Cité surrounded by thirty-two identical houses of stone and brick – and the more

The Baker's Cart *by a late seventeenth-century French artist.*

recent Place des Victoires and Place Vendôme, there were no squares much larger than a cross-roads. A few streets were over forty-five feet wide, among them the rues Saint-Jacques, Saint-Martin, Saint-Antoine and Saint-Denis, but the other six hundred or so were less than fifteen feet from wall to wall and some were less than five. Pavements were unknown and the rain water was carried away only by the uneven slopes of the surfaces.

From morning until late at night these narrow streets and alleyways – made narrower still by the shopkeepers' wares which were piled outside their doors – were thronged by porters and pedestrians, by street vendors vociferously crying their goods, by shepherds and cowherds driving their animals to slaughter, by horsemen and by riders of mules, by men going to work in cloth smocks and leather aprons, by clerks and lawyers in grey and black, by pickpockets and beggars who followed their prey even into the shops, by monks and priests, students with inkhorns at their belts, and proces-

sions of magistrates followed by lackeys holding up the trains of their gowns. Sedan chair carriers and drivers of carts of all kinds forced their way through the throng. There were private carriages, hired carriages and the sprung carriages of nobles with liveried postilions on seats above the glass windows; there were large coaches taking people to and from the provinces; and, between 1662 and when they disappeared through lack of custom in 1667, there were *carosses à cinq sols*, public conveyances carrying eight passengers which left each departure point every quarter of an hour. 'The numerous coaches driven with an amazing rapidity . . . splashing through . . . the mud,' wrote one foreign visitor. 'The total want of foot pavement renders it really dangerous to walk in the streets till you are trained to feats of agility. You are required every instant to dart from one side to the other . . . Accidents are frequent.'

The noise was tremendous and the dirt indescribable. Paris was the 'ugliest, beastliest town in the universe,' wrote Horace Walpole in the next century, when it was far less offensive than it once had been. 'A dirty town with a dirtier ditch calling itself the Seine ... a filthy stream, in which everything is washed without being clean, and dirty houses, ugly streets, worse shops and churches loaded with bad pictures.' This was a far from uncommon opinion. Often pedestrians were compelled to hold their noses and close their eyes. Next to a glittering jewellery shop or one of the many houses where scent, pomade and hair powder were sold, there would be a pile of rotten apples and herring, 'monstrous black sausages in great guts or bladders and boiled sheep's heads'. The streets were filled with excrement, 'filth and even blood streaming from the butcher's stalls'. 'You must call Paris,' the young Nikolai Mikhailovich Karamzin decided, 'the most magnificent, the most vile, the most fragrant and most foetid city.'

Passers-by relieved themselves whenever and wherever the need arose; maidservants emptied the contents of chamber pots from windows with a perfunctory cry of 'Gare l'eau!' Most houses had no latrines or even pits for nightsoil; and even in royal palaces heaps of ordure were piled up in the courtyards and gentlemen could be found defecating behind doors, creating what was described in an official report as 'milles puanteurs insupportables'. Everywhere both ladies and gentlemen indulged in an 'odious custom of spitting about the room, which they certainly do to such an excess that they look like a parcel of Tritons with eternal waterspouts plying from their lips'. Ordinances were frequently issued in attempts to make Paris a cleaner and more hygienic city, but they were universally ignored and it was not until after 1667 when Nicolas-Gabriel de la Reynie was appointed Lieutenant-General of Police that a serious endeavour was made to tackle the problem and householders were ordered to build cesspits and latrines and to sweep the streets outside their front doors. For a time there was a slight improvement, but Paris was soon as dirty as ever. In 1697 an ordinance complained that in certain quarters the inhabitants continued to spill their slops, kitchen refuse and sewage into the streets. Five years later, after a magistrate had fallen to his death while emptying a chamber pot from a high window, a minister complained that the streets were still 'excessively dirty'.

The Lieutenant-General of Police was given wide powers which he used not only in trying to cleanse the city, but also to deal with its high crime rate. In 1642 there had been no less than 342 night attacks culminating in murder in the streets of Paris; in 1660 the sculptor, Antoine Coysevox, and his friends were afraid to return to their lodgings even at an early hour of the evening for fear of assault. The perpetrators of nearly all violent crimes went unpunished, since watchmen rarely entered those parts of the city where such crimes were most likely to occur and the police were constantly hampered by the absence of witnesses in communities in which there had developed an argot quite incomprehensible to the outside world. When criminals were caught they were likely to be incarcerated in the grim dungeons of the Châtelet or the Évêque, the old prison of the Archbishop of Paris which passed to the Crown in 1674, the less uncomfortable Bastille being reserved for those of higher rank, such as the Comte de Solanges who had been committed for incest and was one of only seven prisoners remaining there when the Revolution broke out in 1789. The condemned were brought out into the light from these places to be hanged or burned at the stake before large crowds in the Place de Grève or La Croix du Trahoir. But capital punishment was no deterrent to the coquillards, the sabouleux, the drilles, the robbers, ruffians and vagabonds who haunted the streets.

In his campaign against crime in Paris, the Lieutenant-General of Police forbade the carrying of swords except by those in official positions. He closed cabarets at six o'clock in the evening in winter and at nine in summer. He rounded up prostitutes and had the most troublesome deported to the islands. He provided the city with over six thousand lanterns. Yet in spite of all his efforts, Paris remained a dangerous city. The unwary were still likely to be assaulted after dark by armed robbers who took not only their money but even their clothes and stabbed those foolhardy enough to resist. In the streets – comparatively quiet, except for the miaowing of cats, after the din of the day – criminals appeared in their hundreds from their lairs and prowled in search of prey, not in the least deterred by the eight hundred night-

LE GRAND CAROZEL ROYAL FAIT PAR SAMAIESTE OV LE PRIX DE LA COVRSE
de la Bague et des Testes Fait le 5 6 & 7.me Iuin 1662.

The Grand Carrousel of June 1662.

watchmen in their imposing uniforms laced with silver and gold whom they frequently assaulted and put to flight.

In addition to the professional criminals, there were tens of thousands – an estimated forty thousand – of indigents who existed by begging, occasional prostitution, and what poor living they could make for themselves in the streets. Many of them lived in and around the Cour des Miracles, a slum of dark alleys and rotting houses off the rue Saint-Sauveur. This area, so Henri Sauval, the historian of Paris, wrote, was 'one of the most badly built, filthy and hidden quarters of Paris, as if in a world apart. In order to get there one must wander down shabby, tortuous, stinking little streets . . . I saw a mud-covered house half buried and sagging from age and rotteness which is twenty-six feet square in which nevertheless there are living fifty families with their children, legitimate, illegitimate or stolen. I was told that in this and the other small lodgings around it there lived more than five hundred families huddled on top of one another. Of the women and girls the less ugly prostitute themselves . . . Several paid men to give them children so that they might excite pity and extract alms.'

Elsewhere in other poor quarters like the purlieus of the Place Meubert and the Faubourg Saint-Morrell those who had dwellings of their own lived in cramped, narrow-fronted houses, sometimes of stone but more often of wood and plaster, many of them above small manufactories or shops whose fronts were open to the street – ground-floor windows being rare – and whose upper walls were decorated with a strange assortment of wrought-iron signs indicating the nature of the occupants' trade.

The royal government had always tended to regard the problem of the poor as being best dealt with by repression, so that for comfort or hopes of

French and Italian farce actors in the Théâtre Royal in Paris, 1670.

regeneration the disinherited had to look to the Church or to such humanitarians as St Vincent de Paul whose Daughters of Charity went out into the slums to nurse the sick and feed the hungry. But these acts of compassion were as inadequate in coping with pauperism as were institutions like the Salpêtrière and the Bicêtre in which the destitute were put to forced labour as the price they paid for shelter.

Yet, poor as so many Parisians were, there were few, other than the pitiably destitute, who did not contrive to enjoy themselves when opportunity offered. There were outings in the Cour Saint-Antoine and the gardens of the Arsenal, afternoons spent on the banks of the river watching wine being unloaded at the Pont Saint-Bernard, wood and coal at the Pont Saint-Paul, hay at the Pont du Louvre, the barges sailing for Sens and Auxerre, the washerwomen scrubbing their linen at La Grenouillère. There were the fairs of Saint-Laurent in the Faubourg Saint-Denis, which last-ed for two months from 10 August, and of Saint-Germain which went on from Candlemas to Palm Sunday. There were the firework displays on the Pont Neuf on the feast of St John, the masked balls of *Mardi Gras*; there were countless other parish festivals and the endless variety of the streets.

For those who could afford them Paris offered many other pleasures. It has been calculated that in the 1670s there were no less than 1,847 inns and cabarets in the city and the suburbs, over two hundred of them in the fashionable Faubourg Saint-Germain. A number of these were internationally renowned for their food, the French having already established themselves as masters in the art of gastronomy. On fine days the *beau monde* drove in their carriages along the north bank of the river where for over a kilometre the roadway was wide enough for five or even six carriages to travel abreast, their occupants eyeing each other's clothes with undisguised admiration, jealousy or disdain. Fortunes were spent on clothes by men and women who emulated the fashions of Versailles; and almost equally huge amounts were lavished upon wigs which at one time grew so high that Montesquieu said a lady's face was as far removed from the top of her wig as it was from her shoes.

There were no displays of fashion more splendid than those to be seen when the King came to Paris from Versailles. He did not come often. Indeed, he did not come at all between 1693 and 1700, and he made his last visit in 1706. Yet when he did come the spectacle was as magnificent as it had been in 1660, when he entered Paris with his Spanish bride, accompanied by representatives of the clergy, the city, the guilds of merchants, the magistrates of the courts and the Chancellor in cloth of gold, surrounded by pages, musketeers and Swiss guards, cavalry and gendarmes, all gorgeously apparelled. Equally impressive was the Grand Carrousel of 1682 in the Tuileries gardens where, before more than ten thousand spectators, hundreds upon hundreds of cavaliers paraded about in costumes of astonishing splendour, adorned with jewels and ostrich plumes, as Romans and Persians, Turks and Indians.

In the theatres large audiences enjoyed the comedies of Molière, the operas of Lully and Quinault, and the plays of Corneille and Racine. Exhibitions of paintings and sculpture were held in the Louvre by the Académie de Peinture et de Sculpture which had been granted premises by the King in that part of the palace built in 1661–3 by Le Vau on the Cour de la Reine.

The Académie de Peinture et de Sculpture was but one of the institutions devoted to the arts for which the King found a home in the Louvre. The Académie de l'Architecture was also housed here. So were the Académie Française, which had been founded by Richelieu in 1634, the Académie des Inscriptions et Belles-Lettres, established in 1663, and the Académie de Science founded in 1666. Various members of these and other academies were also found lodgings in the Louvre, among them the engraver, Israel Silvestre, the sculptor, François Girardon, the furniture maker, André Charles Boulle, and the geographer, Adrien Sanson.

It was such men as these and such writers and artists as Nicolas Boileau-Despréaux, Jean de la Fontaine, Jean de la Bruyère, François, duc de La Rochefoucauld and Fénelon LeBrun, Mignard, Rigaud and Coysevox – as well as Molière, Corneille, Racine and the habitués of the salons of Madame de La Fayette and of her friend Madame de Sévigné at the Hotel Carnavalet – who helped to make the Paris of Louis XIV, for all its squalor and violence, the cultural capital of the world.

───────────────────────

While Louis XIV of France was establishing himself as the dominant figure in Europe, the England of the Stuart monarchs was also becoming recognized as a world power. A century before, England had not been a nation of great importance in international affairs. Theirs was the oldest monarchical tradition in Europe, and their sense of national identity was strong. Wales had long since been incorporated into the kingdom; Ireland was a conquered province; Scotland, although not officially part of Great Britain until 1707, had the same King as England when James VI of Scotland became James I of England on the death of his cousin, Queen Elizabeth I, the last of the Tudors, in 1603. Yet sixteenth-century England was not the formidable power that her people liked to suppose. They were, however, envied by other peoples for the relative freedom which they enjoyed.

It had seemed at first that the Tudor dynasty might impose upon the country an absolutist monarchy in the manner of Philip II. But Henry VIII's need to rely upon Parliament to nationalize and reform the Church in England and his successors' dependence upon Parliament to levy taxes helped to strengthen that institution's authority. Charles I's attempt to weaken this authority resulted in civil war (1642–6); while the apparent wish of his second son, James II, to use the monarchy to bring England back into the Catholic fold was to end in the Glorious Revolution of 1688 which allayed all lingering fears of an English monarchical autocracy on the Continental model.

By this time England had taken the place of Holland as the leading trading nation in Europe, and London, which had long been the country's busiest port and by far its largest city, had established itself as the most important commercial and banking centre in the world.

12

London
in the Days of Pepys and Wren 1666–1723

Coming downstairs early one cold March morning, Samuel Pepys, a young official in the Navy Office, was annoyed to find his maids, 'with their clothes on, lying within their bedding upon the ground close by the fire-side – and a candle burning all night'. He was always nervous of fire, and had good reason to be so. On no less than sixteen occasions he recorded serious outbreaks of fire in the journal he kept between 1660 and 1669; and these were by no means all those that erupted in London in those years. For centuries, indeed, the narrow, tortuous streets and cramped, huddled, wooden-framed houses which had characterized London since Saxon times, combined to ensure that the city had been ravaged by conflagration after conflagration. William Fitzstephen, secretary to Thomas Becket, Archbishop of Canterbury until his murder in 1170, had gone so far as to say that the delights of London were overcast by only two curses, the immoderate drinking of fools and the frequency of fires. In 961 a fierce fire had burned out the first Cathedral of St Paul's; and twenty years later another uncontrollable fire had swept across the town from Bishopsgate to the Thames, destroying what little of Roman London had been left standing above ground after the Danes had sacked and burned the town in 851. Large areas of the rebuilt town were destroyed in 1087 in a holocaust which reduced St Paul's once more to a heap of cinders; and in 1153, the flames, sweeping west from Billingsgate, engulfed all the buildings between London

The Great Fire of London in 1666: *an engraving by W. Birch from Thomas Pennant's* Some Accounts of London.

Portrait of Samuel Pepys by John Hayls, 1666.

Bridge and the Fleet River. Reconstructed in stone as the largest cathedral in England, the biggest, in fact, in Europe after those in Milan and Seville and St Peter's basilica in Rome, St Paul's had yet again burst into flames in 1561 when an old plumber had left a pan of coals burning inside the spire while he went to have his dinner. In Pepys's lifetime half the buildings on London Bridge toppled through the flames into the river; a horrifying fire destroyed much of Southwark; and on one single blustery night in 1662 four separate fires broke out in Whitehall Palace, that royal rabbit-warren which King Henry VIII had created around the London mansion of his disgraced minister, Cardinal Wolsey, and which was to be burned to the ground during the hard frost of 1698 when a Dutch laundry-maid left her master's clothes hanging up to dry too close to a charcoal brazier.

Repeated orders were issued to check such carelessness, to reduce the hazards of life in a city in which quantities of combustible material lay piled in the streets, in which tons of straw were stored in stables, wood lay stacked in timber yards against the wooden galleries in the coachyards of taverns, pitch and tar in marine warehouses, kindling in bakeries and cookshops, barrels of tallow, oil and spirits in merchants' cellars. Since

the early Middle Ages citizens had been enjoined not to leave fires burning at night and to keep barrels of water outside their doors. Every ward had been required to provide poles, hooks, chains and rope for the instant demolition of burning houses; and the well-to-do had been ordered to have ladders in their courtyards so that their poorer neighbours might escape through the flames from upper windows. But the constant reiteration of such orders indicates that they were widely disregarded. In Pepys's day a few grab hooks could be seen in the porches of parish churches; there were buckets and ladders in the larger public buildings; there were one or two inefficient water pumps; but these, apart from an ill-organized system of watch and ward, constituted the capital's only fire-fighting arrangements.

No one outside the immediate area, however, was at first much alarmed when in the early hours of 2 September 1666 a fire broke out in Farriner's bakehouse in Pudding Lane and, fanned by a strong wind, soon spread to other buildings in the street. The Lord Mayor in his house in Gracechurch Street looked out upon the scene but soon went grumpily back to bed with the contemptuous observation, 'Pish! A woman might pisse it out.' Pepys, who had seen so many fires like it, soon also went back to bed and to sleep.

But the next morning, on leaving home for his office, Pepys realized that this was no ordinary conflagration. He made for the Tower and from 'one of the high places' there he saw 'an infinite great fire on this and the other side the end of the bridge,' and 'everybody endeavouring to remove their goods, and flinging into the river or bringing them into lighters that lay off. Poor people staying in their houses as long as till the very fire touched them, and then running into boats or clambering from one pair of stairs by the water-side to another. And among other things the poor pigeons I perceive were loath to leave their houses, but hovered about the windows and balconies till they were some of them burned, their wings, and fell down.' That night Pepys went to a little alehouse on Bankside and there 'saw the fire grow', the 'horrid, malicious, bloody flames licking and leaping upon steeple and between churches and houses as far as [he] could see up the hill of the City', forming 'one entire arch of fire from this to the other side of the bridge, and in a bow up the hill above a mile long'. 'It made me weep to see it,' he recorded. 'The churches, houses, and all on fire and flaming at once, and a horrid noise the flames made, and this cracking of houses at their ruine. So home with a sad heart, and there find everybody lamenting and discoursing the fire.'

For the whole of the next day and the Tuesday following the fire raged; and it was not until seamen, brought up from the dockyards, had used gunpowder to blow up whole rows and streets of buildings to open up a gap over which no burning embers could be thrown by the wind, that it was brought under control at last. By then almost four hundred acres within the City walls and over sixty acres outside them had been completely devastated. In addition to St Paul's, eighty-seven parish churches had been effaced. The Royal Exchange, the capital's bourse and trading centre, had been destroyed, together with most of the Guildhall and the whole of the Customs House, two of the city's finest buildings. Forty-four halls of the craft guilds, the City Livery Companies, had been lost as well as 13,200 houses. Ton upon ton of smouldering debris, ash and tumbled masonry lay beneath the pall of smoke. Almost a quarter of a million people, out of a total population which had been estimated at between 350,000 and 400,000 in 1650, were now homeless, many of them camping in tents and huts on the fields outside the city where the King, Charles II, rode out to speak to them, to quell fears of a foreign plot engineered either by the Dutch or the French with whom the country was then at war.

On the day after the fire started, a pupil at Westminster School had seen a foreigner hit over the head with an iron bar; his brother had watched as another was almost dismembered; and a Frenchman who confessed to starting the fire in

Broadsheet showing the Fire of London at London Bridge.

the bakery was hanged at Tyburn. But Londoners were notoriously xenophobic, and always ready to believe the worst of strangers who were frequently hooted and hissed at in the streets. It was 'almost dangerous' for a foreigner to walk about in London on occasions 'if at all well dressed', so one French visitor complained, 'For he runs a great risk of being insulted by the vulgar populace, which is the most cursed brood in existence. [On the Lord Mayor's Day] he is sure of not only being jeered at and being besmattered with mud, but as likely as not dead dogs and cats will be thrown at him.'

Well aware of the attitude of the people towards them, the French were ready to celebrate those 'blessed flames' which had reduced 'the chaos we now call London to a ruinous heape'. Public

Engraving of the Monument to the Great Fire, published in 1676. Designed by Wren and Hooke, the Monument marks the point where the Fire began, 202 feet from Pudding Lane (which is also the height of the Monument).

rejoicings in Paris had been prohibited by Louis XIV, however, the fire 'being such a deplorable accident involving injury to so many unfortunate people'. In Holland protestations of compassion like these were rare. The fire was seen there as divine retribution; and the Dutch told each other without regret that England was ruined, though some newspapers in Amsterdam were forced to admit, echoing opinions in London, that the wholesale destruction of the capital offered a unique opportunity for the erection of a fine new city upon the ruins of the old. 'Truly,' as John Evelyn the diarist put it, 'there was never a more glorious phoenix upon earth, if it do at last emerge out of the cinders.'

King Charles II recognized this himself. He had been well aware how vulnerable to fire London was. In April he had written to the Lord Mayor warning him of the danger, giving him his authority for the demolition of particularly inflammable buildings and urging him to punish those who wantonly contravened the Building Acts. Now that the calamity he had foreseen had overtaken the City, he was determined to turn it to advantage. A man of taste, deeply interested in town planning and architecture, he envisaged a new London as neat and solid as the towns in Holland he had come to admire while he was in exile during and after the Civil War in England, and as imposing as the Paris which Louis XIV was hoping to give to France. Prophesying a wonderful birth for this, his 'native city', he ordered the establishment of a committee, under the chairmanship of the Lord Chancellor, which would discuss its reconstruction as soon as the fires were all thoroughly extinguished. Soon after this a proclamation was issued in his name requiring new buildings to be of brick or stone and new streets to be made wide enough for the convenience of both pedestrians and vehicles. Only those whose claims to sites were undisputed were to be permitted to build on them and then only in conformity with a general overall plan to be officially approved. Unauthorized buildings were to be pulled down.

The City authorities, however, were anxious to begin the work of reconstruction without delay so that commercial life could return to normal as soon as possible. Otherwise many citizens might decide to remain in the outer suburbs and set up business there beyond the control of the City

Livery Companies, escaping the traditional fees and evading the rules governing their conduct. Already, with markets, warehouses, counting-houses and wharves destroyed, trade was at a standstill; contracts could not be fulfilled, nor rents collected. Yet even if all attempts at planning control had been brushed aside, immediate rebuilding on the old pattern would have been impossible. The debris, which was still smouldering hotly in places as late as March 1667, lay so thick upon the ground that it was impossible to tell where houses had stood and where streets had led. On making his way from Whitehall to London Bridge, 'clambering over mountains of yet smoking rubbish ... so hot as made [him] not onely sweate but even burnt the soles of [his] shoes', John Evelyn frequently mistook where he was and lost the way. It took week after week of hard work to cart away the charred ruins and rubbish; and then a long spell of exceptionally severe winter weather made it impossible to build even on sites which had been cleared and of which the ownership was uncontested. The planners, were, however, unable to take full advantage of this welcome respite: the jealousies aroused by competing interests, the difficulties in raising money in an age which had not developed the techniques of long-term borrowing, the problems of tracing the various titles to land when so many deeds and leases had been burned and so many landlords and tenants had died in the plague which had preceded the fire, all combined to make the realization of a comprehensive plan virtually impossible.

Numerous plans of varying degrees of practicality had been put forward. One of them, submitted by Richard Newcourt, the map-maker, proposed a city in the shape of an exact parallelogram with a series of perfectly rectangular blocks of buildings all facing inwards onto a piazza and a church. Another, drawn up by John Evelyn, who was also a Fellow of the Royal Society and had served on several committees since the Restoration of the monarchy, suggested that all the public buildings of the capital should be placed along the river front beside a wide embankment, and laid particular emphasis upon the need for ridding the city of the 'horrid smoke' which, as he had earlier complained, 'obscures our Churches, and makes our Palaces look old, which fouls our Clothes, and

corrupts the Waters'. This plan took the fancy of the King and Queen to whom Evelyn presented it one day at Whitehall Palace where they looked at it, in the company of the Duke of York, in Her Majesty's bedchamber. 'They examined each particular,' Evelyn recorded, '& discoursed upon them for neere a full houre, seeming to be extremely pleased with what I had so early thought on.'

The King also showed great interest in another plan submitted by Christopher Wren, the versatile young Professor of Astronomy at Oxford, who had already displayed striking talents as an architect. Wren's plan recommended that the whole area of central London should be cleared and that a fresh start should be made with wide, straight streets and large open spaces; that a huge piazza with eight roads radiating from it, and a ring-road around it, should be created in Fleet Street; that spacious embankments should be raised on both sides of a widened Fleet River; that a new Royal Exchange and St Paul's Cathedral should serve as the principal of several focal points; and that the Thames riverside, for centuries a jumble of decaying, tumbledown sheds and jetties, laystalls and slimy wharves, should be swept away and replaced by a handsome paved open space – lined with houses and stone steps leading down to the water – making the London waterfronts as attractive as those of Rotterdam or Genoa. This imaginative yet practical plan led to Wren's appointment as one of the Crown Commissioners for the Rebuilding of London.

The Commissioners' discussions began in an atmosphere described by Henry Oldenburg, Secretary of the Royal Society, as 'very perplext'. Some Commissioners, oo he told a friend, 'are for the old, yet to build with bricks; others for a middle way, by [building a new quay along the waterfront] and enlarging some streets, but keeping the old foundations and vaults. I hear this very day there is a meeting ... to conferre about this great work, and to try whether they can bring it to some issue, before the people that inhabited London do scatter into other parts. The great stress will be, how to raise money for carrying on the warre, and to build the citty at the same time.'

Oldenburg was right: the stress, in fact, proved too great. Not only were the planners beset by the difficulty of raising large sums of money for reconstruction and compensation in a time of war;

but they also had to contend with the urgent demands of impoverished tradesmen, shop-keepers and merchants impatient to get back into business, with landlords deprived of rent, with trustees unable to provide for the poor, with lease-holders in dispute with tenants, and with tenants quarrelling with ground landlords, with school-masters who had no classrooms and with governors of hospitals who had no wards. So, for the most part, the old plan of London was restored: narrow streets remained narrow; and tall buildings were crowded into them, condemn-ing the occupants and their descendants to a reliance upon staircases as yet rare in Paris and other European capitals, to a life, indeed, which one French visitor later described as like that of a bird in a cage, running up and down steps, perching like canaries on sticks.

The piecemeal work of restoration was carried on for years, very slowly. Month after month London was crowded with workmen, English labourers and craftsmen drawn from all over the country by regular work and high wages; and foreign craftsmen, mainly from France and the Rhineland, whose work can still be seen in the City's churches and the halls of the Livery Companies. The streets were clogged with carts carrying bricks and tiles, slate and lime, timber and stone. For the new St Paul's alone more than fifty thousand tons of Portland stone were re-quired, in addition to twenty-five thousand tons of other kinds of stone, eleven thousand tons of ragstone, five hundred and sixty tons of chalk, five hundred tons of rubble and countless wagonloads of sand, copper, lead, iron, marble and timber. Work on St Paul's, not begun until 1675, was not completed until 1710 when Wren's son laid the highest stone in the lantern, and by that time a St Paul's workman had become a synonym for slowness. Over half the fifty-one churches rebuilt by Wren were not started until as late as 1676; and the plans for the City's new prisons, as well as numerous other public buildings and rows and squares of private houses, had not even been approved when, two years after the last cellar had ceased to smoulder, the Rev. Samuel Rolle re-ported houses standing 'scatteringly' in streets half built and many of them let to 'Alehouse-keepers and Victuallers to entertain workmen employed about the city'.

Yet when the reconstruction was finished at

Map of the City of London showing the extent of the damage after the Fire.

last, Londoners could justifiably feel proud of much that had been done, of the changes that had been made for the better. A number of fine new streets had been formed: King Street, Queen Street and Queen Street Place, for instance, had

CITTY OF LONDON, WITH THE *SVBVRBES* THEREOF
h extend, by which is exactly demonstrated the present condition of it,
signifijng the burnt part, & where the houses be those places yet standing. *A° 1666*

Annotations of remarkable places

A Ludgate   W. Dukes Palace
B Newgate   X Custom house
C Aldersgate   Y Bedlame
D Cripple gate   Z. Sion Colledge
E Moore gate   a Temple Staires
F Bishops gate   b White Friars Staires
G Algate   c Black Friars Staires
H Essex House   d Puddle dock
I The Temple   e Pauls Wharfe
K Dorset House   f Broken Wharfe
L Bridewell   g Queene Hythe
M Baynards Castle h 3 Cranes
N Christchurch Cloysters i Stiliard
O S Barths: Hospitall k Colharbour
P Charterhouse   l Old Swan
Q Guildhall   m Belins gate
R The Stokes   n Tower wharfe
S Royall Exchange o Artillery Yard
T Gresham Colledge
V Leadenhall

87 S Hellins
88 S Ethelborough
89 Allhallows in the Wall
90 S Bottolphs by Bishopsgate
91 S Bottolphs by Aldgate
92 S Brides
93 Temple Church
94 S Dunstans West
95 S Andrew in Holborne
96 S Fulcher
97 S Bartholomew
98 S Bartholomew
99 S Bottolphs by Aldersgate
100 S Giles by Cripplegate
* S Martin by Canwicke Street

Scale of a halfe English mile

been laid out to open up a main thoroughfare between the Guildhall and the river, for part of the way following the line of the former dreary and evil-smelling Soper Lane where the soap-makers used to live. The Fleet, which had never been a fast flowing river even in Roman times and had since become a shallow, silt-choked, rubbish-filled abomination, as noisome as a sewer, had been straightened, widened and dredged and once more opened to shipping before being arched over and used as an underground sewer. A fine new Royal Exchange had been built by Edward Jerman who had also designed several of the Livery Companies' splendid halls. The Guildhall, whose massive exterior walls had survived the fire, was reconstructed on an even grander scale than that of the medieval building. The Custom House was rebuilt by Wren whose Cathedral and several of whose churches, their stone and lead steeples rising dramatically above the surrounding roofs, remain as enduring tributes to his genius. And on every side were what a foreign visitor described as 'sound and goodly houses, as fair as any in Europe', built in accordance with building regulations which, for once, were rarely evaded.

These regulations governed not only the types of houses which could be built but also the materials of which they could be constructed. In the interests of 'uniformity and gracefulness', houses were to be of four types. In the six 'high and principal streets', the houses were to be of four storeys, except those of the 'greatest bigness' which could be set back behind courtyards. In lesser streets, they were to be of three storeys; in by-lanes and alleys of two. Façades must be flat and straight; and, although balconies were permitted for houses with forecourts, there were to be no more of these overhanging narrow streets. The waterspouts of the past were to be replaced by drainage pipes to convey water down the sides of buildings into gutters in the streets from which nearly all the huge water cisterns, for long an exasperating obstruction to traffic, were to be

Marble bust of Sir Christopher Wren by Edward Pierce.

banished. Shop fronts were also subject to regulation, and all signs were to be set back against the wall rather than hung out on creaking iron bars and rotting poles, a constant danger to unwary passers-by.

Few shopkeepers paid attention to this particular regulation; and until 1762 when an Act was passed forbidding the practice, they continued to hang out their signs at right angles to the streets on wrought iron brackets which, massive though they were, were often not strong enough to support the huge and heavy boards; and these would sometimes crash to the ground on a windy night, occasionally bringing entire fronts of buildings with them, killing and maiming pedestrians. Most of the building regulations were observed, however, and, when they were not, the transgressor ran the risk of having the offending part or even the whole of the building demolished. For the first time since the days of Londinium Augusta – when the city had been not only the largest town in Britain, and the fifth largest in the Western Roman Empire, but one of the most pleasant to be found anywhere north of the Alps – the streets of London were, if not as wide as they had been then, fairly straight and regular, and the buildings in them both sound and handsome.

Beyond the City walls, Westminster and the expanding suburbs were also being transformed in the 1670s and 1680s and the foundations of central London and the West End we know today were being laid. Houses for the rich were being built – most of them in the style made fashionable before the fire by Inigo Jones – in Bloomsbury and north of St James's Palace, around the Haymarket and along the road which led to the village of Knightsbridge. Among the most successful developers was Henry Jermyn, Earl of St Albans, a devious, ingratiating and unscrupulous courtier who was widely rumoured to be the husband of the King's widowed mother, Henrietta Maria. Whether secretly married to her or not, he certainly exercised the most pervasive influence over her, becoming successively her Master of the Horse, private secretary and the colonel of her bodyguard, at the same time gaining complete control over her finances. The King, who found St Albans useful and was prepared to reward him accordingly, granted him a lease of a large field to the north of the avenue leading from St James's

Palace where, on a surface of powdered cockleshells, His Majesty played pall–mall, a game rather like croquet, with his mistresses. In this field St Albans arranged for the building of the aristocratic houses in St James's Square, and for the laying out of elegant streets around them. These he called Jermyn Street after himself, King Street and Charles II Street after his patron, Duke Street and Duke of York Street after his patron's brother, and Babmaes Street after his patron's faithful servant, Baptist May. He also built houses along the King's pall–mall alley which, officially known as Catherine Street in honour of the Queen, Catherine of Braganza, became more generally known as Pall Mall. He constructed a market to serve the new area; and he had a church, St James's, designed by Wren to face on to Jermyn Street with its northern windows overlooking the road to Knightsbridge.

This road was soon to be known as Piccadilly in teasing reference to a large house near a windmill which had been built by a tailor and collar-maker named Robert Baker whose fortune was supposed to be largely based upon the sale of pickadils, the high-ruffed collars then in fashion, and whose house was consequently known to the local wags as Pickadilly Hall. And along Piccadilly mansions even more imposing than Baker's now appeared. Clarendon House was designed by Roger Pratt for the Earl of Clarendon who sold it for about half its enormous cost to the Duke of Albemarle, an improvident young man who was obliged in turn to sell it to a consortium of bankers and speculators headed by Sir Thomas Bond, a denizen, like St Albans, of the Queen Mother's Court. Soon afterwards, in 1680, Bond began the development which was soon to cover its gardens with the buildings of Bond Street and Albemarle Street. And at about the same time the gardens and grounds behind Clarendon House's neighbours – Burlington House, built for the Earl of Cork and Burlington, and Berkeley House, designed for Lord Berkeley of Stratton – were developed with streets of houses that still commemorate their

Detail from an engraving of St James's Park by Johannes Kip. In the foreground is a very early milk-bar – two milkmaids selling cups of milk to passers-by.

titles and the names of their families.

To the east other fine houses were being erected in Bloomsbury where the principal landowner was the Earl of Southampton, the son of Shakespeare's patron. As Lord Treasurer, Southampton had tried to stop the Earl of St Albans's development in St James's Square, fearing that grand houses there might draw purchasers away from the plots he himself intended to offer for sale around a square he had formed in front of Southampton House. But he need not have worried: his own development was quite as successful as St Albans's, although the Russells rather than his own family, the Wriothesleys, benefited from it. For Southampton died in 1677 and, having no sons, his property came into the hands of his wife's step-daughter, Rachel, whose son was the second Duke of Bedford and grandson of the man who had developed Covent Garden. The Duke and Duchess of Bedford, their fortune immensely increased, decided to move to the higher ground of Bloomsbury which was 'esteemed very healthful' and was certainly now more fashionable than the Strand. So they demolished their house there and moved to Southampton House which became known thereafter as Bedford House and which, when its own turn for demolition came, provided sites for parts of Bloomsbury Square, Russell Square and Bedford Place.

While land in St James's, Piccadilly and Bloomsbury was being developed for the rich, houses for the less well off were being built elsewhere. Near Robert Baker's Pickadilly Hall stood Shaver's Hall, a celebrated early seventeenth-century gaming-house, run by a former barber and surrounded by bowling alleys, tennis courts and tree-lined walks. The profits of the gaming-house had slumped during the Civil War, had vanished altogether during Cromwell's Commonwealth, and had not recovered at the Restoration. A shrewd and unscrupulous gambler, Colonel Thomas Panton, 'an absolute artist at the card table either upon the square or foul play', was able, therefore, to buy the property cheaply and, with some additional land acquired from the Baker family, to undertake an extensive redevelopment of the area. He was so successful, indeed, that other owners and speculators were encouraged to follow his example, among them Henry Coventry, a secretary of state, and Edward Wardour.

Wardour Street led into the area known as Soho, presumably after the hunting cry which had for long been heard in the fields here. In this area were several large houses including Monmouth House, Leicester House, Fauconberg House, Carlisle House and Newport House. But buildings on a more modest scale had already started when Wardour Street was laid out; and in the 1670s and 1680s it progressed rapidly as thousands of foreign immigrants flooded into the neighbourhood, many of them Huguenots from France, giving it the cosmopolitan flavour which it was to retain for centuries.

Conspicuous among the developers of Soho were Richard Frith, a rich builder who had helped Sir Thomas Bond erect Bond Street, and a masterful, persuasive physician, Dr Nicholas Barbon, whose father, Praise-God Barbon (or Barebones), had given his name to one of the Commonwealth's parliaments. Barbon lived in splendid style in a house in Crane Court to which he would summon freeholders, tenants, carpenters and masons, and, while his manner alternated between imperious bluster and insinuating charm, would persuade them to agree to his suggestions. Some of his schemes were sound, others not; many of the houses his contractors built were solid; a few fell to pieces; his methods were frequently questionable, on occasions actually criminal. Three of his most spectacular developments were those of Red Lion Square; of the area south of the Strand which the noble families who had once lived there were now abandoning for sites further west, as the Russells had done; and of the estate of the Duke of Buckingham. This, at Buckingham's insistence, Barbon developed in a way that would preserve the Duke's memory forever, using his Christian name and every syllable of his title in the nomenclature of the new streets – George Street, Duke Street, Buckingham Street, even Of Alley – though the name of this last has now been changed by an unamused authority to 'York Place formerly known as Of Alley' in commemoration of Buckingham's predecessors as owners of the land, the Archbishops of York.

Samuel Pepys came to live at No. 12 Buckingham Street in 1679 and remained there until 1688 when he moved to No. 14. Previously he had lived in Seething Lane in the City and it was here that he had gone to work in the nearby Navy Office and

Soho Square in the 1750s : engraving by Sutton Nicholls.

OVERLEAF *A London coffee-house, 1668.*

had set forth upon those jaunts which are de-scribed in his journal and provide so vivid a picture of life in the London that was being rebuilt around him. He entertained guests to dinners 'most neatly dressed' by his maid. 'We had a Fricasse of rabbits and chicken,' he recorded after one merry party, 'a leg of mutton boiled – three carps in a dish – a great dish of a side of lamb – a dish of roasted pigeons – a dish of four lobsters – three tarts a lampry pie, a most rare pie – a dish of anchoves – good wine of several sorts; and all things mighty noble and to my great content.' He went to coffee-houses, to taverns and wine-houses, where it was possible to get a good meal for threepence, and as often as he could out of sight of his wife, he dallied with accommodating women, as he did with Betty Martin, a linen draper in Westminster Hall whose husband, a would-be ship's purser, was 'a sorry little fellow': 'And I do so towse her and feel her all over, making her believe how fair and good a skin she has; and endeed, she hath a very white thigh and leg but monstrous fat.' He went to church, and there, too, he contrived to sit by pretty girls and

'did labour to take [them] by the hand and the body'. He went to the theatre, sometimes arriving three and a half hours before the play began to 'get a good place' in the pit and paying a poor man to keep his seat for him. He walked through the streets and the markets with the cries of the tradesmen and hawkers ringing in his ears: 'Pan-cakes!' 'Hot baked warden pears and pippins! Hot!' 'Dumplins! Dumplins! Diddle diddle, dumplins ho!' 'Crab! Crab! Any Crab!' 'Long thread laces, long and strong!' 'Oysters! Oysters!' 'Buy my fat chickens!' 'Oh, rare shoes! Here's your nice shoes!' 'Here's your rare socks, four pairs a shilling!'

The streets, like those in Paris, were crowded with sedan chairs and carriages of all kinds. There were about five thousand privately owned coach-es, many of them appallingly cumbersome and frequently sticking in muddy ruts, and some seven hundred public hackney-carriages, dread-fully uncomfortable vehicles with leather straps

TOP *Covent Garden Market in the early eighteenth century by Balthazar Nebot.*

ABOVE *The River Thames in the bitterly cold winter of 1677, looking eastwards towards London Bridge : painting by Abraham Hondius.*

instead of springs and in place of glass windows sheets of tin perforated with small holes. There were public wagons carrying twenty passengers and drawn by eight horses, there were brewers' drays and dung carts and butchers' wagons, and while these rattled over the cobbles and screeched against the walls and posts as they moved in one direction, herds of cattle and droves of turkeys were being impatiently driven in another.

Those who wished to escape the hubbub of the streets could respond to the watermen's cries of 'Oars! Oars! Will you have any oars?' and go by river. There were thousands of wherries on the Thames, regulated in size and rowed by licensed watermen; but despite the controls to which they were subject the watermen were a rude and rough set of men relishing the custom, already ancient and long to continue, of greeting their fellow-oarsmen and passengers in passing boats with the most alarming threats and fanciful insults that could be devised. It was a dangerous life as well as a hard one. Each year on average about fifty watermen were drowned at London Bridge alone where the turbulent waters rose to a frightening height as they rushed between the piers. Some passengers remained in the craft as it hurtled under the bridge. One of these, a Frenchman known to Pepys, appeared to be in a state of extreme fear 'when he saw the great fall. He began to cross himself and say his prayers ... though as soon as he was over, he swore, "*Morbleu! C'est le plus grand plaisir du monde!*"' But most passengers preferred to get out of the boat at the Three Cranes in Upper Thames Street, leaving the waterman to shoot the bridge on his own, and then embark again at Billingsgate.

Besides, alighting here enabled visitors to see London Bridge itself, the ancient, top-heavy structure which seemed in danger of imminent collapse as carts and carriages rumbled constantly across it over the narrow roadway and between the bulging houses and haberdashers' shops whose projecting backs, overhanging the water, were supported on great wooden beams and whose upper storeys were joined together by iron tie-bars to prevent them toppling backwards into the river.

London Bridge was one of the principal sights of the City until the houses on it were demolished between 1758 and 1762. Another was the lunatic asylum, Bethlehem Royal Hospital, known as Bedlam, where the inmates were placed in cells in galleries like caged animals and anyone paying a twopenny entrance fee could watch their strange antics and make fun of them. A visit to Bedlam might be followed by a visit to the Tower, the Norman fortress and prison where there was always a chance of catching sight of a celebrated face at one of the barred windows. Here also, in the menagerie, there were lions, tigers, leopards and a two-legged dog; and, in the museum, such fascinating curiosities as 'the entire Skin of a Moor, tanned with the hair on'. From Tower Stairs it was a pleasant journey upstream to Paul's Wharf, the nearest river steps to St Benet's Hill, the approach to St Paul's Cathedral, the City's 'crowning glory'. There was, indeed, so much to see in London that, as a Swiss visitor wrote home in 1698 to his father in Geneva, 'You might stay here a lifetime and not know half of it.'

———————————————————————————

Far away to the east another country was rising to greatness. This was Russia, for centuries considered in the West a sprawling backwater of little importance in the affairs of Europe. In the fifteenth century the gradual expansion of the princely state of Muscovy had begun to accelerate when Ivan III, who waged war against the Tatars of Kazan and of the Golden Horde, inaugurated the reconquest of the Ukraine from Poland and Lithuania, and annexed the republic of Novgorod. This expansion of the Muscovite dominions continued under his successors; and by the time of his grandson, Ivan IV, known as 'Grozny', the Terrible, the Grand Princes of Muscovy, masters of an area as large as the rest of Christian Europe, could with justification call themselves Tsars of all the Russias. Yet although Ivan, who died in 1584, had been intent upon gaining free access to the Baltic and opening up trade with Europe, a century later Russia was still a power largely unknown to the West, conservative and backward. Its capital was Moscow, a city of wood and with streets paved with wood, a dirty, muddy city, though one whose white-walled and golden-domed churches, whose three splendid cathedrals and citadel of the Kremlin, whose beautifully carved and painted window frames, doorways and gables lent it a strangely appealing beauty. On the morning of 30 May 1672 the bell in the Tower of Ivan the Great in the Kremlin square proclaimed the birth of an heir to the Tsar Alexis who was to fulfil an ambition of opening up a window on the West by forsaking Moscow for another capital of his own foundation.

13

St Petersburg
in the Days of
Peter the Great
1703–1725

At the beginning of the eighteenth century the Tsar of Russia, Peter the Great, took a strange and momentous decision. He determined to move the capital of his immense kingdom westward from Moscow, which had long been the centre of government, to a pestilential area of swampland on an island at the mouth of the Neva River where it debouched into the Gulf of Finland. It was said that one day in 1703, when he was thirty years old, he snatched a halberd from the hand of one of his soldiers and cutting two strips of turf, laid them crosswise with the words, 'Here there shall be a new city.' He then dropped the halberd, seized a spade and began to dig the first embankment himself. His astonishing resolve, which was to have consequences almost as revolutionary as those brought about by the Bolshevik government when it re-established the capital in Moscow, was prompted by a desire for what an Italian traveller, Francesco Algarotti, described as 'a window on to Europe'. For his travels had led the Tsar to conclude that only by using the techniques of Western countries, by learning and assimilating their methods of manufacture, would he be able to consolidate a power based on autocracy and serfdom.

Throughout the court quiet voices could be heard expressing misgivings and despondency at the Tsar's extraordinary intention of building a city on an island from which his enemies, the Swedes, would certainly drive the Russians as soon as they could. But Peter was a single-minded

The Peterhof, built by Alexandre Jean Baptiste Le Blond for Peter the Great.

Peter the Great by Jean-Marc Nattier (detail).

man of forceful character and commanding presence. Six feet seven inches in height, his arms were unusually long, his hands powerful and rough, the skin scarred by the hard physical labour that he undertook with such zest and energy. Restless, impatient and decisive, he dominated all around him, his features twitching alarmingly when he was provoked or under stress, sometimes so convulsively that the whole of the left side of his face was contorted by uncontrollable spasms and his eyes rolled up in their sockets until only the whites could be seen. But these convulsions, the Electress of Brandenburg commented sympathetically upon meeting him for the first time, were not in his power to control and were, in any case, curiously at one with his bizarre and unpredictable personality. 'He has great vivacity of mind,' her mother, the widowed Electress of Hanover, concluded, 'and a ready and just repartee, though with all the advantages with which nature has endowed him, it could be wished that his manners were a little less rustic . . . I asked him if he liked hunting. He replied that his father had been very fond of it, but that he himself, from his earliest youth, had had a real passion for

navigation. He told us that he worked himself in building ships, showed us his hands, and made us feel the calloused places that had been caused by work . . . He is a very extraordinary man. It is impossible to describe him or even give an idea of him, unless you have seen him . . . We stayed a very long time at table, but we would gladly have remained there longer still without feeling a moment of boredom . . . He has great qualities and unlimited natural intelligence.'

Peter had been born in Moscow, the son of the pious Tsar Alexis, the second monarch of the Romanov dynasty, and of his second wife, Natalya, daughter of a half Tatar landlord from the remote province of Tarus. His father had had two sons by his first wife, but they were both sickly boys, one of them being partially paralysed, the other dim-witted and half-blind, so that Peter's bursting health seemed all the more remarkable. The elder half-brother, Fedor, died at the age of twenty; the younger, Ivan, was proclaimed joint Tsar with Peter after several members of his family and their supporters had been hacked to death in Peter's presence following an attempt to have him established as sole ruler. Thereafter the two boys appeared together on state occasions; yet whereas Ivan and his ambitious and strong-willed sister, Sophia, lived in state in the Kremlin, Peter and his mother were relegated to a village on the outskirts of Moscow near the German suburb. His education there was very meagre: he learned to read and write and mastered some Latin and Greek; but much of his time was occupied in playing soldiers with the children of both noblemen and peasants who were all required to take the games seriously and to play them with due attention to tactics, fortress building and the capabilities of artillery. Most of his knowledge of these matters Peter acquired from the foreigners in the German colony from which he later also acquired a German mistress.

At the age of seventeen he was married to the daughter of a Russian nobleman who bore him a son; but he did not take to her and soon got rid of her. Soon, too, Ivan died; and Peter became sole ruler of the empire in which he had for some time been recognized as the commanding figure.

He had already decided that he must modernize his country on Western lines and use naval power to assert Russian dominion. Young noblemen were consequently sent to Venice, to Holland and

England to study seamanship, navigation and shipbuilding; and what became known as a Great Embassy of more than two hundred and fifty Russians sailed to all the major European states to study Western methods and to enlist the services of officers, sailors and shipwrights by whose assistance a powerful Russian fleet might be created. The Tsar himself, travelling incognito by sleigh, ship and coach under the name of Peter Mikhailov, reached Holland and set to work in the shipyards of Zaandam. From Holland he went to England where, in a winter so exceptionally hard that the Thames was frozen over from bank to bank, he obtained employment at Deptford. Here he increased his knowledge not only of ships but also of arms, of clockwork and of all kinds of other mechanisms. Here, too, he and his companions behaved so barbarically at Sayes Court, the lovely house of John Evelyn, that when they left after three months the whole place was virtually in ruins with windows smashed, floors ripped up, pictures unrecognizable after being used for target practice and all the chairs gone, presumably chopped up and tossed into the stoves.

Despite the gross behaviour of his retinue, the Tsar was able to induce more than eight hundred skilled workers and technicians, engineers and gunners, architects and astronomers, shipwrights and decorators to enrol in the service of the Russian crown. And when he returned to Russia, where an insurrection which had broken out in his absence was suppressed with ferocious cruelty, these men were put to work to fulfil his dreams of transforming his country into a powerful modern state, of reconquering the Baltic provinces which had been lost to Sweden, and of making St Petersburg a worthy capital for his new empire.

At first he had intended merely to build a port – so that ships trading with Russia would not have to sail as far north as the White Sea and Archangel – and a large fort from which the passage into the Neva, and to the huge Lake Ladoga beyond, could be controlled. The fort, the Fortress of St Peter and St Paul, was to cover most of the island of the Hares at the mouth of the river where, in the summer months, a few Finnish fishermen occupied a huddle of mud huts; and, since it had to be raised above the high-water mark when the waters of the gulf rose in a storm, immense quantities of earth had to be piled on the site from elsewhere. An army of workers, reinforced by Swedish

prisoners, was conscripted for this task. There were no wheelbarrows then in Russia – though the Tsar had certainly seen one at Sayes Court; he had been pushed in one across the ravaged garden and through the splendid holly hedge – so the men had to carry the earth in bags or in their shirts. It was slow and painful work which cost the lives of thousands of those employed on the task. But it continued relentlessly and within five months the outlines of six great bastions had appeared, rising up thirty feet above the waters of the river. Soon afterwards work began on a shipbuilding yard on the left bank of the river, later to become the Admiralty, identified from a distance by the tall wooden spire of its church; this, too, was provided with a strong bastion to protect the site during the repeated attacks that the Swedes unsuccessfully made upon the growing settlement.

For himself the Tsar built a single-storey timber cabin, with a bedroom, dining-room and study, large mica windows latticed in the Dutch style, and with a roof laid with shingle painted to look like tiles. The log walls were also painted and planed so that they gave the appearance of being built of brick. And on a small canal leading off the south bank of the river Peter constructed for his mistress, Martha Skavronskaya, the Lithuanian peasant girl who took the Russian name of Ekaterina, Catherine, and was later to become his empress, a small house also in the Dutch style with a balustrade running the length of the façade, windows separated by Corinthian pilasters and terraces leading down to the water. This fell into complete decay in the nineteenth century but her lover's log cabin, the oldest house in the city, is still to be seen, enclosed by a stone wall erected to protect it by Catherine II.

While bastions were being built, so were ships, at first in the yards above Lake Ladoga, then in the new construction yard on the left bank of the Neva. And as early as 23 September 1704 Peter was able to write to his intimate friend Alexander Danilovich Menshikov, a former stable lad and street seller of hot pies, 'Here, thanks be to God, all goes well. Tomorrow and the day after, three frigates, four snows, a packet-boat and a galliot will be launched.' In the frigate, *Standard*, Peter himself set sail into the Baltic Sea and, measuring the depth with a lead line, he discovered a channel which led from the island of Kotlin, later to be the

naval base of Kronstadt, to the mouth of the Neva and he ordered a fort to be constructed to protect it, himself supervising the laying of its foundations as huge boxes filled with stones were dragged across the ice and then sunk to the bottom of the channel's bed.

To encourage trading vessels to sail to his new port, the Tsar offered all manner of inducements: tolls were reduced to a far lower level than that demanded at Swedish ports; Russian exports were offered at bargain prices provided the goods were taken aboard at St Petersburg rather than at Archangel. The first Dutch ship to enter the port was piloted upstream by Peter himself and granted exemption from Russian customs duties for ever; an English merchantman that followed it was given the same immunity.

After Peter had decided to transform the settlement of wooden huts into a modern stone city, he offered similar inducements to builders and imposed harsh conditions upon the movement and use of materials: all wagons and all vessels entering St Petersburg were required to add a certain quantity of stone to their ordinary cargoes; when a shortage of stonemasons held building up, the construction of stone houses was suddenly forbid-

Peter the Great founding the city of St Petersburg, spring 1703

den in Moscow; and when the supply of timber became insufficient for all the purposes for which it was required, the inhabitants of St Petersburg were forbidden to cut down trees or to heat water for a bath more than once a week so that building work could be continued without interruption. The Tsar made it known that he himself would lay the first stone of any new building and join the owner of the property in a toast to the success of the venture.

Discouraged by its remoteness and by its climate, those who were not compelled to come to St Petersburg to work were reluctant to settle there. But the Tsar made it difficult if not impossible for people to refuse his invitations. In March 1708 he told several members of his family and numerous noblemen, government officials and rich merchants to come for the spring; and most unwillingly they did so, abandoning their comfortable houses outside Moscow, building new ones for what they considered to be outrageous sums in St Petersburg, and paying equally outrageous prices for provisions which had to be transported over great distances by wagon and sledge to the growing city. Determined that St Petersburg should not develop as a city of Old Russia but rather as one to rival London and Amsterdam, the Tsar required that the houses of the new arrivals should be built in the English or Dutch styles, noblemen's houses on the left bank of the Neva – two storeys being required for all those whose owners had more than five hundred serfs – merchants' wooden houses facing them on the opposite bank.

The cost of building and living in St Petersburg was but one of the complaints of the peevish immigrants. Floods were common in the autumn when the waters of the Neva poured through the streets, cascading into cellars, carrying away the flimsier dwellings, and even bearing the masts of ships past upstairs windows. Wolves roamed about both by day and night: as late as 1715 a woman was devoured in broad daylight not far from the Governor General's palace. Fires were constantly breaking out, despite all the precautions taken by the ceaselessly vigilant Tsar who could often be seen hatchet in hand climbing to the top of burning houses to encourage the fire-fighters in their work. 'He incites nobles as well as common people to help in the struggle and does not pause until the fire is put out,' the Danish ambassador recorded. 'But when the sovereign is absent, things are very different. Then the people watch the fires with indifference and do nothing to help put them out. It is no good haranguing them or even offering them money. They merely wait for a chance to steal something.'

If the nobles and merchants considered themselves aggrieved by having to live in so outlandish a place, the men who were drafted to work there had far juster cause for complaint. They perished from cold and exposure, fell ill with dysentery, scurvy, malaria and other diseases, died in their crowded, damp and dirty huts. Yet as hundreds of lives were sacrificed, hundreds of other workers, Cossacks, Siberians, Tatars, Finns, were brought to take up the spades and pickaxes of the dead. 'They were furnished with a travelling allowance and subsistence for six months,' wrote Robert K. Massie in his excellent biography of the Tsar, 'after which they were permitted, if they survived, to return home, their places to be taken by a new draft the following summer. Local officials and noblemen charged by Peter with recruiting and sending along these human levies protested to the

The entry of captured Swedish frigates into St Petersburg : engraving by A. Zubov, 1720. The Admiralty is in the background, and Peter is in the little boat in the foreground.

Tsar that hundreds of villages were being ruined by the loss of their best men, but Peter would not listen ... The actual number who died will never be known; in Peter's day it was estimated at 100,000. Later figures are much lower, perhaps 25,000 or 30,000, but no one disputes the grim saying that St Petersburg was "a city built on bones."'

Yet, ignoring all the complaints and sufferings of his own people and the threats of the Swedes – whose King, Charles XII, remarked with unwarranted bombast that the Tsar could well be left to tire himself out with founding new towns while they reserved for themselves the honour of taking them – Peter never lost faith in St Petersburg, his favourite creation. And after his victory over the

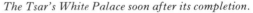

The Tsar's White Palace soon after its completion.

Swedish army at Poltava in 1709, and the subsequent capture of Riga and Vyborg, he was able to consolidate his hold on the Baltic provinces and to concentrate his energies on the expansion of the city he called his 'paradise'.

Already there were about a hundred and fifty large houses in St Petersburg compared with only fifteen five years before; and the Italian architect, Domenico Trezzini, who had been appointed Master of Building, Construction and Fortification in 1703, had built a church within the Fortress and was soon to design the Peter and Paul Cathedral, the Alexander Nevski Monastery and the Tsar's Winter Palace a mile upstream from the Admiralty. After 1713, when Trezzini was succeeded by the German Andreas Schlüter, the city began to grow more rapidly than ever. At that time its centre was Trinity Square near the Tsar's log cabin. Here stood the Church of the Holy Trinity, various government offices, a hospital and the stone mansions of noblemen and ministers; close by was the city's crowded market and the celebrated Triumphal Osteria of the Four Frigates, a tavern which had been opened by a German and was patronized by the Tsar himself, always a heavy drinker, particularly of vodka sprinkled with cayenne pepper. From this centre

The Empress Consort Catherine by Jean-Marc Nattier.

the city now spread on to other islands and across the mainland. On the largest of the islands, Vasilevsky Island, Prince Menshikov, the Governor General of the city, built himself a huge palace, designed by the Italian Giovanni Maria Fontana and the German Gottfried Schädel, with projecting bays at the front, two wings forming a court at the back, and a Dutch roof of iron plates painted red. With its façade broken up by prominent pilasters crowned by stone capitals on each of its three main storeys, its large walled formal garden, its farm and workers' cottages, its private church and landing stage, it was a far more imposing palace than the Tsar's Winter Palace on the mainland. This was originally a modest wooden building, dwarfed by the nearby mansion of General-Admiral Apraxin which stood on part of the site now occupied by the Empress Elizabeth's Winter Palace, and was remarkable only for the naval crown over the front door. It had but two storeys and, because of the need to keep the building symmetrically in line with its neighbours, these were higher than the Tsar, who felt uncomfortable in grand surroundings, would personally have liked. So he had false ceilings constructed inside; and, when the entertaining of important guests had to be undertaken, he borrowed Menshikov's palace for the purpose. His own palace was pulled down in 1721, to be rebuilt in stone. In turn this and its three successors were also later demolished: the Hermitage Museum now stands on the site.

The Tsar's rooms on the ground floor of the Summer Palace were almost as modest as those in the Winter Palace, which was a little further upstream, but the upper floor, which was occupied by Catherine Skavronskaya, who was crowned Empress Consort in 1724, were much grander. These had painted ceilings, walls covered with tapestries or silk, parquet floors and furniture inlaid with ivory. And whereas Peter's favourite room was his workshop, where in a leather jerkin he demonstrated his expertise at his lathe while talking to statesmen and ambassadors about affairs of state, Catherine spent much of her time in her ballroom upon whose walls hung long looking-glasses made in England, representing the first use made in Russia of plate glass in decoration. Here assemblies were held, attended by women on the orders of Peter who was anxious to provide a civilized alternative to those noisy,

Empress Elizabeth's Winter Palace.

drunken all-male parties which up till then had been characteristic of the Russian court and of which one example, held at St Petersburg for foreign envoys in 1715, was reported by Friedrich Christian Weber, the Hanoverian ambassador: 'We were feasted as usual and ... given a well matured Hungarian wine at dinner. We could hardly stand, having drunk such a quantity already, but it was impossible to refuse another pint glass ... This reduced us to such pitiful circumstances that our servants chose to throw one of us into the garden, another into the wood where we stayed until four in the afternoon and where we were sick ... A second debauch followed; this time we fainted away and were put to bed. After one hour's sleep, one of the Tsar's favourites woke us up to visit the Prince of Circassia, in bed with his wife. We had to drink brandy and wine by his bed till four o'clock when we found ourselves at home, with no idea of how we got there.

'At eight a.m. we went to Court to drink coffee but the cups were full of brandy ... We then went to dine, that is to say to get drunk for the fourth time.' On another occasion, having 'gulped down at dinner a dozen bumpers of Hungary wine', Weber was presented with 'a full quart of brandy' which he was forced to drink in two draughts. 'I soon lost my senses,' he reported, 'though I was comforted to observe the rest of the guests, who were lying asleep on the floor, were in no condition to make reflections upon my own skill in

drinking.' At Catherine's assemblies in the Summer Palace it was stipulated that no lady should get drunk, nor should any gentleman before nine o'clock.

The year after the Summer Palace was completed, in 1716, another foreign architect, Alexandre Jean Baptiste Le Blond, came to St Petersburg. The son of a painter and a pupil of André Le Nôtre, who had worked at Versailles for Louis XIV, Le Blond had several distinguished buildings in Paris, including the Hôtel de Clermont, to his credit. Having signed a contract to work in Russia as Architect General for five years, this 'veritable wonder of a prodigy', as the Tsar described him, arrived in the city with a large contingent of French assistants including two draughtsmen, three sculptors, two engineers, two joiners, three stonemasons, a bricklayer, a carpenter, three locksmiths, a chiseller, a founder, two jewellers, a gardener and an inspector of buildings.

With the help of these men, and using Swedish prisoners as labourers, Le Blond constructed the city's main thoroughfare, the Nevsky Prospect, which stretched from the Admiralty to the Alexander Nevsky Monastery; and he carried out numerous improvements to the lovely thirty-seven-acre Summer Garden behind the Summer Palace. This garden had been started years before and planted with trees and flowers from Germany and Holland as well as from all over Russia, and it was already one of the delights of the city. But by the time Le Blond had completed his work there the Summer Garden had been transformed into a far more delightful formal French garden in the manner of Versailles with neat *parterres de broderie* and gravelled walks, Italian, French and Dutch sculptures at the intersections of the paths, with over fifty fountains, with pools and basins, aviaries in the shape of pagodas, a conservatory with orange, lemon and bay trees, a menagerie from which at various times emerged sables, porcupines and a blue monkey. An arbour was imported from Venice; a grotto was adorned with statues by Hans Konrad Ossner.

Le Blond was equally successful with the palace he built for the Tsar on the coast looking across to Kronstadt, a mile or so east of a splendid palace which Prince Menshikov had built for himself at Oranienbaum. Peterhof, as it came to be called, though nothing like as splendid as the palace which Rastrelli created there for Peter's daughter, the Empress Elizabeth, was a fine house with exquisite wood carving by Nicholas Pineau. But it was the surrounding gardens and park and the three summer pavilions in its grounds between the house and the sea, the Hermitage, Marly and

The official unveiling of Falconet's statue of Peter the Great, St Petersburg, 1782.

Monplaisir, which made the place so beguiling. Marly is a modest Dutch house built at the edge of a lake; Monplaisir is also in the Dutch style and, with its French windows opening onto a terrace above the waters of the Gulf of Finland, was the Tsar's favourite of all his houses. It was at the Hermitage, however, that he entertained his guests: here, in the dining-room that occupies the whole of the first floor, the middle of a big oval table sank to the kitchen on the ground floor to be replenished with another course at the ringing of a bell. By each guest were menus on which they marked the dishes of their choice.

The Tsar guarded his privacy jealously at Peterhof. Guests – who were likely to be dragooned into performing some manual task such as planting trees or digging in the garden and were almost certain to be compelled to drink more wine than they wanted – were given cards with the number of the bed they were to occupy and issued with a list of regulations concerning their behaviour which included an injunction against sleeping without first removing boots and shoes.

Le Blond was less successful with his work for Peter on the island of Vasilevsky, though this was not his fault. He and the Tsar had envisaged

creating a city of canals like Amsterdam on the eastern half of the island. There were to be two main canals crossing the whole length of the island and twelve others intersecting them at right angles. All would be wide enough for two boats to pass each other. But they had reckoned without the opposition of the Governor General of the city, Prince Menshikov, who had been given much of the island by the Tsar and considered himself the lord of all of it. He vindictively ensured that the canals were too narrow for boats to pass and so shallow that they silted up with mud. 'On his return to Petersburg after a prolonged absence,' wrote J. V. Stählin-Storckburg who had 'often been surprised' to see how narrow the Vasilevsky canals were, 'His Majesty postponed every other care to pay them a visit. He saw in most of the streets, with much satisfaction, complete rows of houses, built either of wood or stone . . . but was soon overcast when he perceived the pitiful dimensions of both streets and canals. He was struck dumb with astonishment; but his gestures plainly showed how much his contempt and indignation were excited by so egregious a blunder.

'Fearing, however, that he had been deceived in the dimensions of those of Amsterdam, which he had given as a model, he went immediately to the house of Mr Wilde, the Dutch Resident, and asked him if he knew the breadth of the canals of the city. Mr Wilde presented a plan of it to the Tsar, who took out his compass, and having measured the length and breadth of the canals, wrote down their dimensions on his tablets. He then begged the Resident to go with him and see the works that had been finished during his absence. On measuring the first canals he met with, he found that their breadth, and that of the streets added, were not equal to the width of one of the canals of Amsterdam. In a transport of rage he cried out, "The Devil take the undertaking – all is spoiled", and retired to his palace.

'He long remembered the unpleasant feelings of which this blunder had been the cause, and frequently cast an angry look on Prince Menshikov . . . From time to time he went to the island, and having examined for whole hours the streets and canals that were begun, returned sorrowfully without uttering a word . . .

'[One day] after walking over the whole island with the plan in his hand, the Tsar said to his architect, "Well M. Le Blond, what is to be done to carry my plan into execution?"

'"Raze, Sir, raze," answered M. Le Blond, elevating his shoulders, "there is no other remedy than to demolish all that has been done, and to dig the canals anew."

'"I thought so," replied the Tsar, and retired to his boat . . . He never spoke to M. Le Blond again of Vasilevsky Island.'

It was the Tsar's one major disappointment in St Petersburg. As the city grew and became increasingly beautiful he recalled with pleasure the gloomy sentiments of those who had believed his whole scheme both reckless and absurd, who agreed with Prince Narishkin that it was ridiculous to try to rule Russia from its north-western extremity. 'What would you think,' Narishkin asked, 'of an animal that had its heart in its fingernails and its stomach somewhere at the end of its big toe?'

Yet by the time of his death at the age of fifty-two in 1725, Peter knew that his dream had been realized. St Petersburg, his unexpected city, would survive and flourish as the capital of the largest country in the world. His successors were to enlarge and alter it; but it was never to lose the stamp of its creator's extraordinary personality.

———————————————————————————

As Russia grew increasingly powerful under Peter the Great and his successors, the influence of Venice was in sad decline. At the beginning of the thirteenth century, when Byzantium was waning, Genoa, Pisa and the Byzantine city of Venice had all become centres of greater importance. After Genoa had defeated Pisa, and the Venetian republic had overcome Genoa at Chioggia in 1380, it was Venice that eclipsed all her rivals, her ships proclaiming the power of the republic all over the Mediterranean world. During the sixteenth century, however, a long period of economic stagnation began; and by the time Casanova was born in the city in 1725, Venice, a place as devoted to pleasure as Amsterdam was to making money, had started to live on its beauty, its treasures and its prestige.

14

Venice
in the Days of Canaletto and Casanova
1697–1798

A city abandoned to pleasure, Venice was the glittering jewel in the showcase of eighteenth-century Europe, the delightful playground of the Grand Tour. No one could approach it, one admiring visitor thought as he glided towards his first glimpse of it across the smooth waters of the lagoon, without feeling that he was 'entering another world'. Most tourists came here from Milan as their guidebook advised, passing through Verona and Vicenza and then going down the Brenta from Padua in a *burchio*, an elaborately fitted barge, horse-drawn up to the entrance to the lagoon and then towed by a *remulcio* to the custom-house. A gondolier in white trousers and waistcoat with gold rings in his ears and on his fingers would then take the tourist to his hotel or lodgings; and the tourist, lounging on the damask cushions, looking at the bridges and palaces as the gondola drifted along, would feel the excitement of Venice already within him, sensing its spell wrapping itself around him 'at first sight'.

The time to come was during the Carnival which began just after Christmas when, in St Mark's Square, an announcement was made by one of the Doge's officials granting everyone permission to wear masks. Thereafter black or white masks were worn universally by rich and poor alike, by servants and their masters, by working women who could be mistaken for *zentildonne*, and by *zentildonne* who were taken for prostitutes, by patricians, and even by beggars. By the end of the eighteenth century the population of the city had fallen to about 137,000; but

Canaletto, The Feast of San Rocco, *1735 (detail), showing the Doge and Senators in procession.*

during the time of the Carnival the streets were crammed with 30,000 visitors, with 'such a multitude of Jews, Turks, and Christians; lawyers, knaves and pickpockets; mountebanks, old women, and physicians, strumpets bare-faced; and, in short, such a jumble of senators, citizens, gondoliers, and people of every character and condition, that your ideas are broken, bruised and dislocated in the crowd'.

In the daytime there were numerous spectacles to watch: acrobatic displays, bullfights, balloon ascents, wild-beast shows, bear-baitings, puppet plays, burlesques, boxing and wrestling tournaments, fancy-dress parades. There were fortune-tellers and musicians, quacks and harlequins and pantaloons; on Maundy Thursday members of the Smiths' and Butchers' guilds, wearing outlandish costumes, beheaded a bull in St Mark's Square as fireworks roared and sparkled overhead; and a tightrope-walker slid down a rope from the top of the Campanile to present a bouquet to the Doge who received it in his box beside the four bronze horses from Constantinople. On other days there were fêtes to celebrate the various parishes' patron saints; processions of gondolas; wheelbarrow races; displays of the 'Forces of Hercules' in which naked gondoliers, standing in their boats in two rows with planks on their shoulders, balanced tier upon tier of other boatmen one above the other until the whole human barricade collapsed into the canal. At night there were dances and gambling parties, exhibitions in the courtesans' houses, frolics in the streets where eggshells filled with scented water were thrown about by a carnival character known as Mattacino, 'the half-cracked one', dressed as a hen.

John Evelyn was in Venice in 1645 and described the 'folly and madness' of the Carnival which had altered little a hundred years later, as shown by the pictures of Tiepolo: 'The Women, Men & persons of all Conditions disguising themselves in antique dresses, & extravagant Musique & a thousand gambols, & traversing the streetes from house to house, all places being then accessible, & free to enter: There is abroad nothing but flinging of Eggs fill'd with sweete Waters, & sometimes not over sweete; they also have a barbarous costome of hunting bulls about the Streetes & Piazzas, which is very dangerous, the passages being generally so narrow in that

Citty. Likewise do the youth of the severall Wards & parrishes contend in other Masteries or pastimes, so as tis altogether impossible to recount the universal madnesse of this place during this time of licence: Now are the greate banks set up for those who will play at Basset; the Comedians have also liberty & the Operas to Exercise: Witty pasquils [lampoons] are likewise thrown about, & the Mountebanks have their stages in every Corner: The diversion which chiefly tooke me up, was three noble Operas which I saw, where was incomparable Voices, & Musique.'

The Carnival finished towards the end of June. 'At midnight, the marangora and the bell of S. Francesco della Vigna tolled slowly,' Maurice Rowdon wrote in his delightful The Silver Age of Venice, 'and at dawn there was only the coloured trash in the streets ... sweets, oranges, ribbons, pumpkin seeds and confetti trampled on the paving stones ... and an usually complete silence, with Venice's typical night sounds, the lapping of water on stone and the slight boom of boats on their moorings.'

But although the Carnival was over, the pleasures of Venice were not. 'No one gets dressed here until people are going to bed elsewhere,' one visiting Frenchman declared; while it was the English poet and letter writer Lady Mary Wortley Montagu's opinion that no one in the city considered himself old as long as he was not bedridden. There were two hundred cafés, many of them open all night; there were splendid theatres, only one of which ever put on a proper tragedy and did not attempt to try another one; in almost every campo there were magazzeni, wine shops, and pestrini, milk bars serving whipped cream and wafers, where all classes met and drank and gossiped. There were balls in the palaces; parties were held on boats in the canals and in the gardens of the Giudecca; there was gambling in the ridotti, where noblemen held the bank, where stakes were high and where anyone could play from eight or nine o'clock in the morning, men and women alike, provided faces were concealed by masks. There were official gambling houses at the theatre of S. Moisè and at the S. Cassian theatre; and when these were closed in 1774 because of the 'continuous, universal and violent' betting carried on in them, gaming was transferred to cafés and private casinos in palazzi. 'There are usually ten or twelve chambers on a floor with gaming tables

Giovanni Domenico Tiepolo, The Departure of the Gondola, *1760s.*

in them and vast crowds of people,' warned Sir Thomas Nugent in that essential vade-mecum of 1749, *The Grand Tour containing an exact description of most of the Cities, Towns and Remarkable Places of Europe.* 'A profound silence is observed and none are admitted without masks. Here you meet ladies of pleasure, and married women also who, under the protection of a mask, enjoy all the diversions of the carnival, but are usually attended by the husband or his spies. Besides these gaming rooms, there are others for conversation, where wine, lemonade and sweetmeats are sold. Here the gentlemen are at liberty to rally and address the ladies.'

The inordinately rich Englishman, William Beckford, who had been despatched abroad in 1780 by a family concerned by his emotional entanglement both with a young boy and a married cousin, was taken to a *ridotto* overlooking the piazza 'where were a great many lights and a great many ladies elegantly dressed, their hair falling very freely about them, and innumerable adventures written in their eyes. The gentlemen were lolling upon the sofas, or lounging about the apartments.'

If a gentleman, rousing himself from that 'perpetual daze' in which he seemed to pass his time, wished to make love to one of these ladies he would steal away with her, so Beckford said, 'to a little suite of apartments in some out-of-the-way

corner' of which his family were 'totally ignorant' and of which even the gondoliers, 'though the prime managers of intrigue', were 'scarce ever acquainted'. Or, he would make love in a gondola which, by law black since 1562, provided both comfort and privacy in the colourfully decorated interior of its little cabin. Indeed, a gondola was recognized as one of the securest love-nests that Venice could provide. Gondoliers, who never took bribes, were quick to punish any member of the craft suspected of betraying a wife to her husband; while anyone who approached too close to a gondola in which lovers were enjoying themselves was sure to be repulsed: one night, John Evelyn, while conveying a gentlewoman who had supped with him to her gondola 'at the usual place of landing', was fired upon from another gondola 'in which were a noble Venetian and his courtesan unwilling to be disturbed'. Evelyn ran to fetch his weapon, 'until informed of the danger' that would be incurred 'by pursuing it further'.

There were astonishing numbers of courtesans in Venice: at the end of the sixteenth century a man who counted them and gave their addresses listed 11,654, almost ten per cent of the population of the city. Early in the next century

Thomas Coryat, the waggish author of *Coryat's Crudities hastily gobbled up in five Moneths travels*, estimated that there must be at least twenty thousand, 'whereof many are esteemed so loose', he added, 'that they are said to open their quivers to every arrow'. There was a foundling hospital especially devoted to the care of any babies they might be unfortunate enough to bear; but it was rarely full, 'for according to the old proverb the best carpenters make the fewest chips'. Many courtesans were supremely attractive. The French magistrate and scholar, Charles de Brosses, was of the opinion that fairies and angels combined could not have produced beauties like them. Men who could not afford to keep one of their own, Nugent observed, 'join with two or three friends and have one in common amongst them'. Casanova shared a young woman with five or six others who made love to her one after the other until her 'cheeks were flushed with joy'.

'When the nobility have done with their concubines they become courtesans,' Nugent continued. 'Of these there are streets full, who receive all comers and dress in the gayest colours with their breasts open, and their faces daubed with paint, standing by dozens at the doors and windows to invite their customers'. To save her son from 'contracting distempers with common harlots', a rich woman would make a bargain with some poor family for a daughter of the house to become his bedfellow for a sum which depended upon the attraction of the girl. This girl would ultimately join the ranks of the courtesans, and so add one more justification to Venice's reputation as 'the brothel of Europe', the place where you had to beware of the 'Four Ps' – the *pietra bianca*, the slippery white stone of the steps up to the 450 bridges, the *prete*, the *pantaleone*, and, above all, the *putana*, the whore.

As well as being considered the brothel of Europe, Venice also had the reputation of being one of the dirtiest and smelliest of its cities, the heaps of ordure in the *calle* and the refuse and sewage floating down the canals being tolerated by the inhabitants without complaint. John Howard, the prison reformer, advised a fellow-countryman who was staying in the same house as himself not to remain in Venice longer than four

Francesco Guardi, St Mark's Square on Ascension Day, *1723 (detail)*.

Illustration from Casanova's Memoirs *(1945 Berlin edition).*

days; and a later arrival there described the city as a 'stinkpot'. Goethe observed that flat-bottomed boats, manned by country people from the neighbouring islands, occasionally came into the canals and took away the filth which was heaped up in corners by the bridges to use it on their land as manure. 'But there is no regularity or strictness about these arrangements,' he noted, 'and the filthy state of the town is all the more unpardonable because it is as well situated for cleanliness as any town in Holland.'

Samuel Johnson's friend, Mrs Thrale, agreed with him. The Rialto Bridge was 'so dirtily kept and deformed with mean shops that, passing over it, disgust gets the better of every other sensation'. The piazza was 'all covered over in the morning with chicken coops which stinke one to death, as nobody, I believe, thinks of changing their baskets'. And the Doge's Palace 'was made so very offensive by the resort of human creatures for every purpose most unworthy of so charming a place'.

'The very stairs are like a sink,' Baron von Archenholz confirmed. 'Go where you will, you will find whole rills of stinking water, and smell its noxious exhalations. The nobles, who honestly contribute their share, never regard these nuisances, and paddle through them with uplifted gowns.' Even the Basilica was filthy: James Edward Smith thought it must be 'perhaps the most dirty place of public worship in Europe, except the Jews' synagogue in Rome.' William Beckford felt positively poisoned by the stench inside which, as he put it, 'exhales from every recess and corner of the edifice, and which all the incense of the altars cannot subdue. When no longer able to endure this noxious atmosphere, I run up the Campanile in the Piazza, and seating myself among the pillars of the gallery, breathe the fresh gales which blow from the Adriatic'.

Some of the nobles' *palazzi* were about as dirty as the Doge's Palace. But not many foreigners were aware of this, since they were rarely invited into rooms other than those set aside for gambling; and, when they were, they were extended the most meagre hospitality. Venetian nobles 'do not know what it means to offer a meal,' Charles de Brosses complained. 'I have sometimes been at a *conversazione* at the Procuratress Foscarini's, a house of enormous wealth, and she is an extremely charming lady. As the only titbit, at 3 p.m., i.e. at about eleven o'clock at night in France, twenty valets bring in on an immense silver platter, a large sliced pumpkin known as *anfouri* or water-melon, a detestable dish if ever there was one. A pile of silver plates accompanies it; everyone grabs at a slice, washes it down with a small cup of coffee, and leaves at midnight with empty head as well as empty stomach to sup in his own lodgings.'

To give the patricians their due, Charles de Brosses might have added that they did not eat a great deal themselves; and when they did give a great banquet the rich food provided was served more for the pleasure of their guests than for their own: gluttony, it was generally agreed, was not among their vices. Nor, despite appearances, was indolence a universal fault among them. There were at the beginning of the eighteenth century 1,731 nobles entitled to take part in the deliberations of the Grand Council; and many of those who did so were extremely conscien-

tious. The Council met every day of the week, including Sundays and every public holiday with only two exceptions (2 March and 31 January, St Mark's Day), from eight o'clock until midday in summer and from midday until sunset in winter; and there were those who could pride themselves on not having missed a session in a lifetime.

Yet it could not be denied that ever since the fall of Crete in 1669, Venice had become increasingly less a respected mercantile power than a tourist attraction, less populous, less rich. There were still profitable industries with an international reputation, well regulated by the city's guilds or *scuole*. The workers in these industries were woken before dawn by church bells ringing the *mattutin*; and those who slept through the sound of these were sure to be roused by the boom of the basilica's huge bell which was tolled at sunrise. Already the food shops were open; carts were taking fish throughout the city from the fish-market on the Grand Canal; stall-holders were doing business on and around the Rialto where wine boats were being moored at the Riva del Vin; dealers in brocade and velvet were laying out their wares in the Piazza and auctioneers were asking for bids for ducks and chickens; ladies were getting dressed, having their teeth filled, practising their piano lessons, undertaking the duties and enjoying the pleasures depicted in those delightful scenes of social life by Pietro Longhi. Children were kicking balls about across the narrow bridges and playing skittles in the *calle*; beggars, 'saucy and airy and odd in their manners', were taking up their stations; gondoliers were calling and shouting at each other, though hardly ever coming to blows. Venice was not a violent city: murder was as rare there as it was common in Rome and there were fewer robberies than in any other Italian city of comparable size. According to Carlo Goldoni – who was born in 1707 in Venice where many of the best of 250

LEFT *Pietro Longhi,* The Dentist, *c.1745.*

OPPOSITE ABOVE The Barber's Shop, *by a follower of Pietro Longhi,* c.1745

OPPOSITE BELOW The Coffee House, *by a follower of Pietro Longhi,* c.1745.

Giovanni Battista Tiepolo, A Young Couple Visiting a Pregnant Friend, *an undated sketch (detail).*

plays of which he was author were performed at the Teatro San Samuele, the Sant' Angelo and the San Luca (now the Goldoni) – everybody sang in Venice. 'They sing in the *campi*,' he wrote, 'in the streets, along the canals. The merchants sing while offering their goods; the gondoliers sing while they wait for their masters; the workers sing on their way to their workshops.'

From these workshops Venice's lace and metal-work, tapestry, pottery, cloth and, above all, glass were exported all over Europe. Indeed, glass manufacture on Murano was so important to the economy and credit of the republic that the island had its version of the Doge, the Podestà, and a *nuncio* in Venice to represent its interests. On the

other hand the arsenal, though still 'the greatest and most beautiful' in Europe, was far from being the scene of constant activity it once had been. In 1645 over two thousand workers, *Arsenalotti*, had been employed there. John Evelyn believed it to be the 'best furnish'd' arsenal in the world. He saw galleries full of armour and saddles, guns and ropes, grenades and chains and grappling irons, courts piled high with 'Cannon bullets . . . Ordinance on Carriages . . . prodigious Mortar pieces'. On the other side of the canal were forges where men were 'continually at work on Ankers and Iron work'.

'Neere it is a Well of fresh Water,' Evelyn continued in growing wonderment, 'which they impute to Rinoceros's hornes which they say lie in it, & will preserve it from ever being empoison'd. Then we came to where Carpenters were building their Magazines of Oares, Masts etc for a hundred Galleys and Ships ... Then the foundry [where guides pointed out a cannon which had been entirely made while the Doge was having his dinner] ... and over that armes for 800,000 men ... In a word 'tis not to be reckon'd up what this large place containes of this sort.'

The workers, healthy, energetic and well paid, were staunchly patriotic. They put out fires without payment, defended the harbour and manned lifeboats. By 1766, however, their number had declined to less than 1,500 and was diminishing every year; and to most observers it seemed that those who did remain passed their days in idleness.

Indeed, William Beckford thought that most Venetians had more holidays than working days and that for the young noblemen every day was a holiday and most of the hours of daylight spent in bed. In the early morning, to be sure, the Grand Canal was lively enough, its waters covered with rafts and barges filled with fruit and vegetables. 'Loads of grapes, peaches and melons arrived, and disappeared in an instant, for every vessel was in motion; and the crowds of purchasers hurrying from boat to boat formed one of the liveliest pictures imaginable. Amongst the multitudes I remarked a good many whose dress and carriage announced something above the common rank; and upon enquiry I found they were noble

Venetians just come from their casinos, and met to refresh themselves with fruit before they retired to sleep for the day.'

The expensive clothes by which the noblemen were distinguished were casual yet highly elegant. Sumptuary laws had never been too strictly observed in Venice. In the seventeenth century it had been asked if the frills and furbelows on men's costume indicated a desire to change sex; while the immensely tall, uniquely Venetian pattens on which ladies had hobbled about, 'half as high again as the rest of the world', defied all regulations to bring their height down to the permitted measurements. Although severely regarded by the more staid of the eighteenth-century senators who walked the streets in their silk and fur-lined ankle-length togas – coloured black, red, cream or violet according to their rank – Venetian ladies delighted in finery, even in their underclothes. Their hoops and bustles and the tight stays that thrust their bosoms into high relief were covered with extravagantly flowered silks and quilted satins, with flounces and pleats and ermine and gold and silver thread. Shoes were painted in brilliant colours. Veils were edged with lace and sparkled with jewelry. Jewels glittered also in their

Francesco Guardi, Il Parlatorio delle Monache, *showing the daughters of patricians entertaining guests behind the grille of the San Zaccaria convent in St Mark's Square.*

Canaletto, The Bacino di San Marco from the Giudecca, *1735–40.*

hair which was often dyed and usually powdered, splashed with scent and decorated with flowers, with locks of hair and even portraits in miniature of admirers. Enormous hats were garnished with fruits and leaves, butterflies and stuffed birds. Faces were rouged and patched; necks, usually not well washed, though well rubbed with creams and dabbed with the scent that was so liberally sprinkled over everything else, were encircled by necklaces and adorned with pendants that fell down upon powdered breasts. On certain days the wearing of a black robe and long veil were required by the authorities; but the accessories worn with them were no less extravagant and colourful for that, even in church.

Churchmen were often as attentive to their dress as noblemen. 'The *abbé*, with his right both to preach and marry,' as Maurice Rowdon said, 'wore polished shoes with bright red heels and gold or silver buckles. More often he was, like Casanova, fashionable to the point of foppery. His

preaching . . . brought him love letters . . . You saw few priests in company only because they were hidden by their dominos . . . The Venetians laughed and talked during Mass. Women showed bare shoulders, they flirted and kissed. The confessional was a place to get rid of the dark mental effects of debauchery or gambling.'

Nuns were considered to make delightful lovers. Certainly Casanova found so. The nun he met in Venice, where he was born, the son of an actor, in 1725, was a deliciously sensual creature, who enjoyed the bodies of women as well as those of men, and who gave him as much excitement as any girl he had known. Another nun, Maria da Riva, fell in love with the French Ambassador with whom she had so torrid an affair that the Inquisition forbade her to see him any more. This prohibition had no effect, so she was exiled to Ferrara where she soon married someone else. The Inquisition in Venice was usually, however, readier to find excuses than to condemn, and excessively severe Inquisitors tended not to last long: Cardinal Ugo Boncompagni, the future Gregory XIII, was recalled from Venice because he was considered too unrelentingly strict. Admittedly, Veronese, one of the leading painters of the Venetian school in the sixteenth century who was employed in the decoration of the Doge's Palace, was summoned by the Inquisition to defend his *Last Supper* which had been commissioned by the convent of SS. Giovanni e Paolo and which contained such profane details as a servant with a bleeding nose, St Peter carving a joint, a dwarf and a jester holding a parrot on his wrist. But when Veronese protested that painters were entitled to take the same liberties that poets and madmen do, the inquisitors, prompted by the civil authorities, agreed to take no further action provided the name of the picture (now in the Accademia) was changed to *Feast in the House of Levi*. By the eighteenth century decisions of the Inquisitors in Venice had to be approved by the senators who were required to be present at their meetings and were entitled to withdraw from the conference chamber should a severe decree be contemplated and thus prevent it from becoming law.

Nor were the Inquisitors able to prevent Venice's convents from becoming finishing schools for the daughters of patricians who could be seen at Mass behind the grille, as Charles de Brosses saw them, laughing and chatting to each other, pretty and animated, with the décolletage of actresses. They were given lessons, but none too demanding; and they waited for the day when they would catch the eye of a suitable man who would ask an older nun about her and then perhaps take her away to marry her. After marriage she would choose a *cisisbeo*, or male chaperone, a dutiful attendant of her own class who would see to her wants and comforts from the time of her morning toilet until she came home from the opera or gambling table at night, and who might, though probably would not, become her lover.

The picture by Guardi in the Ca' Rezzonico, *Il Parlatorio*, shows some of these girls entertaining their guests behind the grille of the S. Zaccaria convent in St Mark's Square. It was a picture by an artist not so much admired by foreign visitors as his contemporary, the Venetian-born Antonio Canale, known as Canaletto, who, the more topographically accurate of the two, painted so much for tourists that there are now only two examples of his work in the whole of Venice.

Indeed, when the age of the Grand Tour as an aristocratic institution came to an end at the beginning of the nineteenth century, there was scarcely a large country house in England that did not possess its picture by Canaletto, or one in his manner, to awaken memories of gondola rides down the Grand Canal under the Rialto Bridge, past the graceful palaces between the churches of S. Silvestro and S. Samuele, beneath the Ca' Rezzonico, where Robert Browning was to die in 1889, by the Accademia where no bridge stood until 1854, round that supreme masterpiece of the Venetian Baroque, Baldassare Longhena's Santa Maria della Salute, out into wider stream between Piazzo San Marco and Palladio's lovely façade of San Giorgio Maggiore, and then across to the lonely islands of the lagoon as the boatman sang the old barcarole:

> *Coi pensieri malinconici,*
> *Non te star a tormentar.*
> *Vien co mi, montemo in gondola,*
> *Andaremo fora in mar.*

'Don't stay to torment yourself with melancholy thoughts. Come with me. We shall step into the gondola. Let us go forth upon the sea.'

For the eighteenth-century English tourist, the delights of Venice were rivalled by those of Vienna where, according to one visitor in the 1740s, 'there is no place in the world where people live more luxuriously'. The Habsburgs had then been ruling as archdukes, kings and emperors for nearly five centuries. For much of that time, more often by means of judicious marriages than by military conquest, they had been adding to their dominions until the head of the family was not only Emperor of Austria but, 'by God's grace', Apostolic King of Hungary, King of Bohemia, King of Galicia, Lodomaria, Lombardy, Venetia, Illyria and Croatia, King of Jerusalem and Grand Duke, Duke, Margrave, Prince or Count of some thirty other domains inhabited by almost forty million people. Vienna remained the lively, charming capital of the Habsburgs until their rule ended in the upheavals of the First World War.

15

Vienna

in the Days of Franz Josef 1848–1916

As revolution spread fast across Europe in 1848, the simple-minded, epileptic Austrian Emperor, Ferdinand I, was taken hastily from Vienna to the Archbishop's palace at Olmütz in Moravia and was there induced by his forceful ministers, the Princes von Schwarzenberg and Windisch-Graetz, to abdicate in favour of his eighteen-year-old nephew. The pathetic old Emperor, whose most often remembered remark was 'I am the Emperor and I want dumplings', submitted passively. 'God bless you,' he said to his young successor as he placed his hands upon his head and made the sign of the cross, 'Be brave. God will protect you. This is done gladly.' Then he went quietly away to his room, and afterwards, as he wrote in his diary, 'I and my dear wife heard Holy Mass in the chapel . . . and after that [we] packed our things.'

His family, the Habsburgs, the oldest dynasty in Europe, had ruled in Vienna since the thirteenth century. Bounded on the west by the wooded foothills of the Alps, the Wienerwald, and to the north and east by the river Danube and the plain of the Marchfeld, Vienna lay at the intersections of ancient trade routes from the Baltic to the Adriatic and from the Alps to the plains of Hungary. Founded by the Celts in the fourth century BC it had become the Roman garrison town of Vindobona, one of the main strongholds in the frontier defences by which the Romans repulsed for centuries the advancing hordes of barbarians. From about 1200 the town began to gain in importance through its position as a

W. Gause, Court Ball *(detail), 1900.*

trading centre on the river and as a producer of fine wines; and in 1278 it fell into the hands of a highly talented soldier, Count Rudolf of Habsburg, who had been crowned German King in 1273. Thereafter Vienna grew and prospered within the shadow of the Habsburg palace, the Hofburg. And despite plague, fire and assault by the Turks, it maintained from the sixteenth century onwards its reputation as one of the great capitals of Europe and of the world.

Vienna celebrated the Turks' second defeat in 1683 – they had failed to take the city under Suleiman the Magnificent in 1529 – with an outburst of Baroque building which was to last for over seventy years. Old churches and public buildings were given Baroque façades; new Baroque palaces appeared beyond the city walls, pre-eminent among them the Belvedere, designed by the Italian-born Lukas von Hildebrandt for

Portrait of the Emperor Franz Josef by Winterhalter, 1865.

Prince Eugène of Savoy, and Schönbrunn, built by another master of Baroque who drew his inspiration from Italy, Johann Bernhard Fischer von Erlach. The Belvedere – in effect two palaces separated by a terraced garden designed by the Parisian landscape gardener, Dominique Girard – contained the Prince's sumptuous living-rooms in the lower palace and grand reception-rooms for entertaining in the upper one. Both palaces were riotously decorated with gilt and marble, plasterwork and elaborate carving, far more ostentatious than Schönbrunn where the Empress Maria Theresa brought up her sixteen children, including Marie Antoinette who, in 1755, had been born in an armchair to which her mother had retreated from her desk when the labour pains briefly interrupted her examination of state papers.

When Napoleon occupied Vienna in 1806 and again in 1809 he made Schönbrunn his headquarters, ordering that the French imperial eagles should be fixed to the gateway where they still remain, and, as was his custom in occupied capitals, demanding other changes throughout the city, among them the demolition of stretches of the city wall. After Napoleon's fall, representatives of the victorious powers met in Vienna which became for a time the playground and dance hall of Europe. Balls were given in Schönbrunn and in the ballrooms of all the other palaces, beneath the white galleries of Josef Emanuel Fischer von Erlag's Winter, or Spanish, Riding School, and in the halls of the Hofburg. When one of the diplomats attending the Congress of Vienna of 1814–15 was asked in French how the deliberations were proceeding, '*Comment marche le Congrès?*' he replied, '*Le Congrès ne marche pas, il danse*'. 'After the departure of the sovereigns, the orchestra began to play waltzes,' Count de la Garde recorded of one characteristic festivity during the Congress. 'At once an electric stimulus seemed to be communicated to the entire assembled multitude ... One can scarcely conceive of the power which the waltz exercises. As soon as the first bars are heard, countenances brighten, eyes come alive, a tremor of delight runs through everyone. The graceful spinning-tops take shape, start to move, interweave, overtake. One has to have seen the ravishingly beautiful women, aglow with flowers and diamonds, drawn along like bright meteors by this irresistible music.'

Music had long been the delight of Vienna. Many of the finest works of Mozart, who had been appointed to succeed Gluck as chamber composer to the Emperor Josef II in 1787, had been first performed in the city where he died in 1791. His friend Haydn, who brought the late eighteenth-century Viennese classical style to a brilliant climax, had at one time sung in the cathedral choir and also died in the city in 1809. Beethoven, who had first come to study in Vienna in 1786, died there in 1827 and was buried after a funeral at which there were twenty thousand mourners including, as a torchbearer, Franz Peter Schubert, already a commanding figure in the divide between classical and romantic music, whose only public concert was given in Vienna the following year. Several of the city's rich noblemen maintained their own private orchestras and some actually travelled with them. It was entirely appropriate, therefore, that when the Emperor Franz Josef decided in the boom years after 1857 to do for Vienna what Baron Haussmann was doing for the Paris of Napoleon III, and to indulge in one of the nineteenth-century's most dramatic essays in town planning, the building of the Ringstrasse, he should have envisaged a magnificent opera house as one of the principal ornaments of the enterprise.

The Emperor was then still in his twenties. He was not a man of high intelligence or discernment but he had a strong sense of duty and a personal charm that was captivating. 'I like the young Emperor, I must admit,' wrote Queen Victoria after meeting him in England. 'There is much spirit and boldness in his warm blue eyes, and he

View of Vienna with its bastions and a military parade at the time of the accession of Franz Josef by Rudolf Hille, 1848.

shows a certain agreeable gaiety when the occasion arises. He is slender and graceful, and even in the midst of archdukes, all in uniform, he can always be recognized as their head. There is a certain something about him that lends authority.'

He retained that authority always. His ministers were allowed no influence beyond the confines of their departments, and he made it clear that criticisms of his policies were as unacceptable as criticisms of himself. As a young man this made him respected rather than liked, though by the end of his sixty-eight-year reign his virtues of courage, honesty, humanity, and his strength in adversity after the execution of his younger brother, Maximilian, Emperor of Mexico, the suicide of his son, and the assassination of his beloved and wayward wife helped to endear him to the majority of his subjects. When it suited him to be so he could be autocratic and unapproachable; and, while he allowed much freedom to the architects and artists whom he employed, his censure could be devastating: his remarks upon the design of the new Opera House, combined with the jibes of the Viennese while it was being constructed, drove the architect, Eduard van der Null, to suicide in 1868.

The Opera House was built between 1861 and 1869 in the French Early Renaissance style, and in striking contrast to the other grand buildings which faced onto the Ringstrasse. For the Emperor and his advisers had decided to have no

ABOVE *The Österreichische Postparkasse (Postal Savings Bank) built between 1904 and 1906 to the designs of Otto Wagner.*

OPPOSITE *The Opernring, c.1910, showing the State Opera House on the right.*

uniform architectural plan but to punctuate the two-and-a-half-mile course of the new wide boulevard with monumental edifices in widely different styles. The City Hall, the Rathaus, was to be flamboyant neo-Flemish Gothic with Renaissance overtones; the University, a pastiche of early Tuscan Renaissance; the Börse, neo-Classic-Renaissance; the Votivkirche, a church erected to celebrate the Emperor's survival of an assassination attempt by a disgruntled tailor, was to be mock Gothic; the national theatre, the Burgtheater, opposite the Rathaus, neo-High Italian Renaissance with touches of the Baroque; the parliament building, almost a parody of Grecian and Roman motifs; the lawcourts, the Justiz Palast, German Renaissance; the large four- and five-storey apartment blocks, in the Baroque style of the aristocratic palaces of the old city. Statues, adopting idealized poses, were to be placed along the thoroughfare at suitable intervals and double avenues of plane trees, lindens and chestnuts planted to give shade to the passers-by.

The whole concept took thirty years to realize, and during that time was harshly criticized as often as it was praised. Camillo Sitte, the Viennese architect and town planner, condemned what he called the rage for great open gaps that isolated both buildings and people. Otto Wagner, who had himself designed several of the Ringstrasse's buildings in a Neo-Renaissance style, came to believe that functionalism, a non-derivative style and the use of modern materials should be the bases of architectural design, and that the Ringstrasse was a monumental disaster. (His subsequent stations for the City Railway of Vienna and his Postal Savings Bank were to be recognized as important landmarks in the history of modern architecture). Wagner's views were to receive wide enthusiastic support from a rising generation of young artists who in 1897 formed the Wiener Sezession, the Austrian manifestation of *Jugendstil*, the German variant of Art Nouveau. It was a violently anti-historical movement, seeking a style totally enfranchised from past influences. One of its key figures was the painter, Gustav Klimt, whose figure *Nude Veritas* of a young girl holding up a mirror to modern man became a symbol of the Sezession. Wagner considered Klimt the greatest artist who had ever lived. Another influential figure in the movement was Josef Olbrich, a young assistant to Wagner, who in 1898–9 designed the building to house the exhibitions of the Sezession, a block-like structure suggesting a temple in which art was to be a substitute for religion for the intellectual agnostic élite of Vienna.

For all the faults and absurdity that the Sezession found in the Ringstrasse, the new boulevard did at least clear away the last remnants of the medieval ramparts and enabled Vienna to expand beyond the circumference of the inner city which it defined.

And expand the city did. In the Middle Ages its population had been about 20,000. By 1830 it had increased to almost 320,000, by 1848 to about 400,000, and by 1869 to well over 600,000. Before Franz Josef's reign was over it had reached nearly 2,250,000; a second ring-road known as the 'Gürtel' had been created, and for this an outer line of defences constructed in the eighteenth century had, like the medieval ramparts, been demolished. The rapid growth in population reflected an increase in economic activity and industrial and financial wealth, a process already well advanced by the beginning of the epoch between the Congress of Vienna and 1848. This epoch was known as the age of Biedermeier after a character created by the writer Ludwig Pfau, a typical representative of the bourgeois class which, for years existing humbly between the

A late Biedermeier room : watercolour by R. Alt, 1870.

A Viennese tavern scene by Neder.

aristocracy and the common people, was then aspiring to wealth and influence. Yet, although the more successful of this new class, bankers, industrialists, wholesale traders and state suppliers, had been ennobled, and although with the rise of industry the older nobility were becoming progressively poorer, while the *nouveaux riches* were growing increasingly wealthy, Viennese society, if not entirely segregated, was still rigorously separated, except at certain times and places such as the great feast days of St Anne and St Bridget, during the carnival season, the *Fasching*, which took place between Christmas and Lent, and on the Prater, Vienna's main park. Even the wives of the Emperor's ministers would not be accepted at court or received in the ballroom of the Hofburg unless they could produce sixteen quarterings of nobility in their families' coats of arms.

At the apex of this social pyramid were the *Erste Gesellschaft*, the First Society of the nobility. 'Our society,' recalled one member, Baron Hübner, in his memoirs, 'bothers very little about politics. If they are mentioned it is only in order to criticize whatever is being done ... Our women are tall and well built with expressive faces and quick wit, holding their heads high, noses in the air, fond of bright colours for their dresses, made in Paris but not always chosen with taste, talking very loudly and all at the same time, saying whatever passes through their heads in that French peculiar to the drawing-rooms of Vienna.'

Below the *Erste Gesellschaft* came the *Zweite Gesellschaft*, the rich financiers and entrepreneurs whose wives entertained the leading artists, writers and politicians of the day. It was considered permissible for members of the First Society, even archdukes, to attend the parties and receptions of the *Zweite Gesellschaft*; but it was most unusual to see their wives at such functions, the female members of the two societies meeting only at the racecourse or at charity concerts and subscription balls.

What might be termed a Third Society was composed of the petty bourgeoisie who made a golden rule of the quality of *Gemütlichkeit*, that comfortable, cosy, easygoing friendliness which coexisted in them with a temperament of sometimes extravagant emotionalism. These were the people who could be seen sitting at the tables of the cafés of the inner city near the Opera or St Stephen's Cathedral, the Stephansdom, sipping the coffee which was served in a variety of strengths or colours or puffing at a state monopoly cigar. On Sundays they set off in family parties by coach or train for excursions in the Vienna Woods, calling for a beer at a tavern or at the garden or courtyard of a wine-grower for a *Heuriger*, a glass of new wine, usually served by the owner of the vineyard who announced its arrival by hanging out a pine branch which had to be withdrawn when all the new wine had gone.

The revolution of 1848 saw the rise of yet another class, the proletariat. Many of this class lived in blocks of tenements beyond the Gürtel, known as *Bassena-Wohnungen* because water for the occupants on each floor had to be drawn from the cold water tap of a communal basin on the landing. Next to the *Bassena* was a communal lavatory. There were no bathrooms. Indeed, the sanitary arrangements in Viennese households of every class would have been considered wholly unacceptable in almost every other European capital. When Franz Josef's consort, the Empress Elizabeth, daughter of the Bavarian Duke Maximilian Josef, came to Vienna, she was horrified to discover that Schönbrunn, that 'gloomy palace', in the words of her biographer, Joan Haslip, 'with its long, echoing corridors, the everlasting tramp of soldiers on guard, and the detectives hiding behind hedges in the garden', had not a single bathroom. Nor had the Hofburg.

Yet in the realm of social legislation and municipal administration Vienna at that time was as advanced as any city in Europe. Karl Lueger, the leader of the Christian Socialist Party, who was to be largely responsible for transforming the city of his birth into a modern metropolis, was eventually accepted as mayor by the Emperor who for long refused to accept his election on the grounds that he was a dangerous revolutionary. On assuming office he annexed the suburbs, opened schools and hospitals, laid out parks and gardens and took over the tramways and the electricity and gas services in the city's name. It was mainly due to his efforts that universal suffrage was introduced in Austria and that, while the Nationalists under Georg Schönerer were eroding it from the right and the Social Democrats under Viktor Adler from the left, the long hegemony of the German-orientated liberals was broken.

In the fields of science and medicine the Viennese also set examples to Europe: in 1930 the Nobel prizewinner, Karl Landsteiner, by identifying the major blood groups, made blood transfusion a routine medical practice. Robert Bárány also won the Nobel Prize in 1914 for his work on the physiology and pathology of the balancing apparatus of the inner ear. Alfred Adler, the psychiatrist whose system of individual psychology introduced the term 'inferiority feeling', was a product of the University of Vienna Medical School. And his great contemporary, Sigmund Freud, the founder of psychoanalysis, also attended the University of Vienna and, before he moved to London, lived on the mezzanine floor of Number 19, Berggasse. The rooms are now a museum where can be seen Freud's pictures, including an engraving of Fuseli's painting of 1781, *The Nightmare*, the celebrated couch in the consulting-room, and photographs of friends and colleagues, among them the Viennese philosopher Otto Weininger, author of *Sex and Character* (1903), who shot himself at the age of twenty-three; Stefan Zweig, the writer, born in Vienna, also in 1881; Wilhelm Fleiss, the physician who helped Freud analyse himself; and Nathan Weiss, a hospital colleague who hanged himself in a public bath ten days after returning from his honeymoon.

'*Civilization and its Discontents*, the title of one of his later books, is a splendid indication of the tensions within Freud's life in Vienna,' wrote David Pryce-Jones who was himself born in the city. 'Ambivalence like his – a desire to enjoy the capital city but to nag it to death – is a kind of electricity specially generated in Vienna. Ernest Jones, Freud's hero-worshipping pupil from England, noted that consciously Freud loathed Vienna. "There was no beloved 'Steffel' for him, only 'that abominable St Stefan,'" Jones quoted

Heinrich Tomec, The Admiral Tegethoff Monument
with the Ferriswheel (Pratersturm) in the Riesenrad
Fairground, Vienna, *1903.*

Freud as saying ... Yet it was difficult to make Freud travel, and only the Nazis put an end to the lifetime he spent in Vienna, forty-six years of it in the Berggasse ... His theories spring straight from his environment. The "pleasure principle" and "pain principle" – what better reflections could there be of the positive and negative aspects of living in Vienna? The "life force" in conflict with the "death wish" – what is that but a caricature of the Empire as it struggled with its own decadence.' Pryce-Jones goes on to suggest that Freud's identification of totems and taboos is especially apposite, since Vienna was, and is, alive with taboos. 'The entire society was regulated, consciously and unconsciously, by awareness of what was done and what was not done. Daily life, clothing, manners, upbringing, forms of address were hedged about with taboos. The whole class structure was one mammoth taboo.'

Among the photographs at 19 Berggasse is one of Arthur Schnitzler, who was born in Vienna in 1862 and whose stories and plays reflecting and analysing Viennese bourgeois life moved Freud, so he confessed, 'with an uncanny feeling of familiarity'. They also moved and entertained a whole generation of Viennese whose love of the theatre was legendary and several of whose favourite dramatists, including Franz Grillparzer and Hugo von Hofmannsthal, achieved international reputations. The Viennese also loved opera; and, although Mozart, Haydn, Weber, Beethoven and Schubert were all dead when Franz Josef ascended the throne, and Johann Strauss died the year after his accession – to the distress of the French composer Berlioz, who lamented, 'Vienna without Strauss is like Austria without the Danube' – a new constellation of composers arose in their place. Among these were Hugo Wolf, master of the *Lied*, who studied at the Vienna Conservatory; Anton Bruckner, who wrote several of his greatest symphonies in the city where they were at first received with less enthusiasm than hostility; Gustav Mahler, who was Artistic Director of the Viennese Court Opera; and Johannes Brahms, who was appointed Director of the Vienna Gesellschaft der Musik-freunde in 1872 and who could often be seen shambling along in his shabby clothes from his lodgings at No. 4 Karlsgasse to his favourite tavern, the Red Hedgehog, his head bent forward, his hands clasped behind his back like Beethoven,

a plaid shawl secured by a safety pin over his shoulders, a cigar in his mouth, looking as though it might at any moment set fire to his enormous beard. These were to be followed in our own century by Arnold Schönberg who was born in Vienna in 1874 and his pupils, Berg and Webern, both also Viennese.

Although Bruckner had not at first been appreciated, nearly all good music was welcome in Vienna, but that which most stirred the senses of the Viennese of every class were the waltzes of Josef Lanner and the Strauss family; for the Viennese, with the singular exception of their most famous composer of waltzes, Johann Strauss the Younger, who could not dance himself, were passionate dancers, and their churches and palaces and great public buildings were scarcely more famous or more frequented than the dance halls which could be found in almost every quarter of the city, from the Sperl, the Tivoli and the Apollo, to Dommayer's Casino, the Mond-schein, the Coliseum, the Sofiensaal and the Dianabad-Saal where the 'Blue Danube' was first played in 1867.

Caricature of Johannes Brahms after Otto Böhler.

While the dance halls catered for a wide spectrum of the Viennese public, every great family in Vienna gave its private ball in its own palace; and at the height of the celebrations of the *Fasching* a grand court ball was given by the Emperor in the Rittersaal, a huge white and gold room lit by glittering chandeliers on the first floor of the Hofburg. The guests, officers in gorgeous uniforms, duchesses with bosoms covered in diamonds, noblemen in violet cloaks trimmed with sable and fastened with silver clasps, passed through the courtyard between lines of hussars in scarlet shakos and green cloaks. Upstairs in the Rittersaal the Master of Ceremonies struck the floor three times with his staff, the doors were opened, the men stood to attention, the women curtsied, and the Emperor, in the uniform of a field marshal, entered the room accompanied by a procession of archdukes and archduchesses.

Beneath the Rittersaal in the Graben, a wide open space, half street half square, once the moat around the Roman camp, the humbler citizens enjoyed their more modest pleasures, drinking, talking, reading newspapers in the coffee-houses, playing billiards, eating vanilla crescents or congress doughnuts or chocolate cake. At Demel's in the Kohlmarkt, founded by a pastry-cook in 1785 and acquired by Christoph Demel in 1857, the customers sat at marble-topped tables beneath looking glasses on walls of painted plasterwork and were addressed by the staff in the third person, as indeed they still are. At Sacher's in the Kärntnerstrasse they ate surrounded by red plush; and here in the hall is the framed supper menu that the Emperor's heir, Crown Prince Rudolf, wrote in his own hand in 1889 shortly before he shot his mistress at the royal hunting lodge at Mayerling and then killed himself: 'oysters, turtle soup, lobster *à l'Américaine*, *truite au bleu* with a Venetian sauce, quail stew, chicken *à le française*, salad, compôte, chestnut puree, ice, Sachertorte [a chocolate cake, a speciality of the house], cheese and fruit. With this, Chablis, Mouton-Rothschild, Röderer Champagne, Sherry Superieure.'

The meal and the death that followed it provide a fitting epitaph for Franz Josef's Vienna, for the Viennese in the midst of their pleasures never quite abandoned the sense of misgiving and the hint of despair which so often, at some tragic turn in their private affairs, would lead them to suicide. And there seemed, at the turn of the century among their writers, to be a premonition of impending disaster, a mood which one of them described as a 'Gay Apocalypse'. On 29 June 1914 at Sarajevo, the Archduke Franz Ferdinand, the Emperor's nephew and heir to the throne, was assassinated with his wife on a ceremonial visit. It was the spark that precipitated the First World War and swept away forever the *belle époque* of Franz Josef. He died in 1916 when the outcome of the War was still undetermined. The last of the Habsburgs, his successor Karl I, left Vienna after the War; the Republic was declared on 12 November 1918. The way was clear for the entry of the dictators.

As the nineteenth century drew to a close and the twentieth began its revolutionary course, cities all over the world started to expand dramatically. For ever-growing populations, blocks of flats and apartments had to be constructed and new suburbs created; parks had to be laid out and shops and department stores built, as well as hotels and railway stations, offices and showrooms, schools, hospitals and banks, museums, art galleries, town halls and law courts; while all the public services needed by the people had to be supplied and the demands of their private transport to be met. In cities which did not or could not spread outwards the densely packed buildings grew higher and higher, though skyscrapers were unusual outside America before the Second World War. After that war the appearance of most large cities, even of those untouched by the conflict, began to change again as much was swept away in the general enthusiasm for the Modern Movement. The following chapters attempt to give an impression of six modern cities, two in America, two in Europe, one in Asia and one in Australia at periods when their peculiar characteristics were most pronounced.

PART III

THE MODERN CITY

16

New Orleans
'The Crescent City'

'Our town is very beautiful,' a young French nun told her father soon after the foundation of New Orleans. 'The streets are very wide and straight. The houses are well built, whitewashed, panelled and filled with sunlight, with roofs of shingles that look like slate ... They sing a song which proclaims that New Orleans is as beautiful as Paris.'

Not long before, in 1682, the intrepid French explorer, René Robert Cavelier, Sieur de La Salle, had sailed down the longest waterway of the north American continent, the Mississippi River, and into the Gulf of Mexico. He had symbolically taken possession of the whole region and had named it Louisiana after his sovereign, King Louis XIV. Two years later he had been appointed governor of the territory and had been given instructions to establish settlements there; and, although he was killed by one of his own men during a mutiny in 1687, French interest in colonizing the area was maintained and settlements were founded at Biloxi and Mobile. A third settlement was established in about 1718 by a French Canadian aristocrat and various Canadian *aventuriers des bois* who chose as its site a place some eighty miles from the mouth of the Mississippi just south of a large, brackish lagoon later to be called Lake Pontchartrain in honour of one of

New Orleans in 1841, painted by W. J. Bennett after a sketch by A. Mondelli.

the French King's ministers. They called the place New Orleans after Philippe, duc d'Orléans, Regent of France and principal holder of the royal charter granted by the King for the development of the region.

The site, its founders had decided, would serve both as a river port and a seaport, ideal for exchanging goods from Europe and the Caribbean for cargoes of hides, tobacco and indigo shipped down river from the hinterland. Its earliest dwellings were rough palmetto huts erected between the river's edge and the forest; but soon a French engineer laid out the neat town, divided into sixty-six squares, which the French nun described, its streets named after French nobles, popular saints or important buildings or landmarks: Bourbon Street, for example, St Louis Street, Barracks Street, Rampart Street and Canal Street. Trim as the town appeared, however, and conveniently as it was sited on a fine waterway in an area of astonishing fertility, New Orleans had many problems: there were constant incursions by hostile Indians and devastations caused by hurricanes; mosquitoes were a persistent torment; the water level was so close to the rich alluvial topsoil that underground cellars were

René Robert Cavelier, Sieur de la Salle.

almost unknown, and even today the municipal authorities have to provide numerous pumping stations to keep the city dry; while regular epidemics of yellow fever as well as malaria were to take a dreadful toll.

The French were, therefore, quite thankful in 1762 to cede the colony to Louis XV's cousin, King Charles III of Spain, though less than forty years later Napoleon forced the Spanish government to restore Louisiana to France, a step which so alarmed the American President, Thomas Jefferson, that he quickly entered into negotiations with the French to buy the territory so as to safeguard the free navigation of the Mississippi River. Napoleon was in such urgent need of funds to finance his war against the English that these negotiations soon resulted in the famous Louisiana Purchase of 1803, the running down of the French flag in New Orleans and the hoisting of the American flag in its place.

The transfer did not at first meet with the approval of most of the inhabitants of the city who had been governed with justice and efficiency by the Spanish administration. Urchins followed American newcomers in the street, shouting insults and chanting rude songs; while the old native families of French and Spanish extraction would have nothing to do with the *Américains coquins*, merchants, travellers, entrepreneurs and politicians whose arrival in their city they deeply resented.

It was a city in which they took great pride. After a terrible fire in 1788, it had been almost entirely rebuilt. The wooden shingles of the roofs had been replaced by tiles; street lighting had been introduced; new suburbs, including that of the Faubourg Ste Marie, had been built; the first of several theatres had been opened, the first of the city's newspapers published; and restaurants had opened to cater for the tastes of this most cosmopolitan of the New World's cities. For there were not only in New Orleans people of French and Spanish blood; Germans had arrived from a colony of farmers who had settled about thirty miles up the river in an area later known as the German Coast; hundreds of refugees from areas disrupted by the American War of Independence had followed them; with the increase of agricultural and commercial activity tens of hundreds of black slaves, mostly from the Caribbean islands, had arrived; and after one of the city's planters

New Orleans in the 1860s.

had discovered a method of granulating sugar there seemed no limit to the amount of work that could be found for them.

Marriage between the races was widespread, though the offspring of such marriages were destined to occupy positions in New Orleans society determined largely by their colour. The mulatto was the child of a European and a Negro. A quadroon, the child of a mulatto and a European, would grow up to look down upon the mulatto whose mother was a Negro; the octoroon, the offspring of a quadroon and a European, would feel superior to a *griffe*, the child of a Negro and a mulatto, who would in turn regard as inferior the pure-blooded Negro.

Many half-caste women were extremely beautiful and when Harriet Martineau, the English writer and economist then thirty-two years old, came to New Orleans in the 1830s she was assured by ladies she felt could not possibly be mistaken that the 'connection between white men and quadroons' was 'all but universal'. 'The quadroon girls of New Orleans are brought up by their mothers to be ... the mistresses of white gentlemen,' Miss Martineau wrote in *Society in America*. 'They are highly educated, externally, and are, probably, as beautiful and accomplished a set

of women as can be found. Every young man early selects one, and establishes her in one of those pretty and peculiar houses, whole rows of which may be seen in the Ramparts. The connection now and then lasts for life; usually for several years. In the latter case, when the time comes for the gentleman to take a white wife, the dreadful news reaches the quadroon partner, either by letter entitling her to call the house and furniture her own, or by the newspaper which announces the marriage ... Some men continue the connection after marriage.'

So-called 'quadroon balls' were regularly held in order that white men could select women as mistresses, some of whom occasionally became their wives. These balls were conducted with the utmost decorum, the quadroon girls being accompanied by their mothers as chaperones. They were held at first in the Condé Street ballroom, where from their seats in the tiered boxes, the chaperones warily watched the behaviour of the young men in their long, brightly coloured coats and elaborately stitched boots; then at the St Philip Theatre, where the first theatrical performance in English was given in 1817; and finally, until the 'quadroon balls' were abandoned towards the middle of the century, in the Théâtre d'Orléans whose dance floor was said to be the best in America.

Including the Negroes and coloured people, the population of the city, which had reached five thousand by 1785, doubled by the end of the century, despite the recurring epidemics of yellow fever; and by 1810, when New Orleans had become the fifth largest city in the United States, it had risen to twenty-four thousand. Many of the new arrivals were either slaves or free *gens de couleur* who had fled from the slave revolution in Santo Domingo; many others came down the Mississippi from the north, most of them, after 1812, by steamboat.

Before the advent of the steamboat, merchandise had been floated down river in small craft, flatboats or keelboats, which, if not broken up and sold as timber, were either punted or hauled up again. The boatmen engaged in this work were a rough, unruly lot who, from their riverfront tenements and quays, roistered their way through the taverns and brothels of the quarter known as 'The Swamp' along Girod Street close to where the grandiose Louisiana Superdrome, that gigantic complex of sports stadium, restaurants, bars,

ballrooms and cocktail lounges, with a roof covering nearly ten acres, was to be built in the 1970s. After the arrival of the steamboat, and until the middle of the nineteenth century when the railways began to take over the business of transportation in the Mississippi River Valley, to go downriver to New Orleans was one of the most luxurious ways of travelling that the world had to offer. Berths were equipped with feather beds and pillows, saloons with thick rugs and carpets, expensive pieces of furniture and grand pianos, crystal and bronze chandeliers. Every male passenger was provided with his own richly ornamented and gilded spittoon. The food provided was exquisite and presented on services of fine china or silver. The only disadvantage was that the captains were so jealous of their boats' reputation for speed that at the sight of a rival they raised so much steam that the boilers were liable to burst and sometimes did so, scalding both passengers and crew. The boilers were fed with pine knots dipped in tar when extra speed was required. But, according to the American journalist and author, Herbert Asbury, 'among the Negroes a firm belief prevailed that the fires were fuelled with well-fattened slaves, and that at a crucial moment in the race a steamboat captain did not hesitate to give the command, "Throw in another nigger!"'

There were sixty steamboats plying the river in

The Mississippi steamboat Mayflower *in 1885.*

1820, over four hundred by 1840 when, thanks to this navigation, the rapid expansion of commerce in New Orleans made it the most prosperous of American cities with a population of well over a hundred thousand. Indeed, it seemed for a time that it might well become the busiest port in the world, with an unparalleled traffic in cotton as well as molasses and sugar. One visitor to the city at this time described the port as being 'covered with human beings of all nations and colors, and boxes, bales, bags, hogsheads, pipes, barrels, kegs of goods, wares and merchandise from all ends of the earth! Thousands of bales of cotton, tierces of sugar, molasses; quantities of flour, pork, lard, grain and other provisions; leads, furs ... and the wharves for miles with ships, steamers, flatboats, arks ... I stepped on shore, and my first exclamation was, "This is the place for a business man!"'

It was also a place for the pleasure seeker. As the city grew and prospered, developing distinct quarters with characteristic architectural styles, it became celebrated throughout the continent for the amusements and excitements it had to offer, for the wild celebration of Mardi Gras when

ABOVE *The Levée, New Orleans, in 1884, from a lithograph by Currier and Ives.*

RIGHT *The Mississippi steamboat* Pargoud, *a stern-wheeler passenger and freight boat, active 1884–98.*

RIGHT, BELOW *The Levée, showing workers unloading cotton from a river boat,* c.1900.

bands of masked figures paraded through the streets, shouting, singing, dancing, throwing confetti and handfuls of flour, making their way to the carnival balls which were held all over the city. As well as numerous theatres, there were all kinds of clubs and gambling rooms, and all manner of eating-houses, from splendid restaurants like Antoine's – still in business in the French Quarter, and now the oldest restaurant in continuous family ownership in America – to the cheap eating places of the Irish quarter, known as the Irish Channel, between Magazine Street and the Mississippi River. There were also scores of brothels, and, after the Civil War, a notorious red-light district named Storyville after Sidney Story, the reformist alderman whose determination to bring prostitution under control was largely responsible for its creation.

The Civil War was a watershed in the history of New Orleans. Louisiana seceded from the Union on 26 January 1861; but the city remained in Confederate hands for scarcely more than a year, and on 1 May 1862 the commander of a Union army of fifteen thousand men marched in to occupy it. This was Major General Benjamin Butler, an attorney and politician before the War and believed to be so corrupt in his administration of New Orleans that he became known as 'Silver Spoons' Butler. With him came equally grasping officers and civilian officials who were said to have made fortunes from illicit deals and profiteering; and after the Civil War was over there arrived a multitude of adventurers from the north and east, politicians known as carpetbaggers because their only property qualifications were the belongings they stuffed into their travelling or carpet bags. As these carpetbaggers began to gain control of the city government New Orleans politics became increasingly corrupt. One Governor, who was eventually impeached and retired to private life with an immense fortune, openly declared, 'I do not pretend to be honest, only as honest as anyone else in politics.'

While political campaigns were regularly accompanied by violence and intimidation, violent crimes were equally commonplace. In the 1860s the British war correspondent, William Howard Russell, was told by a Criminal Sheriff in the city, a 'great, burly, six-foot man with revolvers stuck in his belt', that New Orleans was 'a perfect hell on earth, and that nothing could ever put an end to the murders, manslaughters and deadly assaults till it was made penal to carry arms', a practice adopted by citizens of all classes and occupations. In the infamously criminal areas of the city, along Girod Street in the American Quarter, Gallatin Street in the French Quarter, and along St Thomas Street and Corduroy Alley in the 'Irish Channel', there were innumerable taverns, concert-saloons and groggeries, brothels and barrel-houses which were known to be the haunt of criminals, hooligans and ruffians of every type. Both the barrel-house and the concert-saloon were introduced in New Orleans by the northerners who flocked there after the Civil War. The barrel-house was generally a long room with rows of barrels down one side and tables with mugs and tumblers down the other. Upon the payment of five cents a customer could fill a mug with the dubious, adulterated spirits contained in the barrels; but if he became drunk, as he often did, he was sure to be dragged outside or into a back room and robbed. He was not much safer in one of the lower concert-saloons in which the liquor was served by girls, known as beer-jerkers, who acted also as prostitutes. One of the toughest of these concert-saloons was the Buffalo Bill House run by one Bison Williams who had come to New Orleans from Cincinnati and entertained his customers not only with the obscene songs and dances performed by his serving girls but also with boxing and butting matches, and dog and rat fights.

As well as barrel-houses and concert-saloons there were numerous dance-houses in the city, establishments with bars and dance floors on the lower floor and with cubicles on the upper floors rented by prostitutes. The dance-girls wore nothing but slippers and knee-length calico dresses and, in some places, according to a reporter writing in the New Orleans *Times*, dispensed even with these scanty garments, they and their partners dancing 'in a state of awful nudity'.

Many of these establishments were controlled by the Mafia which was active in New Orleans from 1869, and which in 1890 was responsible for the murder of the police chief, David Hennessy, who was shot as he was walking home. Nineteen Italians were subsequently arrested, and ten were charged. At their trial, however, seven were acquitted and the jury declared a mistrial for the other three, whereupon a mob, encouraged by newspapers and community leaders, forced their way into a prison in Trémé Street and killed every Italian prisoner held there.

The more expensive and smarter of New Orleans's brothels employed small orchestras and bands; and it is often claimed that it was one of these bands, the Spasm Band, who were the original creators of jazz in 1895. Most of the seven young members of this band, and the singer who used a length of gas-pipe as a megaphone, had home-made instruments, including a fiddle made from a kettle, whistles, horns, a harmonica and a drum kit comprising a cow-bell, a kettle and a gourd filled with pebbles. It is also said that Charles 'Buddy' Bolden, a black cornet player and a barber by trade, who was born in New Orleans in 1868, was the first musician in the city to play in the style to be known as jazz. Whether or not either of these claims can be substantiated, it is at least reasonably well established that jazz was being played at Storyville as early as the 1890s and, at the same time, in cabarets and dance-halls, cafés and hotels elsewhere in New Orleans, in the resort areas around Lake Pontchartrain, and on riverboats on the Mississippi. At first this new music was far from widely enjoyed. A newspaper cartoon of the 1890s depicts a jazz band in Basin Street playing on a balcony while men and women hold their ears and shout in protest and dogs roll over and howl. But by the early years of the twentieth century, as anyone who lived in the city can attest, music could be heard, as Vincent Fumar says, 'anywhere and at all times of the day. Whether from mule-drawn advertising wagons or at the social gatherings of the wealthy, ragtime pianists, collective-improvisation groups and "sweet" bands fill the air every day of the year.' And from the city where Jelly Roll Morton began his career as a jazz pianist in 1902 and where Louis Armstrong played his trumpet on the riverboats, Sidney Bechet his clarinet, and King Oliver his cornet in the bordellos of Storyville, jazz spread all over the world.

Storyville was closed in 1917 as a result of pressure by the Federal Government which disapproved of legalized prostitution anywhere near a naval or military base in wartime. But the prostitutes and brothels moved elsewhere and, under the eye of a bribed police, carried on much as before, if more discreetly. By then control of the city had passed, with the help of the Negro

The 'Original New Orleans Jazz Band' with Jimmy Durante at the piano, 1920.

ORIGINAL NEW ORLEANS JAZZ BAND

A street of balconies in the Vieux Carré in 1925.

vote, from the Republican and northern politicians to the Democrats who, once in office, showed little confidence in electoral support by the Negroes and disenfranchised many of them by introducing education and property qualifications. The Democrats retained control for thirty years during nineteen of which, from 1902 to 1921, Martin Behrman ruled the city as mayor. His Regular Democratic Organization, the political machine known as the Old Regulars or Choctaws, provided a mechanism of city government similar to that of Tammany Hall in New York which was largely dependent upon graft but not lacking in efficiency. Behrman changed the executive body from a group of seventeen aldermen each elected by his own ward to a council composed of five commissioners supposedly

elected by the city but in fact selected by himself.

The Democrats were, however, unable to prevent the decline of New Orleans as a commercial centre, which had already become apparent under the Republicans. In the nineteenth century the general indolence of the population, the lack of competitive spirit in the merchant class, and the death rate from disease, which remained abnormally high, had continued to ensure that the city lost its lead to New York. In the twentieth the decline has accelerated: whereas New Orleans had been America's ninth largest city, it was only the twelfth in 1900 and the sixteenth in 1918.

Yet for all its poverty and its high incidence of crime, the city remained, as one visitor put it, the 'most colourful, the noisiest, and the most distinctive city in the whole new world'. Its distinctive character was, and is, due to the contrasting areas which have been formed in the course of its development, and the type of architecture which prevails in each. The French Quarter, often still called by its old name of Vieux Carré, is the heart of the old city. Here, around Jackson Square – named after the general, later President, who fought off a British attack in the war of 1812 – its essential flavour is preserved in an engaging mixture of French and Spanish and American architecture. To the south of the Vieux Carré is the Faubourg Ste Marie, called later the American section and now the Central Business District. This was mostly developed by American businessmen who moved to New Orleans after the Louisiana Purchase of 1803. To the north and north-east two Creole faubourgs sprang up after 1805, Marigny and Trémé, the latter mostly occupied by the well-to-do, French-speaking, free coloured population of New Orleans whose houses are still to be seen. Further immigration in the 1830s and 1840s by Germans and Americans led to the creation of the Lower Garden District upriver from the Faubourg Ste Marie. Several fine Greek revival mansions were built here by architects from England, Scotland and Ireland for wealthy American merchants and bankers. South-west of the Lower Garden District are the Garden District and the Irish Channel. Although begun in the 1830s as a suburb where the increasing number of wealthy American businessmen could erect their showy homes in the Italian Renaissance and Greek Revival styles, the main period of construction of this area was after 1850 and especially from 1865 onwards. The Irish Channel was built along the waterfront for Irish immigrants, most of whom worked as building labourers.

On the other side of the river the district known, for some reason long forgotten, as Algiers, existed as a separate small township of shipbuilders and farmers until incorporated into New Orleans in 1870. Most of the old colonial buildings here were burned down in 1897 and reconstructed as what has been described as a 'sparkling late Victorian settlement that has remained virtually unchanged almost a century later'. Two other relatively new districts are Jefferson City and University City which were incorporated into New Orleans in the 1850s. These owe their development to the World's Industrial and Cotton Centennial Exposition of 1884–5, which was held in the area now occupied

by Audubon Park – named after the American naturalist and artist who once had a studio here – and which proved a financial disaster. This area is characterized by the long, low houses with four or five rooms set on one floor, one behind the other, and known as shotguns, and by similar houses with an upper storey over the back part. 'Invariably,' as the architectural historian of New Orleans, Roulhac Toledano, has written, 'there is a front porch with wide overhang on a full, colonette supported gallery ... Most of these houses were built as rent houses for working-class people by wealthy developers who often constructed an entire block of identical shotguns. When prefabricated woodwork became available in catalogues, the combination of decorative detail created a lavish exhibition of design combinations along the streets. Turned columns, spindles and brackets (fretted, pierced and reticulated) abound and recall Oriental, Middle Eastern and Steamboat prototypes, all turning the uptown streets of New Orleans into a giant puzzle of woodwork.'

Wandering through these streets and across to the Vieux Carré, the visitor to New Orleans cannot fail to be captivated by the atmosphere of the city with its constant echoes of a Gallic-Hispanic and Caribbean past, to share that feeling for it which was experienced by Lafcadio Hearn, by Sherwood Anderson and William Faulkner, and by the Tennessee Williams of *A Streetcar Named Desire*.

Bourbon Street, New Orleans, as it is today.

17

Tokyo
'City of the Rising Sun'

In February 1854 Matthew Perry, an American naval officer, sailed with nine ships into Edo Bay to collect the reply to a letter from the President of the United States which he had delivered eight months before. On that earlier occasion he had shown himself to be a man not to be trifled with. Ignoring Japanese orders to leave, he had insisted that if the government did not instruct an official to receive the letter he had for the Emperor he would deliver it himself by force. And, after a few days of negotiation, he had persuaded the Japanese to accept the letter, leaving them with the strong impression that if they continued to refuse to enter into trading and diplomatic relations with the West, the same sort of fate awaited them as had overtaken China in the recent Opium War. On his return to Japan, therefore, Perry was able to conclude the first treaty between that country and his own and to open the way for the United States and for other Western powers to make further trading agreements with the Emperor.

The Emperor, in fact, was a purely ceremonial figure who lived in seclusion in Kyoto. Real power was in the hands of various noblemen, the heads of families of which the greatest was the house of Tokugawa. These noblemen accepted the overlordship of the Tokugawa who ruled as Shoguns or viceroys in the Emperor's name. For two hundred years, the Shoguns had been in control of the Empire, pursuing an isolationist policy and excluding all foreigners, or barbarians, from the country, other than a few Dutch

Eitai Bridge, a favourite Tokyo beauty-spot, opened in March 1875 (detail).

merchants who traded under the strictest control. Yet, even before Commodore Perry's arrival, there were signs that the days of the hereditary Shoguns would soon be over: Japan was beset by social and economic difficulties; a number of influential samurai were giving voice to an increasing discontent; several noble families openly resented the continuing power of the Tokugawa house; there was widespread feeling throughout the country that to survive in the modern world Japan must take lessons from the Western barbarians and not treat their ideas with the lofty disdain of the Chinese. The country, in fact, would have to be modernized, even at the expense of some of its ancient traditions. Discontent erupted into violence in the 1860s; the last of the Shoguns was forced to step down; the young Meiji Emperor was restored to power, 2,563 casks of imperial sake being distributed in Edo by way of celebration; and in 1869 the city, to be known thereafter as Tokyo, was declared the new capital.

For generations Edo had been divided into two parts, the Yamanote or High City, characterized by its shrines and temples and the large houses of the aristocratic and the rich; and the Shitamachi, the Low City, which was predominantly plebeian, and which, although it, too, had its big houses and its temples, was far more noisy, lively and intimate than the more sedate hilly region of the grand estates clustered around the Shogun's castle, now the imperial palace.

In Edo as a whole there were between 1,000,000 and 1,250,000 people at the beginning of the nineteenth century. It was almost certainly the largest city in the world, bigger even than London

Foreign steamships off Nagasaki, c.1854: Bai-oban colour print by an anonymous artist.

whose population in 1801 was less than 960,000. It was also one of the most congested in the world, the great majority of its inhabitants living in the Low City in cramped dwellings comprising no more than two rooms, measuring only about twelve feet by nine, and built of such combustible materials that most of them lasted for less than twenty years before being consumed in one of the city's numerous fires known as 'the flowers of Edo'. The population of the city had fallen dramatically during the troubled last days of the Shogunate as thousands left the city for fear of what might become of them if they stayed. But the numbers soon began to rise again and within twenty years they were as high as they had been in the most prosperous days of the Shoguns.

Among the new residents were many foreigners. For several years before Edo was officially opened to foreigners preparations were being made to accommodate them in a foreign settlement and to provide for their supposed needs in the area. One of these needs was for a hotel, and it was met by the Hoterukan, an establishment with more than two hundred rooms on three floors and a staff of over a hundred. It was a very strange structure built by a Japanese contractor who seemed intent on providing a design which, while not offending the susceptibilities of Japanese nationalists, would make Europeans and Americans feel at home. Its most notable feature was a tower that might have been constructed for a Japanese castle in the sixteenth century; this looked down upon a Japanese garden complete with tea-house and pagoda; the interior was decorated in the Western style. The whole was soon destroyed by fire.

Close to the Hoterukan was the New Shimabara, a pleasure-quarter equipped with 130 brothels and 84 tea-houses where the services of 1,700 courtesans and 200 geisha were available. This, too, however, did not long survive, partly, no doubt, because so many of those who lived in the foreign settlement were missionaries. The New Shimabara was often crowded with foreigners; but most of them came to inspect it out of curiosity rather than to enjoy the pleasures which it offered, and it was closed within a few months. The district nevertheless remained one in which the needs that the New Shimabara was intended to supply could be satisfied. There was, for example, an institution that purported to be an

Traditional old houses in Oji, Tokyo, c.1910.

English language school run by an English family who called themselves Summer and included several daughters who, 'if indeed they were sisters', so a former Japanese pupil wrote, 'it was curious that they resembled each other so little . . . They were, in any event, an assembly of "she foreigners", most alluring, from eighteen or nineteen to perhaps thirty . . . There was an old woman described as their mother; and there was not a man in the house . . . At the gate with its painted louver boards was a wooden plaque bearing, in Chinese, the legend "Bull's Eye School of European Letters". No one called it by the correct name. It was known rather as "The Summer" . . . The monthly tuition was a yen, and it must have been considerably more for those who had private means. A yen was no small sum of money in those days . . . The matter of private lessons was a strange one, for they took place upstairs during the evening hours.'

The foreign settlement did not maintain its peculiar character for long, since within a few years the original treaties were revised and foreigners were allowed to live where they liked. By then the westernization of Tokyo was well under way, and parts of the city seemed already to foreign visitors to have an atmosphere less redolent of the Orient than reminiscent of America or Australia. This was particularly so of the Ginza district which, destroyed in a disastrous fire in 1872, was rebuilt largely of brick under the supervision of an English architect, Thomas Waters. Before the fire W. E. Griffis, author of the

Guide Book of Yedo, had described Ginza as a characteristic district of the old Tokyo. He passed through one street 'full of folding screens', then through another of dyers' shops, 'with their odours and vats'. 'In one small but neat shop,' Griffis continued, 'sits an old man, with horn-rimmed spectacles, with the mordant liquid beside him, preparing a roll of material for its next bath. In another street there is nothing on sale but bamboo poles, but enough of these to make a forest. A man is sawing one . . . Another man is planing . . . I notice a blacksmith at work: he pulls the bellows with his foot, while he is holding and hammering with both hands. He has several irons in the fire, and keeps his dinner boiling with the waste flame . . . The cooper holds his tub with his toes. All of them sit while they work. How strange! Perhaps that is an important difference between a European and an Asian. One sits down to his work, the other stands up to it.'

After the rebuilding, this district was unrecognizable. Another writer of guide books, the Englishman Philip Terry, author of *Guide to the Japanese Empire*, described it as a 'structural Hodge-podge'; the English traveller and writer, Isabella Bird found it more like the outskirts of Melbourne or Chicago than a city of the East; while the French naval officer and novelist, Pierre Loti, thought that it had '*une laideur Américaine*'. For all their vaunted modernity, the new buildings were slow to find occupiers. Solid yet damp, stuffy and ill-suited to the Japanese climate, they ran, as Edward Seidensticker has observed in his excellent book about Tokyo, *Low City, High City*, 'wholly against the Japanese notion of a place to

Trams and rickshaws in the Ginza, c.1920.

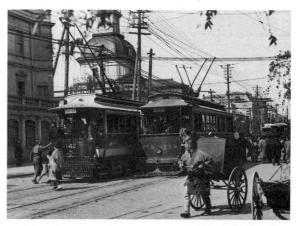

Kuniteru Yamada, The Nihon Bridge, Tokyo, c.*1865.*

OPPOSITE *Japanese transport in the late nineteenth century : woodblock print by an anonymous artist.*

live in. Choice sites along the main street presently found tenants, but the back streets languished, or provided temporary space for side shows, "bear wrestling" and "dog dances" and the like ... As many as a third of the buildings on the back streets remained empty. [Yet] despite the views of Miss Bird and Loti, the new Ginza ... was a huge success as an instance of Civilization and Enlightenment ... Everyone went to look at it ... it was also a great success with the printmakers. As usual they show it in brilliant sunlight with the cherries in bloom; and indeed there were cherries, at least in the beginning, along what had become the widest street in the city, and almost the only street wide enough for trolleys.'

The horse trolley had come into use in Tokyo in 1883, and soon electric trolleys were also to be seen. There were horse-drawn omnibuses as well, and trains ran regularly from Shimbashi Station south of Ginza to Yokohama: the Emperor himself, in Western dress, had travelled on one of the first trains of a railway financed in London, built under the direction of an English engineer and run by a foreign staff. But the most common form of transport was the rickshaw, and this at least was a Japanese invention. In the 1870s there were no

less than fifty thousand rickshaws in Tokyo. At first they were extremely noisy as the iron wheels rattled over the bridges and down the streets, the runners shouting warnings of their approach. They were also at first considered unseemly by the more respectable citizens who objected to the indecorous pictures that were painted on their backs, and the indecently scant clothing of the runners. But soon rubber tyres deadened the rattle of the wheels and the authorities required the runners to wear more than a loin cloth and forbade the decoration of their vehicles in questionable taste. Thereafter it was only the most conservative of Japanese who regretted the passing of the palanquin, and those whose livelihood depended upon water transport – particularly the owners of boating inns and floating restaurants – who considered the rickshaw a tiresome and unnecessary innovation.

While the English architect, Thomas Waters, was at work in the Ginza district, other foreign architects were designing buildings elsewhere. Josiah Conder, the most influential of them all – and, as lecturer in architecture at the university, responsible for the training of a whole generation of young Japanese architects in Western styles and techniques – designed the Rokumeikan, an Italianate government-owned guest-house complete with ballroom, music-room, library and suites for important visitors to Tokyo. A Russian designed the Nikolai Cathedral. An Englishman, William Barton, supervised the construction of the Ryōunkaku, otherwise known as the Asakusa Twelve Storeys. This was well over two hundred feet high, the tallest building in the city, an octagonal red brick tower equipped with Japan's first elevator, an importation from America. The two top floors, provided with telescopes, were for observation. Below them were exhibition rooms and floors on which goods from all over the world were laid out for sale.

Department stores on the Western model, as well as banks and hotels, were soon to be so familiar as no longer to provoke comment. The Mitsukoshi department store and its rival, Shiro-kiya, stood opposite each other at either end of the Nihombashi bridge, attracting customers with large posters and advertisements which would not have looked out of place in New York. There were glass display cases; there were departments selling Western clothes and hats; there were other departments selling watches, for a wristwatch was a sure indication of Civilization and En-

The Imperial Hotel, with a lily pond at the front entrance.

lightenment; yet others displayed leather goods, including briefcases. There were even shopgirls, whereas in the days of Edo there had been only shopboys. The only essential difference between these stores and their counterparts in the West was the tradition that required customers to remove their footwear when entering them and receive in exchange a pair of slippers which was returned when the footwear was reclaimed.

Yet, despite the new buildings going up everywhere, there were still areas of Tokyo where the atmosphere of old Edo could still be sensed. In 1879, the journalist John Russell Young accompanied General Ulysses Grant and his wife on a trip down the river and described a scene which might have been witnessed in the time of the Shoguns. 'We turned into the river ... and went on for an hour or so past tea houses and shops and under bridges, watching the shadows descend over the city. It is hard to realise that Tokio is a city – one of the greatest cities of the world. It looks like a series of villages, with its bits of green and open spaces and enclosed grounds breaking up the continuity of the town. There is no special character to Tokio, no one trait to seize upon and remember, except that the aspect is that of repose. The banks of the river are low and sedgy, at some

points a marsh. When we came to the house of the Prince, we found that he had built a causeway of bamboo through the marsh out into the river.'

Shopping in department stores; visiting the zoo; walking in parks, another innovation first introduced in 1873; reading newspapers, the first of which was published in 1870; going to a gentleman's club – the first of these was founded in 1880 – or attending a beauty school, the fashionable Japanese man and woman in Tokyo was anxious to appear as up-to-date as possible, while shunning the affectations of those extreme forms of Western behaviour and appearance known as 'high collar'. Foreign dress, though expensive at first, soon became *de rigueur* for men and a foreign appearance desirable. In the days of Edo, men had shaved part of the head, letting the hair grow long on the rest so that it could be pulled up into a topknot. But by the late 1890s scarcely any men wore their hair in the old-fashioned way: most went to a barber's shop to have it cut in the new style known as *jangiri*. Women were less eager to change their traditional clothes or hairstyle, but the most adventurous had their hair cut shorter and let it hang down from the head. The mother of the playwright, Hasegawa Shigure, suddenly appeared before her daughter one day with a 'different face'. Her eyebrows, which had formerly been shaved, had been allowed to grow; her hair was dressed in a new way; most strange of all, her teeth, which, like those of other women in Edo – including the Empress until 1873 – had been blackened, were now 'a startling, gleaming white. It was the more disturbing because something else was new. The new face was all smiles, as the old one had not been'.

As the appearance of the people of Tokyo changed, so did their habits. 'So many acts that had seemed natural,' as Seidensticker says, 'were suddenly uncivilized.' A list of misdemeanours committed in 1876 shows that almost half the ten thousand or so offences were described as 'urinating in a place other than a latrine'. Most of the rest were included under the headings of quarrelling or nudity or, in eight cases, transvestism. Orders against mixed bathing were issued in 1860 and repeated in 1870 and 1872; while the bath-houses themselves, which had formerly provided facilities for drinking tea served by young girls and for playing games, became houses of ill repute rather

Devastation in Tokyo's principal streets after the earthquake of 1923.

than places in which to meet friends. Private houses had formerly been identified only by some more or less picturesque description; they now had numbers. Traffic regulations in the past had been lax, yet whereas it had been customary to drive on the right where the narrowness of the passage made rules indispensable, it was now decreed that vehicles should, in the English manner, drive on the left. Visiting cards, lemonade, ice-cream and artificial legs were but a few of the Western products introduced into Tokyo at this time. Chairs were first seen in government offices in 1871, the year in which it became no longer necessary for those entering them to remove their shoes on doing so. Sumō wrestling – whose special status as a Japanese sport was indicated by the name of the huge sports arena in which matches were held, Kokugikan, the Hall of the National Accomplishment – had formerly been reserved for the entertainment of men. The women of Edo had with reluctance eventually been allowed to attend the last day of a tournament. By 1877 they were being admitted every

The ruins of Nihombushi, Tokyo, after the earthquake.

day. And by then baseball had arrived in Tokyo and was soon to rival sumō as a national sport.

Eating habits changed too. In the old days of Edo meat and dairy products were rarely served, and bread was unusual. But after the Meiji restoration beef and pork became favourite foods, despite Buddhist objections and a lingering disinclination to be seen buying it in a butcher's shop. Bread and pastry also became popular: in the shade of the oaks and pines, the cherries and maples planted along the waterways, workers and students alike could be seen eating buns filled with bean jam. Some of the students were in Western dress or in the student uniforms worn in many Western countries, but not all of them: many continued to wear traditional clothes until the Meiji Emperor died in 1912 and the accession of the Taishō Emperor heralded a new era.

Towards the end of the Meiji the passion for Western styles had seemed to be waning, and at the time of the Russo-Japanese War of 1904–5 there were outbreaks of violence against foreigners. The treaty that brought the War to an end on terms considered too favourable for the enemy, and negotiated with the help of American diplomacy, was greeted by rioting in Tokyo. Christian churches were burned down; the American legation was stoned by a shouting mob; and nearly five hundred policemen and firemen were injured, some of them fatally. Yet a few years later, under the Taishō, the pace of westernization increased. Milk bars were crowded with young girls, bus conductresses, typists, telephonists drinking ginger ale and eating sweets and Chaplin caramels, their hair cut short, their eyelids shadowed. Young men, their hair sleeked back with oil and without a parting, sat beside them in blue shirts and green ties, their trousers flared at the bottoms, wearing large spectacles known as *roido* either after Harold Lloyd, the American comedian, or after celluloid. In their conversation they made frequent use of foreign words not only when the lack of a Japanese equivalent made this unavoidable but also because the fashionable people of the High City, which now provided a cultural model for the Low, preferred words like Mama and Papa to the titles of the past.

Cinemas showing American films were also crowded. So were theatres where Western Operas and Western-style musicals were performed. Pav-

lova and Prokofiev attracted large audiences. Einstein came to lecture and the earnest attention of his audiences helped to persuade him that the Japanese were a nicer people than the Americans. Frank Lloyd Wright came, too, to design the Imperial Hotel which was opened in 1922 and succeeded the Rokumeikan as Tokyo's principal international meeting place.

Yet for all its Western atmosphere, Tokyo was in 1922 a far from modern city. Streets in the centre were in poor condition and the crowded roads leading into it in worse; the water supply was so inadequate that over a quarter of the population still had to rely on the often brackish water from wells; and in the Low City water sellers still carried their buckets through the streets. The sewage disposal system was equally inadequate, most householders being required to make private arrangements to have their sewage carted away or sold to farmers who, incidentally, paid more for waste from upper-class than from poorer homes and more for that from men's latrines than from women's. Combustible refuse was burned in the open air, creating in the poorer parts of the city a horribly pervasive smell. Passengers in motor cabs were bumped about so vigorously that their heads often struck the roof. To travel on public transport was to experience a crush and a noisy jostling which would have appalled even a Neapolitan, especially in late summer when the atmosphere is close and heavy.

It was particularly sultry on 1 September 1923 when disaster struck the city. The earthquake itself, its epicentre in Sagami Bay, caused less damage than might have been expected when the first shocks erupted with such violence that the seismographs at the Central Weather Bureau could not record them. But fires soon spread across the city, devouring alike the wooden houses and more solid structures such as the Mitsukoshi department store which, like Frank Lloyd Wright's Imperial Hotel, had survived the initial shocks. When the last tremor died away, nearly three quarters of the buildings of the city had been entirely destroyed or badly damaged; and over a hundred thousand people had been killed. Part of the High City had been spared, but most of the Low City, and with it the heart of old Edo, had disappeared for ever. Modern Tokyo was to rise upon the ruins.

Berlin

'The Babylon of the World'

Towards the end of the First World War, the artist George Grosz, who had served in the infantry and suffered from shell-shock, returned to Berlin where he had been born twenty-five years before. He found a city that 'looked like a grey stone corpse. The houses were cracked, paint and plaster had crumbled away, and in the dull, grimy eye-sockets of the windows you could see the caked traces of tears: the tears of people looking for familiar faces that were never to return.' 'Those were frantic years,' Grosz added. 'I embraced life with open arms and made contact with others equally anxious to turn their backs on the emptiness of the past.'

That past had seen the rapid growth of Berlin as the capital of a nation obsessed by *Borussismus*

PREVIOUS PAGE *George Grosz,* Street Scene (The Kurfürstendamm), *1925.*

BELOW *A street kitchen during Germany's post-war food shortage, 1918.*

which was defined in 1856 by Freiherr von Ketteler, Bishop of Mainz, as an *idée fixe* about Prussia's mission to dominate the world. It was a newly discovered destiny. Of the European towns which grew to be capital cities of powerful states, Berlin came late upon the scene. Originating in an inconspicuous settlement on the River Spree, it was first recorded as a city in 1244; and it was not until the Hohenzollern dynasty had consolidated their hold on the surrounding territories at the beginning of the sixteenth century that Berlin became the capital of Brandenburg, and not until the end of the seventeenth century that it became a place of importance in the time of Frederick William, the Great Elector. Even then its population was scarcely more than twenty-five thousand and of this number five thousand were Huguenot refugees from France. In the next century, during the reign of the most gifted of the Hohenzollerns, Frederick the Great, the city was enlarged and embellished with several fine

buildings including a splendid opera house in Unter den Linden. Yet Berlin was largely a creation of the nineteenth century. At the time of Napoleon Bonaparte's final defeat its population stood at about 197,000. Less than a century later, following the establishment of new industries and a surge in commercial activity, it had risen to well over two million. At the same time the Prussian Kingdom, of which the city was the proud capital, had, under the forceful leadership of Otto von Bismarck, absorbed the other German states, and in 1871 united Germany had been proclaimed an empire. Thereafter the forms of government, the ways of life and the character of the Prussians were to a large extent imposed upon the rest of Germany. The Germans as a whole became renowned for their discipline, their devotion to duty, their energy and capacity for hard work. They were also distinguished by their unbridled national pride and their lack of faith in adversity which could turn their courage into nihilism.

The arrogance of their leaders was reflected in the massive buildings erected in Berlin after the proclamation of the Kaiserreich, such as the Reichstag, the parliament building, the Kaiser Wilhelm Memorial Church and the bloated mansions of the plutocrats in the Hansaviertel. It was these ostentatiously large buildings, surviving symbols of a vanished power, that mournfully greeted the soldiers who, like George Grosz, returned defeated to the city in 1918. They found a people determined to evade the humiliation of their unexpected defeat in the creation of a myth. For the working class the explanation lay in the incompetence of their rulers who must be swept away by revolution; for the officer class and the middle class the blame lay with the politicians who had stabbed their fellow-countrymen in the back; for people in all classes, Germany had been the victim of a war of aggression by nations jealous of her growing power and success.

The appearance of the city itself, if shabby in parts and neglected, had not been changed by the War. The main buildings, the palaces, the opera houses, the Protestant and Catholic cathedrals, the mansions of Unter den Linden, the ministries in the Wilhemstrasse, the houses of the wealthy citizens, the residences of the ambassadors along the Tiergartenstrasse, the cafés of the Kurfürstendamm (or Ku-damm as Berliners affectionately called it), the dingy tenements near the

The Kaiser Wilhelm Memorial Church from the Tauentzienstrasse, 1930.

Alexanderplatz with their two-room flats and communal lavatories in the hall, the ugly working-class suburbs to the north and east of the city, these were all more or less the same as they had been when the War began. But there was a feeling in the air that the life of the city would never be the same again. Berlin was to be the scene of violent political turmoil and intense artistic ferment.

Already, as Grosz discovered, left-wing Socialists, known as Sparticists after the leader of the Roman slave revolt of 73 BC, had occupied those power stations which were not already shut down by strikes. In November 1918, after the Kaiser had left for exile in Holland, they captured the Berlin police headquarters; and the next year, having constituted themselves the Communist Party of Germany, they held a mass demonstration attended by some two hundred thousand people in the Siegesallee – the Victory Avenue, which had been completed in 1910 to commemorate Prussia's defeat of France in 1870 – and they afterwards occupied several public buildings. The newly installed German government were able to parry this threat only by enlisting the aid of the *Freikorps*, troops owing their allegiance

ABOVE *Friedrich Ebert on his way to a Reichstag meeting,* c.*1920.*

BELOW *Hannah Höch,* Cut with the Cake Knife, *1919.*

to ex-officers of the Kaiser's army. With the enthusiastic help of these soldiers the Communist uprisings were brutally suppressed and, on 5 January 1919, their leaders, Karl Liebknecht and Rosa Luxemburg, were both captured and shot. But by calling in the *Freikorps* the Government had unleashed an ungovernable force which later, in the guise of Hitler's storm-troopers, was to help destroy democracy in Germany quite as thoroughly as the Communists would have done.

Owing to the disorders in Berlin, the German National Constituent Assembly of 423 members met in the Thuringian city of Weimar on the river Elbe and in 1919 selected Friederich Ebert as the first President of what became known as the Weimar Republic, conferring wide powers upon the President who, though elected for a term of seven years only, was enabled under the famous Article 48 to suspend civil rights in times of emergency and to assume dictatorial powers. This was a proviso which Hitler was to find extremely useful when he was consolidating his power.

While Berlin was still in social upheaval, the city also witnessed an astonishing artistic upheaval which displayed its most eccentric outbursts in the Dada movement. This movement, which prepared the way for Surrealism, seems to have been given its name at a cabaret in Zürich in 1916 when a paper knife, stabbed into a French-German dictionary, lighted upon the French word for hobby-horse which struck the young artists present as sounding ideally absurd for their anti-aesthetic creations. When the movement blossomed in Berlin it became more overtly political, while its protest activities and public meetings became more shocking and provocative to the bourgeoisie whom it was intended to enrage.

At the first Dada exhibition in Berlin, held at the Burchardt Gallery in 1919, the life-size figure of a general suspended from the ceiling appeared to float above the heads of the crowd. Established artists were outraged by the exhibition, complaining angrily that 'nothing was being treated seriously or with proper respect any more, even the avant-garde'. The outcry against the exhibition was such that a court order was obtained to close it down.

The activities of the Dadaists, nevertheless, became even more outrageous. The writer, Franz

Mehring, recalled how one of the Dadaists' numerous periodicals, *Jedermann sein eigner Fussball* (*Every Man His Own Football*) was sold in the streets: 'We hired a char-à-banc of the sort used for Whitsuntide outings, and also a little band, complete with frock coats and top hats, who used to play at ex-servicemen's funerals. We, the editorial staff, paced behind, six strong, bearing bundles of *Jedermann sein eigner Fussball* instead of wreaths. In the sophisticated west end of the city we earned more taunts than pennies, but our sales mounted sharply as we entered the lower-middle-class and working-class districts of north and east Berlin ... "Every Man His Own Football" entered the Berlin language as an expression of contempt for authority. The periodical even looked like becoming a best-seller – and would have, if we had not been arrested on our way home from serenading the government offices in the Wilhelmstrasse ... *Jedermann sein eigner Fussball* was permanently banned, and we were charged with seeking to bring the Armed Forces into contempt and distributing indecent publications.'

George Grosz, who contributed some of his most savage caricatures to the periodical – which was celebrated also for its use of the Dadaist innovation, photomontage – described another Dada demonstration, 'a race between six typewriters and six sewing machines to the accompaniment of a swearing contest'. On this occasion Ben Hecht, who had been sent to report upon the Berlin phenomenon by the *Chicago Daily News*, was awarded the charter of an Honorary Dada in the shape of a beer mug half filled with sand. 'However, during the uproar that, as at all other Dada meetings, followed this one, and at which Dadaists did battle with their enraged audience, the symbolic charter was wrenched out of Ben's hands and used as a weapon.'

Less ephemeral than the achievements of the Dadaists were those of the composer Kurt Weill and the playwright Bertolt Brecht whose three-year collaboration produced the musical comedy *Aufstieg und Fall der Stadt Mahagonny* (*Rise and Fall of the City of Mahagonny*), which was a *succès de scandale* in 1927, and *Die Dreigroschenoper* (*The Threepenny Opera*), a play with music based on Gay's *Beggar's Opera* with the eighteenth-century scenes and characters transformed into representative figures in the Berlin underworld of the 1920s. Indeed, Berlin at this time was

A rehearsal of the Threepenny Opera *at the Schiffbauerdamm Theatre, 1928. The actors are, left to right: Erich Pono, Roma Bahn, Harold Paulsen and Kurt Gerron.*

celebrated for its major theatrical productions, the extraordinary Expressionist staging techniques of Erwin Piscator and the massive presentations in the huge theatre converted from a circus by the architect Hans Poelzig for Max Reinhardt. Here three thousand spectators were able to admire such spectacular shows with their unexampled crowd scenes as *Danton's Death* by Georg Büchner and Reinhardt's sensational production of *Orpheus in the Underworld*.

In these years there were no less than forty theatres in Berlin as well as three opera houses. Otto Klemperer was at the Kroll Theatre, conducting concerts and opera, from 1927 to 1933; while Bruno Walter was conducting at both the Staatsoper and the Lindenoper. The Berlin opera was then undoubtedly among the best in Europe, with one of the largest repertoires anywhere. Sixty-six different operas were performed in 1926–7, and at the Staatsoper, after almost a hundred rehearsals, Kleiber conducted the world première of Berg's *Wozzeck*. After the Staatsoper was renovated and reopened in 1927, Berlin opera became even more admired and some of the productions of Wagner were considered superior even to those of Bayreuth. At this time the Berlin Philharmonic Orchestra, under the baton of Wilhelm Furtwängler, was probably the best orchestra in the world.

It was also the heyday of the Berlin film industry which gave to the world such masterpieces of the cinema as *The Cabinet of Dr Caligari*, *M*, *Metropolis* and *The Blue Angel*, the film that made an international star of Marlene Dietrich who sang '*Ich bin von Kopf bis Fuss auf Liebe eingestellt*' ('From head to foot I'm hooked on love') in a night club like scores of others in Berlin. In these places 'beauty dancers' performed naked, transvestite hostesses with painted faces leered and pouted, and the denizens of German night life both native and foreign talked and drank and eyed each other in the murky light through the smoke of cigarettes. Christopher Isherwood, who was gathering the material that was to be used in *Mr Norris Changes Trains*, *The Berlin of Sally Bowles* and *Goodbye to Berlin*, fell in love with a boy named 'Bubi' at Cosy Corner in the Zossenerstrasse, while W. H. Auden wrote: 'Berlin is the buggers' daydream. There are 170 male brothels under police control. I could say a lot about my boy, a cross between a rugger hearty and Josephine Baker. We should make D. H. Lawrence look rather blue. I am a mass of bruises.'

The freedom of expression and absence of

Clerks entering a Berlin bank with large baskets to collect wages, July 1923.

shame in Berlin in the days of the Weimar republic were accompanied by much economic hardship and moral degradation. The uncertainties of the political situation, the burden of reparations imposed upon Germany by the Treaty of Versailles, the constraints placed upon the regeneration of German industry, all combined to make the finances of the state extremely precarious. It needed but a single dramatic incident to precipitate a crisis. The spark was provided in the spring of 1922 by the assassination of Walther Rathenau, the Jewish financier and Foreign Minister, by anti-semitic terrorists. Immediately the mark began to slide out of control. Postage stamps quickly rose from 75 pfennigs to 30,000 marks and were soon selling for millions and billions. A loaf of bread which in 1918 cost just over half a mark was selling by November 1923 for 201 billion marks. Foreign currency was virtually priceless: when the inflationary spiral had reached its height one United States dollar was worth more than four trillion marks. By the middle of 1923 the Reichsbank was keeping 300 paper mills and 150 printing firms busy in supplying Germany with money. 'I have known days when I had to pay 50,000 marks for a newspaper in the morning and 100,000 in the evening,' recalled Stefan Zweig. 'I sent a manuscript to my publisher on which I had worked for a year; to be on the safe side I asked for an advance payment of royalties on ten thousand copies. By the time the cheque was deposited, it hardly paid the postage I had put on the parcel a week before. On streetcars one paid in millions, lorries carried the paper money from the Reichsbank to the other banks, and a fortnight later one found 100,000 mark notes in the gutter; a beggar had thrown them away contemptuously. A pair of shoelaces cost more than a shoe had once cost, no, more than a fashionable store with two thousand pairs of shoes had cost before. To repair a broken window cost more than the whole house had formerly cost, a book more than the printer's works with a hundred presses. For £20 one could buy rows of six-storey houses on Kurfürstendamm, and factories were to be had for the old equivalent of a wheelbarrow.'

The principal sufferers were the middle-class pensioners and the working class. The government itself benefited by being able to pay off its internal debt and Germany was in 1924 as free from debt as she had been in 1870, that is to say, as the historian A. J. P. Taylor has pointed out, in as favourable a financial position at the end of a lost war as she had been at the end of her victorious war against France. There were also, among the wealthier industrialists and merchants, profiteers who, by buying when everything was so cheap, increased their fortunes to a gigantic size; and there were, of course, black marketeers who contrived to do well out of the crisis.

The moral deterioration which accompanied the financial chaos has been described by many observers. 'Berlin was transformed into the Babylon of the world,' wrote Stefan Zweig. 'Bars, amusement parks, red-light districts sprang up like mushrooms. Along the entire Kurfürsten-damm powdered and rouged young men saun-tered, not all of them professionals. Every high school boy wanted to earn some money, and in the dimly lit bars one might see government officials and men of the world of finance tenderly courting drunken sailors without any shame. Even the Rome of Suetonius had never known such orgies as the perverted balls of Berlin, where hundreds of men dressed as women and hundreds of women as men danced under the benevolent eyes of the police. In the collapse of all values a kind of madness gained hold, particularly in bourgeois society which until then had been unshakeable in its probity. Young ladies proudly boasted that they were perverted. To be sixteen and still under suspicion of virginity would have been considered a disgrace at any school in Berlin.'

'The times were certainly out of joint,' George Grosz confirmed. 'All moral restraints seemed to have melted away. A flood of vice, pornography and prostitution swept through the entire country ... The streets were wild ravines, haunted by murderers and cocaine peddlers, their emblem a metal bar or a murderous broken off chair-leg ... War cripples, real or sham, hung around every street corner ... "Je m'en fous!" was what everyone thought. "It's time we had a bit of fun." The shimmy was the latest craze ... Instead of first and second violinists we now had banjo and saxophone players, forced grins fixed in place ... I made careful drawings of all these goings on ... I almost grew rich and Erwin [Piscator] actually hit the jackpot simply by making faces and showing our bare behinds to the rich and mighty ... It was chiefly because they

were so bored with their lives that the rich enjoyed drinking to their own downfall. They would say "Prosit! Drink it down ... Go on Erwin, let's have it straight from the shoulder! No need to mince your words with us."

' "You stinking rich capitalist swine!" '

' "Ha! Ha! Say that again. I just love to hear you say it! Here, take a blank cheque, fill it in for any amount, any amount you like ..." '

Outside, a group of men in white shirts marched up and down, shouting in unison: 'Up with Germany! Down with the Jews.' They were followed by another group, also in disciplined ranks of four, bawling in chorus, 'Heil Moscow! Heil Moscow!' Afterwards some of them would be left around, heads cracked, legs smashed and the odd bullet in the abdomen. The city was dark, cold and full of rumours.

It was a city waiting for dictatorship. On May Day 1929, after a new Chancellor, Gustav Strese-mann had gained the confidence and cooperation of the Allies and re-established the value of the mark, there were further violent clashes between Communists and police in Berlin: and, after five days of fighting in barricaded streets, over twenty people lay dead and 150 seriously wounded. The next year, during a period of acute depression in which the numbers of unemployed reached three million, Hitler's National Socialist party gained five and a half million votes and well over a hundred seats in parliament. The Communists also increased their vote, and this induced the army and the industrialists to back Hitler. In October 1931 Hitler was received for the first time by the President, Field Marshal von Hindenburg. The interview lasted for seventy-five minutes and the former corporal spoke for sixty of them. After his visitor had gone, the old Field Marshal decided that he was a 'queer fish'.

In the election of July 1932, however, the Nazi vote soared to 13,745,000 after Hitler's storm-troopers, previously banned by the President for their acts of violence but now given free reign, had marched through the streets of Berlin intimidat-ing all opposition. The next year President von Hindenburg, convinced that only a government headed by Hitler would have a chance of success, conferred the Chancellorship upon him. Then, by extremely adroit political manœuvring and the use of skilful propaganda which presented the burning of the Reichstag building in Berlin as part

*Sixty thousand Communists, wearing their full military
regalia, taking part in a parade in a Berlin park, 1926.
The salute is taken during the march past by their
President, Ernst Thaelmann, the Communist candidate
for Germany's presidency.*

of a Communist conspiracy, Hitler persuaded the
German parliament to vote him powers that
granted him a virtual dictatorship.

In the summer of 1934, the long-standing feud
between Hitler and two of his chief lieutenants,
Ernst Roehm and Gregor Strasser, both of whom
urged a more revolutionary development of Nazi
action, came to a head. The army, whose support
Hitler considered indispensable, had become resentful of the growing power and disorderly
conduct of the storm-troopers – who now numbered two and a half million men – and were
alarmed by the revolutionary doctrines of their
leaders. So the Führer, as he was already known,
was able to come to a secret agreement with the
chiefs of the armed services; and on the night of 30
June–1 July, 'the Night of the Long Knives' as it

came to be called, Hitler, with the help of
Himmler's S.S. and Goering's special police, had
a large number of storm-troopers, certainly more
than a hundred, assassinated. Roehm was dragged
out of bed in a hotel and shot; Strasser was seized
at his home in Berlin and killed a few hours later in
the Prinz Albrechtsrasse Gestapo gaol.

Although the murdered men were for the most
part brutal thugs, a wave of revulsion spread
across Europe against a regime which so callously
disposed of its own supposedly loyal supporters.
In Berlin, however, there was no overt protest.
And when President von Hindenburg died in his
eighty-seventh year in August that year, it seemed
both natural and inevitable that Hitler should take
over the powers of head of state and commander-
in-chief of the armed forces. On 19 August
ninety-five per cent of Germans who had
registered went to the polls and ninety per cent of
those voted in favour of the Führer's assumption
of power.

Abroad the protests gradually died down; and
admiration for the new and evidently efficient

regime began to be widely expressed all over Europe. After meeting Hitler, Lloyd George, the former British Prime Minister, decided he was a great man. Thousands who went to Berlin for the Olympic Games in August 1936 were also deeply impressed by what they saw. No efforts were spared to present a magnificent spectacle. Sumptuous parties and dinners were given by the Nazi leaders. At one of these, staged by the Minister for Popular Enlightenment and Propaganda, Josef Goebbels, three thousand foreign and German guests were entertained at a garden party on the Pfaueninsel, the Peacock Island. On a terrace lit by five thousand lanterns overlooking the lake, they were served the finest food and wines that Germany could produce, while the Berlin Philharmonic Orchestra played for them, accompanied by singers from the State Opera and stars of the Berlin Ballet. The paths through the Island's woods were illuminated by girls from the city's cabarets and variety theatres dressed as torchbearers and page boys in powdered wigs and tight trousers. As the evening wore on, these girls

A propaganda parade of the Hitler Youth in Berlin, August 1934.

joined in the dancing and before long, according to Frau Goebbels's biographers, 'one saw drunken, reeling figures with shrieking girls under their arms or on their knees, trying to make off with them into the underbush. Adjutants feverishly tried to maintain order, and fretful aides from the ministry did their best to pacify the spirits that had been aroused. But the strong-arm men from the beer-hall brawls of north-east Berlin [officers of the *Sturmabteilung* who were among the guests] had long ago learned how to defend themselves from outside interference. Jaws were punched; people were kicked; bottles flew through the air; tables were overturned. The ambassadors, ministers, generals and captains of industry took flight. Thus Goebbels's feast on the Pfaueninsel turned into the greatest scandal in Berlin during the Third Reich ... The Minister was in a rage, the Führer indignant.'

This, however, was a rare mishap. The

The Olympic Games, Berlin, 1936 : the flame is carried into the packed stadium.

Olympic Games were a triumph of propaganda, even though Hitler could not conceal his annoyance when four gold medals were won by the black American athlete, Jesse Owens, and turned his back as the German spectators stood to applaud and cheer the American's victory. Foreign observers went home with further highly favourable reports: the people of Berlin had been most friendly; there had been no savage attacks in the Press upon the decadent democracies of the West; no action had been taken against Catholics and Protestants critical of the regime; Jews had not been molested and signs reading *'Juden unerwuenscht'* ('Jews Not Welcome') were removed from shops, beer gardens, hotels and theatres.

These signs were soon replaced. Already Jews had been excluded from public employment and their marriage to Aryans had been forbidden. Now attacks against individual Jews became more frequent and were usually ignored by the police. A number of prominent Jews left the country but for many escape was impossible, and a large number of those who could have fled stayed on in the vain hope that their persecution would soon cease. In

fact, it grew even more cruel. And on the night of 9–10 November 1938 a government inspired pogrom was provoked by the murder of a German diplomat by a Jew in Paris. That night, 'Crystal Night', glass shattered in the windows of Jewish-owned shops, synagogues were set on fire, private houses were broken into and their contents hurled into the street, Jewish men and women were assaulted and murdered. Official figures listed thirty-six dead and the same number seriously wounded, but the real numbers were much greater.

While Hitler was considering a solution to the problem presented by the hated Jews, he was also planning a new and more glorious Berlin as a memorial to the Nazi era. In the 1920s, inspired by the Berlin-born Walter Gropius and his workshops in the Weimar Bauhaus, architects in Berlin were endeavouring to fulfil Gropius's declared aim of co-ordinating 'all creative effort and achieving in a new architecture the unification of all training in art and design', of creating the 'collective work of art – the Building – in which no barriers exist between the structural and decorative arts'. Gropius himself in 1921–22 designed Sommerfeld House in Berlin whose decorations, carved by Bauhaus students, were to become characteristic of the Art Deco style. And in 1928 he retired as Director of the Bauhaus to return to private practice in Berlin; but in 1934, finding the Nazis, who had already closed the Bauhaus, intolerable, he left Germany for England. Almost all the leading writers, artists, musicians and scientists of the time had already followed or were to follow his example and left a country in the grip of a regime whose supporters could pile up tons of literature in the street beside the State Opera House and set it alight. Grosz and Paul Klee left, Bertolt Brecht and Kurt Weill, Max Reinhardt and Erwin Piscator, Heinrich Mann and Paul Hindemith, Arnold Schönberg, Bruno Walter, Erich Kleiber and Otto Klemperer, Alfred Döblin, Albert Einstein and the architects Erich Mendelssohn and Ludwig Mies van der Rohe.

For the fulfilment of his own grandiose architectural plans, Hitler turned to Albert Speer, whom he asked to design the 'biggest building in the world', a domed assembly hall with 180,000 seats, a cupola four times the size of the United States Capitol, surmounted by a gigantic eagle. This vast hall was to be surrounded by other immense buildings, all of them massively monumental and, like the Egyptian pyramids, reflecting the power of the nation's rulers. Few of these concepts ever got further than the sketches and architectural drawings which Hitler continued to study until the very end of his life, and nearly all those buildings which were created at his instigation were destroyed in the War that he made inevitable. At the end of that War over fifty thousand people in Berlin had been killed by Allied bombing and a further hundred thousand civilians had died in the desperate battle for the city launched by the Russian army on 16 April 1945. And around the garden of the bunker in which Hitler's corpse was burned, the city that he had dreamed of making the capital of an empire lasting for a thousand years lay in tumbled ruins.

The beginning of the Nazis' persecution of the Jews in Berlin: notices are put up to boycott Jewish shops and goods, April 1933.

19

Moscow
'A Model Communist City'

On an estate at Gorki some eighteen and a half miles south of Moscow where he had been living for ten months recuperating from a stroke, Vladimir Ilyich Ulyanov, better known as Lenin, died of a cerebral haemorrhage at ten minutes to seven on the evening of 21 January 1924. His body was brought back by train to the Paveletsky station in Moscow and the coffin was then carried on the shoulders of some of his friends to the Trade Union House, formerly a club for nobles, where it was placed on a high bier in the Hall of the Columns. There it lay in state for seventy hours while from the freezing cold of the street outside tens of thousands of people from many parts of Russia filed past in a final act of homage. Then the coffin was carried to a temporary mausoleum in the Red Square where a vast throng waited; but, with the temperature at thirty-five degrees below zero, few of those in the dense crowd took off their hats as the coffin passed by, raising their gloved hands instead to salute the departed hero.

While most of the principal Bolshevik leaders took part in these obsequies in Moscow, there was one notable absentee. This was Lev Bronstein, or Trotsky, who was in the Caucasus, said to be undergoing a cure. He was undoubtedly, after Lenin, the most popular among the chief Bolsheviks and might have been expected to step into his shoes. His failure to return to Moscow for Lenin's funeral seemed to the Muscovites inexplicable and inexcusable. He himself later claimed that he had been wrongly informed about the date and advised to remain at Tiflis to

The Kremlin from Red Square.

Lenin and Stalin in Gorki, August/September 1922

continue his treatment. Responsibility for this misinformation, so Trotsky said, rested with the General Secretary of the Communist Party, Joseph Vissarionovich Djugashvili, known as Stalin.

Stalin was born in the provincial Georgian town of Gori in 1879, the son of a drunken cobbler and a devoutly religious washerwoman who had hopes that he would become a priest. He was sent to the church school at Gori, where he was taught Russian which he always spoke with a Georgian accent, and then attended the Tiflis Theological Seminary. Far more interested in revolutionary politics than in religion, however, he studied in secret the works of Karl Marx and by the time he was twenty-one he had joined a Georgian revolutionary organization and three years later was a member of the Bolshevik faction of the Russian social democrats. After the revolution of 1917 his rise in the party was rapid; and, although Lenin had begun to have doubts about him during his last illness, Stalin skilfully contrived to defeat all his rivals in the struggle for power after Lenin's death. Lenin's two fellow-members of the Politburo, the powerful policy-making committee of the Communist Party, Grigori Zinoviev and Lev Kamenev, were dismissed, disgraced and eventually executed. Other opposition leaders were banished into eternal exile. Trotsky was stripped of his citizenship, deported in 1929, and, on

Stalin's orders, later murdered in Mexico where he had found refuge. By then Joseph Stalin's authority in Russia was supreme and from his office in Moscow he exercised a power as absolute as that of Peter the Great.

The Moscow which the Bolshevik leaders had inherited from the Tsars, and had once again made the capital of Russia, was a city surrounded by the waters of six rivers. It had begun its existence as a settlement at the foot of a hill, the Borovitsky Hill, on the north bank of the Moskva River. Here a fort had been built in the twelfth century by Prince Yuri Dolgoruky and thereafter the place grew and prospered, its importance much increased when the Metropolitan of the Russian Orthodox Church moved his see here from Kiev and when Ivan III, the Great, extended the frontiers of the surrounding empire. Ivan reconstructed the castle of the town, the Kremlin, which he enclosed within massive walls and towers designed for him by Italian architects, walls, which still encircle the Kremlin, built of brick and extending for almost one and a half miles. Several stone churches had already been built within the walls; and to these were now added the five-domed Cathedral of the Assumption which was completed in 1479 to the designs of Aristotele Fioravanti of Bologna, who used the twelfth-century cathedral at Vladimir as a model, and the Cathedral of the Archangel Michael, designed in the style of the Italian Renaissance by Alevisio Novi of Milan and finished in 1509. French as well as Italian architects came to work for the Tsars in Moscow, providing it, in the seventeenth century, with some of its most distinctive Baroque architecture, while England and Dutch merchants travelled to the growing city to trade, and from Scotland came soldiers recruited for service in the imperial armies. All were referred to indiscriminately as 'Germans' and even before the days of Peter the Great, whose curiosity about the West was first aroused here, the population of the so-called 'German colony' in Moscow had risen to at least fifteen hundred. Most of the rest of the city's population consisted of artisans, tradesmen and labourers who rose in revolt on several occasions against the harsh conditions in which they were required to work and live.

Despite Peter the Great's transfer of the capital to St Petersburg, Moscow remained a trading centre of great importance in the eighteenth century and continued to expand. New churches and hospitals were built; the monumental Senate building in the Kremlin was designed by the most notable architect of the period, Matvei Kazakov, who seems also to have had a hand in the Pashkov Palace which, mainly the work of the architect Vasily Bazhenov, was built on a hill overlooking the Kremlin in 1784–7 and now houses the Lenin Library. Both Bazhenov and Kazakov also designed several of those characteristic noblemen's houses which, facing the street or standing behind a winged forecourt, two or three storeys high, with gardens and servants' quarters at the back, towered above the small wooden houses in which the majority of Moscow's people still lived.

Two-thirds of these houses were destroyed by fire when the city was set alight by its inhabitants during Napoleon's occupation in 1812; and a Committee for the Construction of Moscow had to be established to build a new city amid the charred ruins of the old. The Commission's chief architect was Osip Bove who designed, among many other buildings, the Triumphal Arch and the Church of the Virgin of All Sorrows. These are recognizably works in an eighteenth-century tradition. But after Bove's death in 1834 the prevailing classicism was rejected in favour of an eclecticism in which different styles were sometimes combined in the same building, as in Konstantin Thon's Great Palace in the Kremlin (1838–49), which associates classical and Russo-Byzantine features, and his enormous Cathedral of Christ the Redeemer (1839–83). Alongside these new imposing public buildings, which included the Bolshoi Theatre rebuilt in 1843 after its destruction by fire, splendid new mansions were constructed for rich industrialists who had made their money in mining, textiles and other industries. And as these industries flourished, as Moscow became the second largest manufacturing town in Russia after St Petersburg, and as new railway stations were built – including the Nicholas, now the Leningrad, Station – the population of the city, which had been no more than two hundred thousand at the end of the previous century, had more than trebled by 1872.

This fast increase in the number of inhabitants led to the construction of row upon row of small houses, apartments and even barracks for the accommodation of the poor on the outskirts of the

General view of Moscow, c.1910, with the Temple of the Saviour in the background.

city, creating suburbs in as striking contrast to the administrative and business centre and the opulent residential districts of the well-to-do, as the charm of the flower market at the foot of the Kremlin contrasted with the filth of the surrounding streets whose pavements rose up in cracked bulges or disappeared into holes filled with stagnant water. The growth of the city progressed with no effective planning and with that characteristic Russian predilection for schemes too ambitious to be properly executed. The Russian writer, Pushkin's friend, Chaadayev – whose excoriating attack on Russian isolationism and cultural sterility was to lead to his being declared insane by the Tsar – gave examples of this predilection in two objects which remain among the principal sights of Moscow, the Tsar Cannon, cast in 1586 and one of the largest ever made, and the Tsar Bell, the world's biggest bell, displayed at the splendid white 250-foot-high Ivan the Great Bell Tower. 'In Moscow,' Chaadayev said,

A queue for a shop in a Moscow street in one of the poorer suburbs of the city, March 1921.

ABOVE *Peasants joining the collective farm at Chegorani village, 1931.*

'every foreigner is taken to see the great cannon and the great bell – the cannon which cannot be fired because of its immense size, and the bell which fell down before it was rung. It is an amazing town in which the objects of interest are distinguished by their absurdity; or perhaps that great bell without a tongue is a hieroglyph symbolic of this huge, dumb land, inhabited by a race calling themselves Slavs as though wondering at the possession of human speech.'

Yet if Moscow was remarkable for its unrealizable schemes and dreams of grandeur, it was remarkable, too, for its theatre and its music. The decorative possibilities of the theatre, for instance, were inspiringly revealed by Sava Mamontov, a merchant prince, who established an art school at his country house and recruited the leading artists of his day to provide the settings for operas which he produced in his own theatre. 'For

OPPOSITE Death to World Imperialism: *Communist poster by D.Moor.*

the first time scenery and costume designing was entrusted to easel artists who were within a short time to sweep away the specialists with their stereotyped ideas and their heavily built-up sets, and to substitute youth, colour and freshness,' Arnold Haskell has written. 'Painting took its place in the theatre, and the scene with its costumes, carefully graduated patches of colour, became a living canvas ... It is thanks to Mamontov that such works as *Boris Godounov*, *Khovantchina*, *La Pskovitaine*, *Sadko* and *Snegourotchka* were recreated, and it is here for the first time that the genius of Chaliapin was revealed.' The impresario Serge Diaghilev made frequent visits to Moscow to see Mamontov and the productions which he inspired and, with his painter friends Leon Bakst and Alexander Benois, he later, under Mamontov's influence, revolutionized the production of opera and the ballet throughout Europe and America. At the same time the presentations of the Bolshoi Theatre went from strength to strength, while the Tchaikovsky Conservatory, founded in 1866 by the pianist Anton Rubinstein, provided teachers of the stature of Tchaikovsky himself, of Rachmaninov and Khachaturian.

Men and women receiving instruction in geography at the Pedagogical Institute of Geography, as part of Stalin's state education scheme.

Concerts organized by the Russian Musical Society and performed by the Moscow Philharmonic Orchestra were given in the halls of the Club of the Nobility, the fine classical building in which Lenin's coffin had been placed, in the Manezh, a converted military riding school (now the Central Exhibition Hall), and in the Tchaikovsky Concert Hall, home of the USSR State Symphony Orchestra. The productions of the Bolshoi Theatre were rivalled by those of several other theatres, including the Moscow Art Theatre, founded in 1898 by two intellectuals, Konstantin Stanislavsky and Vladimir Nemirovich-Danchenko.

These productions were not, however, for the poor; and, as the First World War approached, the contrast between such slums as those around the Khitrov market – where Tolstoy, determined to see the worst the city had to offer, was surrounded by ragged, hungry, shivering and importunate derelicts – and the ostentatious mansions of the old aristocracy and of the newly

rich merchants and industrialists, was no less disturbing than it had ever been.

In 1912 the young diplomat, R. H. Bruce Lockhart, arrived in Moscow as Vice-Consul and for three days lived in 'a turmoil of entertainment'. He was invited to luncheon parties and to racecourses, he attended gala performances at the theatre, shook hands with long-bearded generals, 'exchanged compliments in French with the wives of Moscow merchants', and attended 'an immense dinner given by the Haritonenkos, the sugar kings of Moscow'. The whole huge Haritonenko palace was a 'fairyland of flowers brought all the way from Nice. Orchestras seemed to be playing in every ante-chamber'. Scores of waiters served vodka and delicious food. Then, when his appetite was sated with *zakuski* and reindeer tongue, a footman handed him a card with a plan of the table and his own place at it. A huge dinner was served; course after course, wine after wine appeared until eleven o'clock when a ballet was performed in another vast room on a higher floor and a violinist played Chopin nocturnes. Then there was dancing, followed by supper, and, at four o'clock in the morning, the guests were driven away, well wrapped in fur rugs, in troikas drawn by Arab horses.

Bruce Lockhart took a room at the Metropole Hotel. 'As I walked through the hall to the restaurant,' he recorded in his memoirs, 'my first impressions were of steaming furs, fat women and big sleek men; of attractive servility in the underlings . . . of great wealth and crude coarseness . . . I had entered into a kingdom where money was the only God . . .

'The restaurant itself was a blaze of light and colour. The long high room was surrounded by a balcony on all sides. Along the balcony were gaily lit windows and doors opening into private rooms – known in Russian as 'kabinets' – where, hidden from prying eyes, dissolute youth and debauched old age trafficked roubles and champagne for gipsy songs and gipsy love . . . The restaurant itself was a maze of small tables. It was crowded by officers in badly cut uniforms, Russian merchants with scented beards, German commercial travellers with sallow complexions and close-cropped heads. And at every table a woman, at every table champagne . . . At the end of the room was a high balustraded dais, where an orchestra, resplendent in red coats, crashed out a Viennese waltz with a frenzy which drowned the popping of corks and the clatter of dishes and finally by its increasing furore subdued the conversation . . . As I drank my first glass of vodka and for the first time ate caviare as it should be eaten – on a warm "kalatch" [a warm roll with a handle like a basket] I realised I was in a new world in which primitiveness and decadence lived side by side.'

Five years later that world was swept away in the revolution that brought Lenin, and ultimately Stalin, to power. In their early years in government, the Bolshevik leaders were faced with harrowing problems. While excited avant-garde poets and theatrical producers staged their mass re-enactments of revolutionary victories in the streets of Moscow, while artists produced propaganda posters in Cubist and Futurist styles and painted revolutionary slogans on palace walls, social reformers preached the liberation of women, free love and the destruction of the family, shouting, 'Down with the capitalist tyranny of parents!' and while young Communists exuberantly boarded the city's crowded trams without any clothes on as a demonstration of their rejection of the bourgeois life, there was widespread hunger, even starvation. Many of the five million

men in the Red Army who had had to be demobilized after the end of War had turned to banditry for a living. The sailors at the naval base of Kronstadt, who had led the insurrection against the provisional government which had been set up after the abdication of the Tsar in March 1917, turned against their new Bolshevik masters, denouncing the autocratic rule of the Central Committee of the Party, and had to be suppressed by units of the Red Army and the security service, the *Cheka*. All around Moscow peasants were resisting the Party's policy of requisitions by armed uprisings. Faced with a crisis of such magnitude, Lenin, while maintaining his political power intact, had decided on retreat in economic practices. The New Economic Policy, which lasted from 1921 to 1929, restored a market economy, cut back on social services and the nationalization of industry, and permitted greater social freedom. The effect of this policy in Moscow was striking. In a short time the city began to resemble its old self, 'with peasant women selling potatoes in the markets,' as Professor Sheila Fitzpatrick has written, 'church-bells and bearded priests summoning the faithful, prostitutes, beggars and pickpockets working the streets and railway stations, gypsy songs in the nightclubs, uniformed doormen doffing their caps to the gentry, theatregoers in furs and silk stockings. In this Moscow, the leather-jacketed Communist seemed a sombre outsider, and the Red Army veteran was likely to be standing in line at the Labour Exchange. The revolutionary leaders,

A physical culture parade in Red Square, 1934.

quartered incongruously in the Kremlin or the Hotel Luxe [now the Central Hotel in Gorky Street] looked to the future with foreboding.'

By the late 1920s, however, when Stalin's opponents and rivals had all been defeated, he was able, after tactical shifts in policy during his struggle for supreme power, to impose his own Stalinist rule upon the party and the country, condemning dissent from its undeviating line, accusing opponents of treason. He inaugurated an intensive industrialization programme and enforced the collectivization of agriculture, compelling peasants to work on state farms, arresting, exiling and shooting the recalcitrant or having them worked to death in labour camps, continuing to export grain while famine spread across the Ukraine, pushing through a social reorganization that may have cost as many as ten million lives.

Terror, which had been used by Lenin on a limited scale and for limited purposes, became an accepted instrument of government, a horror without end and often without discernible reason. It reached every class in society – aristocratic relics of the old regime, industrial managers forced to confess to invented crimes to serve as scapegoats for failures in Stalinist policies, intellectuals, religious leaders, politicians. A series of purges from 1933 to 1939 almost entirely eliminated the leading figures in the Party of the 1920s. Not even the chief executioners were spared. The infamous head of the OGPU, the

Members of a team of Moscow underground workers, 1 May 1934.

Unified State Political Administration, G. G. Yagoda, and N. I. Yezhov, the equally terrible head of the NKVD, the People's Commissariat of Internal Affairs, were both swept away. In 1937 it was the turn of Marshal Tukhachevsky and other Red Army Generals. A number of victims were eliminated by means of show trials in Moscow, following abject confessions of guilt, others more quietly disposed of by trials in camera or without any trial at all.

The arrests usually took place at night or in the early hours of the morning and were followed by incarceration in one of Moscow's gaols for political prisoners, the Lubyanka, the Lefortovo, the horrendous Sukhanovka, a former monastery, or the Butyrka. All were overcrowded: in the Butyrka in 1937 there were 140 prisoners in a cell designed for 24; in a women's cell, there were 110 in a cell supposed to hold 25. The only way for them to lie down was sideways, squashed together on the floor between the latrine buckets. And in all torture was regularly used to extract confessions, though most prisoners, as Alexander Solzhenitsyn says, had no idea what they were supposed to be guilty of. 'There was a feeling among them that people were being arrested for no reason at all . . . Interrogations were usually conducted at night . . . They shone lights in the prisoner's face . . . They made use of the hot air systems to fill the cell first with icy-cold then with stinking hot air. And there was an airtight cork-lined cell in which there was no ventilation and they cooked the prisoners . . . The heat was turned up until your blood began to ooze through your pores. When they saw this happening through the peephole, they would put

Moscow 'Arbatskay' underground station.

the prisoner on a stretcher and take him off to sign his confession.'

Beyond the prisons' walls meanwhile, Moscow was changing and developing. In spite of widespread inefficiency, Stalin was succeeding in creating a formidable military and industrial state and a capital with the facilities to train men and women to maintain and increase its strength. Technical education, in particular, was vastly expanded. Large numbers of schools, institutes, colleges, and university buildings appeared; and, at the same time, new office blocks and ministries were built. The Commissariat of Agriculture was completed in 1933 to designs by A. V. Shchusev in the then favoured Constructivist style which emphasized the functional aspect of architecture and required that a building should reflect its means of construction. The Gostorg Building, also in the Constructivist style by B. M. Velikovsky, was finished in 1927, pioneering the use of ferro-concrete and glass. And the building designed by I. I. Rerberg and now used for

meetings of the Supreme Soviet was opened in 1934. The following year – the year in which the metropolitan underground was inaugurated, with its lavishly decorated marble stations and fast trains – the government produced a General Plan for the reconstruction of Moscow.

This plan proposed that the main development area should be to the southwest of the city where, after the war, the vast complex of the new Moscow University and several other skyscrapers were built. Here stood the huge Mosfilm Studios, begun in the 1920s when Eisenstein, director of *The Battleship Potemkin* and *Alexander Nevsky*, worked in them, later to be joined by Sergei Bondartchuk who made the most successful rendering of *War and Peace*, and Grigori Chukhray, director of *Ballad of a Soldier*.

While building continued at an increasing rate to cater for the needs of a population which was rising fast and was to reach four million five years after the General Plan was inaugurated, Moscow still contrived to retain its open aspect with broad avenues called Prospekts, with enormous squares, wide streets beside the broad Moskva River, and with fine parks of which the elongated Gorky Park along the left bank is the most celebrated, though by no means the biggest.

The ordinary people of the city, however, were quite unable to enjoy this sense of space at home, living accommodation being so inadequate that two families often had to share a single room and sometimes three families, or even four. In his memoirs, Dimitri Shostakovich writes that if a room was large, it would be divided into three or four sections. 'And there was no talk of luxury like an apartment. An apartment could hold ten or fifteen families. There was a housing shortage, what could you do? ... And it's easier to make a statement or, to put it bluntly, a denunciation about your neighbour, since your neighbour's life is on display. Everything is visible – who came, what time he left, who visited him, who his friends are. What a person cooks for dinner is also visible, since the kitchen, obviously, is communal.'

Shostakovich goes on to record that a comedy about this communal living called *Squaring the Circle* was put on at the Arts Theatre. The ageing actor and director, Konstantin Stanislavsky, who, as founder of the theatre, lived as a privileged member of the élite in a large eighteenth-century house off Gorky Street, came to a rehearsal and could not understand the plot. 'Why,' he asked, 'are all these people living in one room?' It was explained to him that this was common enough in Moscow; but he could not believe it. 'This is a true story about one of the great directors of our times,' Shostakovich comments sardonically. 'Now it's clear that Stanislavsky lived in his own world. He was an exalted man with an artistic soul. He received groceries from an exclusive distributor, as did all geniuses and Party workers bringing outstanding benefit to the state ... The ones who didn't get groceries kept quiet so that they wouldn't end up behind bars for spreading slander, and as for the ones who did get groceries, it's obvious why they kept quiet.'

Foreigners usually experienced the same difficulty as natives in finding decent places to live. Malcolm Muggeridge, who was correspondent for the *Manchester Guardian* in Russia in the 1930s, first took up quarters in the Nora Moskovkaya Hotel newly built for tourists. Then a long search began for other accommodation. This 'involved visiting numerous apartment blocks where rentable rooms were allegedly available. They invariably turned out to be part of a room, with, at best, the possibility of hanging a blanket to curtain off the portion offered to us, and the use of corporate cooking and washing facilities ... This was how the majority of Soviet citizens lived ... Only important officials like the Sokolnikovs and rich writers like Ehrenburg, enjoyed the luxury of apartments to themselves. Ehrenburg's flat actually had some Impressionist paintings – otherwise banned in the USSR – hanging in it. He also had a country residence near Moscow.'

Tired of walking around the Red Square beneath the Red Flag flying above the Kremlin and by visits to the anti-God Museum in the cathedral – where a pendulum swung to demonstrate that the force of gravity was above any supposed divine law and where fossilized saints were on display to refute the fraudulent claims that they had been miraculously preserved against the ravages of time – Muggeridge, for comfort, turned to the streets 'where the endless stream of anonymous people were somehow companionable, as the pendulum God and the refrigerated saints were not. Grey-faced; as winter came on, in padded coats and felt boots, their footfall mysteriously silent in the snow – they seemed to be coming from nowhere. Just drifting inscrutably along. There was little to look at in the shops except wooden cheeses and cardboard imitations of plenty to come. No neon lights, no spelt out pleasures; no whiff of flesh or snatch of music as a swing door opened and shut. All drab and grey and restrained. And yet I had a feeling, stronger than I can possibly convey, that what was happening in Moscow must happen everywhere. That it was the focal point or pivot of our times, whose essential pattern was being shaped there.'

To another journalist in Moscow at this time, A. T. Cholerton of the *News Chronicle*, it was the 'sheer philistinism of the regime that appalled him, its total humourlessness, its abysmal taste, its dreadful buildings, its flat, heavy representational paintings of Lenin and Stalin, like portraits of Lord Mayors in Manchester Town Hall; the long-winded cant and dull hatred which hung like an oppressive cloud over it.'

Yet, when the German armies approached the city in the late summer of 1941, the resistance of the Muscovites was heroic. At first there had been disarray among the leaders and symptoms of panic among the people. Buildings were no longer heated; water supply was intermittent; bombardments of the city caused great damage. Food grew short and shops were looted. But the strong resistance of the Russian army induced Hitler, against the advice of his generals, to suspend the advance of his Centre Army Group; and the respite enabled the Russians to build defensive zones around the city. As torrential rains turned the roads into quagmires, slowing down the resumed German advance, it was announced in October that Stalin had taken personal control of the defence of the city. The whole of the Kremlin disappeared under a camouflage of green branches; the streets were blacked out at night; the tunnels of the Metro became a vast underground shelter.

On 3 November 1941 a Swedish press report described how the Red Square now resembled a huge stage 'with scenery spread out on the ground. The stone pavement of the square has been decorated with roofs, chimneys, house fronts with windows, etc. This is a camouflage measure against air raids. Most of the windows of the buildings in the city have been covered or simply painted blue. Everywhere in Moscow one can observe the "home defence's" constant drilling, in which they practice street fighting. The inhabitants receive instruction in building barri-cades. Machine-guns are set up at street corners and on roofs. The public learns for the first time that hidden in many buildings at intersections are well-equipped machine-gun nests which had been installed there during construction of the buildings.'

On 7 November, as a demonstration of defiance the traditional parade to celebrate the October Revolution of 1917 was held as usual; and later that month frost and snow added to the difficulties and hardships of the German armies. But, despite the appalling weather and their heavy casualties, the Germans reached the suburb of Khimki. In December, however, the Russian troops of the Far Eastern Armies began to enter the line which was gradually pushed outwards as they went over to the attack. And it was soon clear that the invaders were about to suffer their first major defeat of the War. The danger to Moscow gradually receded and thereafter the city became an immense arsenal as well as a supply of manpower for the forces: seven hundred thousand of its inhabitants went to the Front. The great crisis of the regime was over; and the work of reconstruction which was to transform its capital was soon to begin.

A ski batallion leaving for the front, December 1941.

20
New York
'A Stroke of Genius'

1883 was a memorable year for New York. On New Year's Day Theodore Roosevelt, who had been born in the city twenty-five years before, was nominated as candidate for the office of Speaker in the New York State Assembly and so, rising like a rocket, as he put it himself, began that quick ascent to the Presidency which he was to reach in 1901. That same year witnessed the opening of the Brooklyn Bridge, the longest single-span suspension bridge of the time and the first to use steel cables, which, crossing the turbulent waters of the East River, joined Brooklyn to Manhattan. 1883 was also the year in which New Yorkers celebrated the centenary of American independence.

In 1783, following the defeat of their forces under Lord Cornwallis at Yorktown in Virginia two years before, the British had finally agreed to recognize the American nation with its first capital at New York. Over two and a half centuries before, the island of Manhattan, which is the centre of what was to become for a time the biggest city in the world, had first been sighted by Europeans during a voyage of exploration down the eastern seaboard of North America made by Giovanni da Verrazano, a Florentine navigator in the service of the King of France. Thereafter French vessels had entered the mouth of the river in which Manhattan stands to trade with the Iroquois Indians who lived on the island in long wooden houses sheathed in elm bark. The river became known as the Hudson after the English explorer who in 1609, seeking a route from

Modern view across Brooklyn Bridge

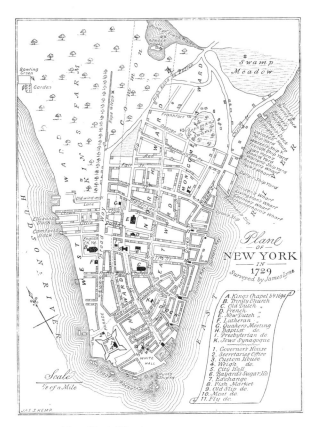

ABOVE *New York City in 1729.*

Europe to Asia by way of the Arctic Ocean, sailed upstream as far as the site of the modern town of Albany near which he established a stockaded fort. Hudson was then in the service of the Dutch East India Company; and it was one of the Dutch governors of the settlement that developed from this fort, Peter Minuit, who, in 1626, purchased for sixty guilders' (about twenty-four dollars') worth of trinkets what was to become the most expensive piece of land on earth – the island whose northern end was occupied by the Indian tribe of the Manna-Hatta.

At the south end of this island the Dutch built a town, New Amsterdam, whose fortified northern boundary marked the line of the future Wall Street. Beyond the stockade, in open country, they established their farms, called boweries, and raised crops of beans, barley and wheat. Across the East River, a channel that links New York Bay with Long Island Sound, they worked more farms and orchards in rough country which they called Breukelen (Broken Land). The township here was to become known as Brooklyn and was to grow

into the largest of New York's five boroughs after Manhattan, the others being Queen's, the Bronx and Staten Island.

Yet although the Dutch have given some celebrated names to New York, notably the Roosevelts and the Vanderbilts, their sway did not last long. One of Peter Minuit's successors as Governor, Peter Stuyvesant, the son of a Calvinist minister, an ill-tempered, one-legged, despotic man was so disliked in the colony that when in 1664 the King of England, Charles II, sent Colonel Richard Nicolls out to America to claim the territories at the mouth of the Hudson River, the Dutch settlers ignored Stuyvesant's call for volunteers to defend it against the troops disembarked from the British warships. Charles II, maintaining that the entire coast of America from New England to Virginia belonged to the British Crown, granted the territories to his brother, James, Duke of York, so New Amsterdam became New York; and the colony, whose inhabitants had numbered about 1,500 under the Dutch, prospered under the British. The Dutch recaptured Manhattan island in 1673; but they were driven out again by the British the following year and when the War of Independence began in 1776 New York's population had risen to 25,000. By the time the War was over, and American independence had been recognized by the Treaty of Versailles of 1783, its population had increased to 33,000 as compared with the 28,000 of Philadelphia and the 18,500 of Boston.

Yet it was not the British, just as it had not been the Dutch, who created the New York in which Theodore Roosevelt grew up. More than any other in the world's history, this city was the product of a mingling of nationalities, cultures and civilizations; for throughout the second half of the nineteenth century, from all over Europe immigrants had streamed into New York to escape from poverty or oppression at home, drawn by the promise of freedom and the hope of wealth in the New World. They had sailed past Bedloe's Island, named after its first Dutch owner, Isaac Bedloo; and on this island those who came in the years after 1886 had passed by the colossal statue of Liberty holding aloft her beacon, over three hundred feet high, as a light to dispel the darkness of the past and to welcome the immigrants in accordance with the often quoted words inscribed in bronze inside the pedestal:

'Keep, ancient lands, your storied pomp!' cries
  she
With silent lips, 'Give me your tired, your poor,
Your huddled masses yearning to breath free,
The wretched refuse of your teeming shore.
Send these, the homeless, tempest-tost to me.
I lift my lamp beside the golden door.'

Those principally responsible for the statue
were appropriately cosmopolitan: the words are
those of Emma Lazarus, a poet born in New York
of Spanish-Jewish stock; the base upon which
they are inscribed was paid for by subscriptions
raised by a campaign conducted by the *New York
World*, America's largest newspaper, owned by
Joseph Pulitzer, an immigrant from Hungary; the
statue itself was sculpted by Frédéric-Auguste
Bartholdi, a Frenchman whose countrymen had
presented it to New York as a token of their
sympathy for the Americans in their struggle for
freedom; it was unveiled in the presence of
President Stephen Grover Cleveland, a man of
old colonial stock whose forebears had emigrated
from Ipswich, England in 1635.

BELOW *A slum dwelling, 1896*

Although the French had supported the Americans so warmly in their fight for liberty, they had
never numbered largely among the immigrants to
New York in the nineteenth century. Nor had the
British, except in times of severe agricultural
depression at home. It was the Irish who constituted the main influx of immigrants in the
1840s after a devastating potato famine had resulted in widespread starvation in a country
where nearly half the entire population depended
largely upon the crop for their sustenance. In less
than eight months of 1847 nearly sixty thousand
Irish immigrants were disembarked on Staten
Island in the harbour mouth, five and a half miles
from New York. Perhaps as many as a million
people altogether emigrated from Ireland within
the six years before 1851, most of them to America
and the majority of these to New York.

Many of them arrived ridden with typhoid,
typhus or ship fever. A doctor who went down
into the hold of one immigrant vessel discovered
scores of shrunken, half-naked figures crouching
in the berths from which they had been too weak
to rise since the voyage began, 'wallowing in their
own filth'. They were transported to the quarant-
ine buildings which covered about thirty acres of

ground on the north-eastern point of the island; but there, according to an Englishman who had joined his Irish fellow-immigrants at Liverpool, they had to endure conditions no better than those aboard ship: the roofs leaked and the straw on the iron beds was sodden; the food was inedible; the sanitation appalling; the staff were either indifferent or 'downright cruel'.

The buildings were so overcrowded, and the medical inspection of the arrivals so perfunctory, that thousands of immigrants were passed as healthy and allowed to proceed to New York where epidemics of fever were constantly breaking out, not only in those areas in which the new arrivals congregated but also, in the words of the Chief of Police, 'among those whose social position was such as to lead to the supposition that they would be exempt'.

Even if he escaped typhoid or typhus, the immigrant was unlikely to evade the clutches of the New York swindlers who lurked in their hundreds to prey upon him. First of all there were the so-called passenger brokers who undertook to hold themselves responsible for immigrants in return for a sum paid by the ship-owners who were legally obliged to pay a fee for any passenger who appeared unlikely to earn a living. The city officials connived at this practice, some of them making a financial profit out of it – 'the entire business', so an Immigration Commissioner reported, 'became a private traffic between a set of low and subordinate city officials, on the one hand, and a band of greedy, unscrupulous brokers on the other.'

The brokers, having given their bond for an immigrant, thereafter virtually disposed of his life and labour, making contracts with one or other of the cheap boarding-houses where he and his family were lodged, or themselves establishing houses where, in the words of an investigating committee, the inmates lived in 'a state of misery and wretchedness not to be borne or countenanced by any civilized community'. They were crammed together, up to ten in one small room, overcharged for both inadequate food and coarse spirits distilled from Indian corn and coloured to look like brandy; and they were overcharged, too, for storing their possessions in damp cellars from which all that they owned was as likely as not to be stolen.

As well as with the passenger brokers and

bondsmen, the immigrant had to contend with the 'runners' who swarmed on the docks, often fighting each other as they rushed towards the quays, pouncing on the new and nervous arrivals and, making all manner of improbable promises, taking them and their luggage off to some cheap lodging-house whose owner, usually an Irishman himself, paid the runners for the opportunity of fleecing 'the cattle' brought to him. Those few passengers who did not intend to stay in New York were offered rail and boat tickets for other destinations, being charged as much as five or six times the normal fare, or sold tickets issued by companies that had long gone out of business or had existed only in the imagination of corrupt printers. But, while most German immigrants moved up river and then travelled west, most of the Irish remained in New York, unwilling to separate themselves from their gregarious fellow-countrymen, preferring to live together in the squalor of town slums – drinking whiskey in their groggeries whose walls were papered with pictures of Irish heroes, condemning the perfidy of the detested English, and enjoying their balls and wakes – rather than adventure outside their enclosed communities, as Henry Ford's father, a rare exception, did when he came over from Ireland in 1847 and travelled far west to clear a forest in Michigan. 'It has been a strange accident,' wrote Thomas D'Arcy McGee, who had emigrated in 1842 and become a newspaper editor, 'that a people who in Ireland hungered and thirsted for land, who struggled for conacre and cabin even to the shedding of blood, when they reached the New World, in which a day's wages would have purchased an acre of wild land in fee, wilfully concurred to sink into the condition of a miserable town tenantry, to whose squalor even European sea ports would hardly present a parallel.'

So the Irish quarters of New York became appallingly squalid and overcrowded as, year after year, immigrants poured into lodging-houses, into tenements in the former homes of rich merchants who had moved to more salubrious areas, into cellars in which almost twenty thousand people – some four per cent of the population – were living in 1849, into converted schools and chapels and into those ramshackle

New York City Elevated Railroad, 1880s.

ABOVE *Immigrants crowded into the lunchroom at the Ellis Island Detention Center, whilst awaiting approval of their entry into America, 1923. The Center was closed less than a month later.*

LEFT *An Italian mother with her three children after arriving on Ellis Island, 1905.*

wooden 'barracks' which were built by speculators on several floors, leaning against less insubstantial buildings, and let out in single rooms to tenants, hundreds of whom had to use the same steep, unlit, creaking, rotting staircase.

Sanitary conditions were dreadful. Since the city was surrounded by water and could expand only to the north, new arrivals were obliged to live in already congested localities, usually by the waterfront; and since there was as yet no adequate system of public transport most had to find accommodation within walking distance of their work. There had been a time in the recent past when the present Theatre District south of Central Park had marked the northern limits of the city and here those noxious trades such as horse-skinning and bone-boiling had been carried on; here also were the city's slaughter houses and glue factories. But the rapid expansion of New York

northward had meant that these trades were now undertaken in an area where thousands of people lived, and the effluent from workshops, factories, shambles and hog-pens added to the problems presented by a primitive system of sanitation that allowed huge heaps of ordure to be piled up in the streets and sewage to be carted by contractors to the waterfront and to be shovelled into the river. Even in those parts of the city where the more prosperous citizens lived, pigs, described by the New York *Sun* as being as 'dangerous as hyaenas', wandered about in their hundreds, snuffling in the gutters and occasionally knocking down unwary passers-by. Stray dogs, too, were numerous and many of these were mad: in less than three months of one summer in the 1840s over fifteen hundred dogs were clubbed to death in the streets. Yet, as the *Sun* observed, the dogs seemed to know the hours when they were likely to be in danger, and they hid until they thought it safe to reappear and then came out again in droves, adding to the filth that already befouled the pitted, rutted streets.

But although both the Commissioners for Immigration and the City Inspector responsible for sanitation were faced with virtually impossible tasks, conditions gradually improved. From 1855 all immigrants were landed at a single pier under the watchful eyes of police; the hospital on Staten Island was enlarged and modernized; accommodation for immigrants who could find no work was provided at the expense of the city; fraudulent runners and passenger-brokers were arrested and several were prosecuted; and in 1867 the construction of tenement houses was regulated by law.

Soon afterwards the great wave of Italian immigrants began; and by 1878, for the first time, there were more Italians entering New York than emigrants from any other country. A few years later, when the first Italian Prime Minister to visit the neglected south of his country, Giuseppe Zanardelli, reached Moliterno, he was taken aback by the mayor who welcomed him on behalf of the 'eight thousand people of this commune, three thousand of whom are in America and the other five thousand preparing to follow them'. By 1927 over half a million Italians were living in New York, most of them in the area south of Greenwich Village known as Little Italy.

Jews also came to New York in large numbers in the late nineteenth and early twentieth centuries, escaping from a succession of pogroms in Russia, Romania and Poland and from poverty elsewhere. As late as 1880 there were no more than a quarter of a million Jews in the United States; by 1924 there were four and a half million. The German and Sephardic Jews were the most

A Jewish trader with his barrow of ancient hats and a bottle of restorer beside them.

successful in their adopted country, several of the Germans founding the great banking houses of New York, while most of the Lithuanian and the Hungarian Jews tended to remain poor.

By 1902 Ellis Island, then the centre of Immigration Control for New York, was dealing with immigrants at the rate of eight thousand a day. Although the more talented and robust were able to make their way in the highly competitive freedom of the new society, for many the poverty and deprivation of the old continent were rediscovered in the new, and for these immigrants the only comfort was to be found in the sympathetic company of fellow-exiles of their own race. In the early years of the century, as Alistair Cooke has written, 'you could have gone to New York's Lower East Side ... and looked on the roaring maelstroms of any street scene as proof positive that the immigrants of many nations were already bubbling together in the melting pot. Yet if you went closer and listened, you would know that they were all bubbling within the confines of Little Italy or Little Russia ... sooner or later, the ones with health and energy, and gumption or cunning, would want to break away altogether or at least find some dependable link with the big alien society around them. They frequently found it in a character who haunted the docks and the employment agencies and the factories, a man whose headquarters was the local political clubhouse and whose daily beat was up and down the wobbly staircase of the tenements'.

These neighbourhood politicians, as often as not Irishmen or Jews, regulated the lives of the people and became a byword of corruption. Tammany Hall, the Executive Committee of the Democratic Party in New York, which was named after a Delaware Indian chief famed for his love of freedom, was used by several extremely undesirable characters as a means of self enrichment. One of these was William M. Tweed, a man of Scottish origins who entered New York politics under a cloak of respectability by ousting a notoriously corrupt mayor but who thereafter, with his minions in the various departments of the municipal government, succeeded in robbing the city of sums estimated at a minimum of forty-five million dollars and probably as high as two hundred million. He died in prison in 1878, having spent six years in the utmost comfort attended by a masseur and eating meals sent in by the best restaurants in New York. Yet Tammany Hall had its worthier manifestations of 'honest graft', vote-catching through the rendering of genuine humane services to the community. George Washington Plunkitt, an Irish ex-butcher who was a Tammany Ward boss, made a fortune not over scrupulously from harbour transport and as a contractor; but at the same time he was a tireless benefactor to those in need and, in exchange for their ready votes, brought much comfort to Irish, Jews and Italians alike.

Yet if politics was a means of enrichment for some, far greater rewards were to be obtained in the realms of finance, commerce and industry. The flood of cheap labour brought in by immigration and the almost limitless supply of raw materials presented unparalleled opportunities for the resourceful entrepreneur. New York never became an important industrial centre like Buffalo; its major manufactures in the earlier years were for the garment trade. But because its port was the largest on the eastern seaboard it was from the beginning a main communication centre, and it soon became, and has since remained, the principal financial centre of the United States. This was largely due to John Pierpont Morgan, a banker of genius, whose reorganization of various family interests in 1895 gave rise in New York to J. P. Morgan and Company, one of the most influential banks in history, worthy of comparison with those of the Bardi and Medici in Florence.

Fortunately for New York, Morgan and other millionaires like Andrew Carnegie and Henry Clay Frick, who made fortunes in steel, Cornelius Vanderbilt whose huge wealth originated with the profits of the Staten Island Ferry, and the Rockefellers who founded the Standard Oil Company in Ohio, all chose to spend a large part of their riches on beautifying New York whose fine modern buildings testify to the positive influence of private patrons in comparison with the far less impressive results achieved in so many other cities by municipal or government spending or the speculations of developers whose main interest was profit. The architecture of New York is, indeed, one of the great manifestations of building in the world's history, as remarkable in its way as the pyramids of Egypt, the temples of Athens or the churches and palaces of Rome. It is far from being a unified or homogeneous architecture, as might be supposed by the traveller who views the

The construction of the Empire State Building, 1931 : a workman signals to his mates below.

harmony of its great rectilinear towers from the deck of a ship steaming down Long Island Sound, for the rich Americans who have provided it with so many of its finest buildings developed different tastes on their travels and were determined to indulge them.

J. Pierpont Morgan, for example, was an admirer of the arts and architecture of the Italian Renaissance, and the Morgan Library, which was built to the designs of Charles McKim in 1906, well reflects this interest. Frank Woolworth, the store millionaire, on the other hand, had admired the Houses of Parliament in London, and decided to construct a Gothic tower 792 feet high with soaring gargoyles aloft. Designed by Cass Gilbert and completed in 1913, the Woolworth Tower, apart from the Eiffel Tower in Paris, was the tallest building in the world until 1930 when it was outstripped by the 1,045-foot-high Chrysler Building constructed in the Art Deco style with a stainless steel spire reminiscent of the radiator cap of the car upon which Walter Percy Chrysler's fortune was based. A year after the Chrysler Building was completed, the famous Empire State Building, appeared, and this was taller still by 205 feet, a requirement of the head of the syndicate responsible for it, Alfred Smith, a former governor of New York. It is also in the Art Deco style, a total departure from the style of the Flatiron Building, which resembles a big slice of a palazzo of the Florentine Renaissance stretched out like a harmonica. The earliest of New York's tall buildings and one of the first of any size to be

The Flatiron Building.

constructed on a steel frame, it was finished in 1902 and is now dwarfed by its neighbours.

While the Empire State Building was nearing completion, work began on the Rockefeller Center on a seedy, midtown site where building continued for twenty-nine years under the direction of John D. Rockefeller, Junior, and then for a further thirteen years after his death in 1960. The sixteen years it took to build Frank Lloyd Wright's Guggenheim Museum (1943–59) seems brief in comparison. When the Rockefeller project was at last completed, fourteen immense tower blocks had been erected between Fifth Avenue and the Avenue of the Americas and 48th to 51st Streets. The daytime population of this vast complex, which includes the seventy-storey building of the Radio Corporation of America, numbers about 240,000 people served by thirty restaurants and countless shops and places of entertainment. The Center had originally been intended to provide a new home for the Metropolitan Opera; but the financial crisis of 1929 had obliged the 'Met' to withdraw from the project, leaving Rockefeller to carry on alone.

The Wall Street Crash was a cataclysmic and revealing episode in the history of New York. It occurred at the end of a decade during which production and employment were both rising; and, though wages were not increasing appreciably, prices were not going up either. There were still many poor, but there were increasing numbers of people who were well off and becoming rich or, if not, were determined to become so and become so quickly. The stock market seemed an ideal way to achieve this ambition: prices of stocks were rising and continuing to rise. As a journalist pointed out in the widely-read *Ladies Home Journal* under the headline 'Everybody ought to be rich', it was quite simple to make money. All that was required was investment in sound common stocks. It was confidently asserted in 1929 by no less an authority than Professor Irving Fisher of Yale that stock prices had reached what look like 'a permanently high plateau'. The markets of the New York Stock Exchange remained strong throughout the summer. And then on 5 September a distinguished economist voiced an alarming warning at the Annual National Business Conference: 'Sooner or later a crash is coming, and it may be terrific.' It did come and it was terrific. On a single day the following month almost thirteen million shares were sold, many of them, in Professor Galbraith's words, 'at prices which shattered the dreams and the hopes of those who had owned them ... Often there were no buyers, and only after wide vertical declines could anyone be induced to bid.' During the next few days prices plummetted still further and millions more shares were sold for any price they would fetch; and now it was not just the less comfortably off who were being ruined but the wealthy also who were being subjected 'to a levelling process comparable in magnitude and suddenness to that presided over a decade before by Lenin'.

Yet the New Yorker was, and is, astonishingly resilient. There were stories of ruined speculators leaping from the windows of skyscrapers. But, in fact, the wave of suicides that followed the crash was a myth; and, although a decade of depression did ensue, there was little evidence in New York that the citizens had lost either their capacity for enthusiasm or their wry, often caustic humour. Within a few months of the crash the windows from which broken men were said to have dived to the pavements below were filled with chattering, waving onlookers as Bobby Jones, the golfing hero who had won both the amateur and open championships in Britain and the United States, received a welcome in a ticker-tape parade to rival that accorded in 1927 to the aviator, Charles Lindbergh, after which New York's Street Cleaning Department was faced with the task of clearing up eighteen hundred tons of paper.

As it was in 1930, so New York remains today the most cosmopolitan city of the modern world, and it still has its national enclaves. East of the Bowery, where drunken derelicts lie in doorways, is Little Italy and east of that the area of cast-iron façades known as SoHo, not after London's cosmopolitan quarter but because it lies south (So) of Houston Street (Ho). To the south is Chinatown which was first settled by the Irish in the mid-nineteenth century and then by the Italians and which, since the Chinese moved in during the 1870s and 1880s, has spread into parts of Little Italy and northwards and eastwards into some formerly Jewish areas. To the north, beyond Central Park, is Harlem, founded by the Dutch and called by them Nieu Haarlem after the town in Holland. This was once a farming community beyond the limits of the city and is now occupied almost exclusively by Blacks in its western part and by Puerto Ricans and other Spanish-speaking immigrants to the east.

It is entirely appropriate that so cosmopolitan a city should have been chosen to accommodate the headquarters of the United Nations. On a site previously occupied by slaughter houses, junk-yards and tenements overlooking the East River on First Avenue and 52nd Street rise the elegant buildings of the United Nations Center which were fittingly designed by an international team of architects headed by Wallace Harrison who was chief architect also of the Rockefeller Center. Michael Leapman, the English journalist who lived in New York for many years, thinks that, despite the problems presented by having so many delegates enjoying diplomatic immunity in their city, New Yorkers are 'proud to have the U N here and appreciate the consequent broadening of their horizons – even if, being New Yorkers, they will not admit to being impressed by anything'. They are, however, impressed by New York itself, and rightly so. For all its crime, the extremes of its climate, the squalor of its poorer areas, it is as Edward Koch observed upon his inauguration as Mayor in 1978, 'a stroke of genius . . . a larder for the hungry, a living library for the intellectually starved, a refuge not only for the oppressed but also for the creative'.

A worried crowd outside the New York Stock Exchange during the Wall Street Crash, 24 October 1929.

21

Sydney

'The Finest Harbour in the World'

Soon after the first shots of the American Revolution were fired at Lexington, the British Government was forced to face the fact that the transatlantic colonies could no longer be considered a convenient dumping ground for criminals who were allowed to escape hanging. For some time these unwanted men were incarcerated in convict hulks moored in the estuaries of rivers; and then in 1786 it was proposed that the new continent discovered on the other side of the world some years before by Captain Cook might provide a more satisfactory answer to the problem. Captain Cook had recorded in his journal that the great quantity of plants which had been collected when his ship lay at anchor off the coast of what he called New South Wales, from its resemblance to the northern shores of the Bristol Channel, had induced the naturalists in his expedition to give this part of it the name of Botany Bay. Its 'series of beautiful meadows abounding in the richest pastures and only inhabited by a few savages', so it was suggested in an official letter addressed to the Lords Commissioners of the Treasury, would prove 'an admirable destination for the savages at present a heavy charge upon their Lordships at home'. Thus it was that Captain Arthur Phillip, a resourceful, firm though humane naval officer, was assigned the task of forming a penal settlement in Australia. Appointed Governor of New South Wales, he sailed from England in the early summer of 1787 in command of a frigate, three store-ships and six convict-ships containing 558 men, 192 women

Sydney Harbour Bridge.

Algernon Talmadge, The Founding of Australia, c.*1935*

and a guard of marines. Eight months later this 'first fleet' as it came to be known in Australia arrived in Botany Bay which, far from being the fertile, pleasant land that Captain Phillip had expected, was a barren area of swamp and sand. He accordingly set sail north for Port Jackson, an inlet of the Pacific which Cook had named after Sir George Jackson, an Admiralty secretary; and here, so he recorded in his first dispatch from New South Wales, Phillip 'had the satisfaction of finding the finest harbour in the world, in which a thousand ships of the line may ride in the most perfect security'. Early on the morning of 26 January 1788 a flagstaff was erected, the English flag raised, volleys of small arms were fired, toasts were drunk to the colony's success, the marines cheered and Phillip christened the cove where this ceremony took place, Sydney in honour of Thomas Townshend, Viscount Sydney, Secretary of State for the Home Department with which the Department of the Colonies was then united.

It was a cheerful enough occasion, but the early history of Sydney was not a happy one. Nearly fifty of Phillip's charges had died on the long voyage; others had escaped; two women had gone off in a French ship. The convicts that remained were sullen and unruly; many were suffering from syphilis, dysentery or scurvy; all were as reluctant to farm the land they were expected to clear as to build a settlement upon it, or to help the guards fight off the constant attacks of natives who had been provoked into hostility. When food supplies ran low they raided the stores; and, undeterred by whipping and the hanging of seventeen of the worst offenders, they pilfered the meagre crops of wheat. 'In the whole world there is not a worse country,' complained the Lieutenant-Governor. 'Almost all the seeds we have put in the ground have rotted ... I think it will be cheaper to feed convicts on turtles and venison at the London Tower than to be at the expense of sending men here ... If the Secretary of State sends out more convicts I shall not scruple to say that he will bring misery on all that are sent.'

More convicts were sent, nevertheless; and, since the transport contractors were paid by the numbers of convicts they took on board and not by the numbers they landed, many died on the way, some of them being actually starved to death for the sake of higher profits. Those who did survive the voyage were as miserable as the Lieutenant-Governor predicted. As soon as the transports laid anchor in the cove, the officers of the colony, followed by the non-commissioned officers and then by the men, came aboard to 'select such females as are most agreeable to their persons'. When these had been taken ashore, the rest of the convicts were disembarked and marched off to begin their seven or fourteen years of work. Many of them worked in chain gangs for up to twelve hours a day and were shut up at night in wooden huts still wearing their heavy iron fetters, often in such cramped conditions that there was not enough room for them all to lie down at once.

The Governor maintained that the colony would never develop satisfactorily unless honest and healthy men and women were encouraged to come out from England with their fares paid for them. A few subsidized settlers did accordingly emigrate, but most of these were judged to be 'not very superior' to the convicts who greatly outnumbered them. Seventeen years after Captain Phillip had been obliged to return home because of ill health, the population of New South Wales was still scarcely more than ten thousand and the great majority of these were convicts, many of them fed with the 'coarsest food', so the *Sydney Gazette* reported, 'governed with the most rigid

A chain gang marching to work, 1831.

discipline, subjected to the stern and frequently capricious and tyrannical will of an overseer', who was often a convict himself. 'I have seen men for mere venial offences scourged until the blood has dripped into their shoes,' a witness told a parliamentary committee. 'And I have seen the flesh tainted on a living human body from the effects of severe flagellation. After being flogged he must go again instantly to the fields.' The convicts contrived, however, frequently to get drunk for, as it was reported without undue exaggeration the 'whole community might be classed into those who sold spirits and those who drank them'.

An attempt to prevent the unlimited importation of ardent spirits was made by Captain William Bligh who was appointed Governor in 1805. But Bligh's efforts were only partially successful, while the fiery temper and overbearing manner which had provoked mutiny aboard the *Bounty* brought about another mutiny in New South Wales in 1808 and the establishment of a provisional government by the local military backed by those civilians with no taste for firm law. Bligh in consequence returned to England, after being released from prison, and was replaced in 1809 by an army officer from an old Scottish family, Lachlan Macquarie, a vain, impatient but capable man who would brook no opposition to his authority and became a virtual dictator in the settlement.

When Macquarie arrived in Sydney, the place had most of the characteristics of the frontier town and the rough sea port. The houses, many of them already dilapidated, had excessively small windows because glass was not available in any other size; their shingle roofs were painted blue because that was the colour of the only readily available paint. Most of the men wore either

Major Taylor, The Town of Sydney in New South Wales, *1823.*

uniform or convict attire; most of the women were dressed without regard to any prevailing fashion. In the area known as The Rocks, west of Sydney Cove where Captain Phillip had landed, dark alleys and courts led down to the water's edge beneath sandstone outcrops. There were thieves' kitchens here, and brothels for seamen and the soldiers of the garrison, rag and bottle shops and

Mrs Elizabeth Macquarie, wife of Major-General Lachlan Macquarie, Governor of New South Wales.

low taverns and hovels in whose foetid air scores of men, women and children died of typhoid and dysentery every year. At that time a ridge of sandstone divided The Rocks into two and it was not for many years that gangs of convicts hacked a passage through this ridge to open up a way to the more pleasant Argyle Place and the Garrison Church of Holy Trinity.

Soon after his arrival in Sydney, Macquarie decreed that convicts must be treated with more leniency, granted tickets of leave, freed from some of the disabilities under which they laboured, and, when their sentences had expired, granted holdings of thirty acres. His hopes that such treatment would make them better citizens were, however, to be largely disappointed. Most convicts preferred to sell their newly acquired land and spend their money on drink and women or the passage home to England rather than settle in Sydney; while the favours granted them discouraged the immigration of free settlers which did not begin on a satisfactory scale until Sir Thomas Brisbane succeeded Macquarie in 1821.

The free settlers who came out in the time of Brisbane and his successors became increasingly outspoken in their demands that New South Wales should no longer be used as a rubbish heap for convicts, that it should become a decent and respectable colony and Sydney a town of which they might be proud. In petitions to the Governor and the Colonial Office in London they complained of the influence that rich and disreputable ex-convicts had managed to acquire, of the disgraceful crime rate, of the incidence of highway robbery for which there were more convictions every year than there were for all robberies put together in England, of the numbers of escaped convicts who had become bushrangers, and of ticket-of-leave men who lived as squatters on the outskirts of town and acted as fences for the robbers and burglars inside it, of the amount of drunkenness and the number of brothels. These protests were received sypathetically in England where transportation was already being condemned as neither deterrent nor reformative: the last convict ship arrived in the harbour in 1849.

By then Sydney had developed into a thriving city with a population of well over thirty thousand. While he was Governor, the forceful Lachlan Macquarie had initiated a remarkably ambitious building programme; and in the twelve years of his administration work had begun on hospitals, schools, barracks, courthouses, parks and churches, as well as a road, three miles long, from Government House to the point overlooking Port Jackson, Mrs Macquaire's Point, which, like the road, Mrs Macquarie's Road, still bears her name. Mrs Macquarie was a small, intelligent, accomplished woman who had little in common with the leaders of such society as Sydney had then to offer. She went for long walks either by herself or accompanied only by her husband's aide-de-camp and a loyal servant he had bought for eighty-five rupees when serving in India. She spent hours on Mrs Macquarie's Point, looking out across the harbour, sitting in a seat cut into the rock which is still called Mrs Macquarie's Chair. Since it was known to flatter her husband's vanity, several places in Sydney were named after him, too, among them Macquarie Place, a small park laid out upon part of Government House's kitchen garden which is now shaded by huge Moreton Bay fig trees and contains the anchor and a cannon from Captain Phillip's frigate, the *Sirius*.

For help in his building programme Macquarie called upon the assistance of a gifted designer, Francis Greenway, a sad man, dogged by misfortune, who had been deported for forgery. Among Greenway's buildings still to be seen in Sydney are the Hyde Park Barracks completed in 1817 as a convict dormitory for nine hundred men, who could be seen trudging the streets to work in yellowish grey canvas uniforms; St James's in Queen's Square, Sydney's oldest existing church; and St Matthew's Church in Moses Street whose foundation stone was laid by Macquarie the year his name was carved beneath the clock on the pediment of Hyde Park Barracks, 'L. Macquarie, Esq. Governor, 1817'.

Hyde Park itself, once a haunt of bushrangers

The Circular Quay, Sydney, c.1890.

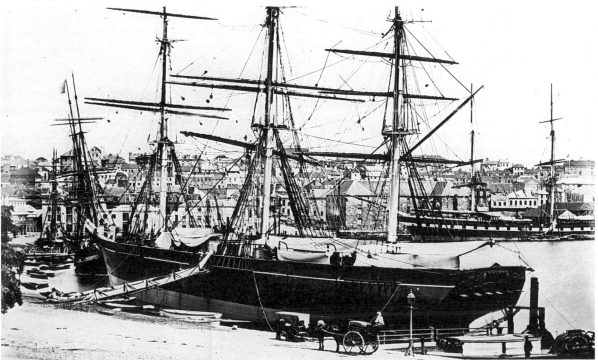

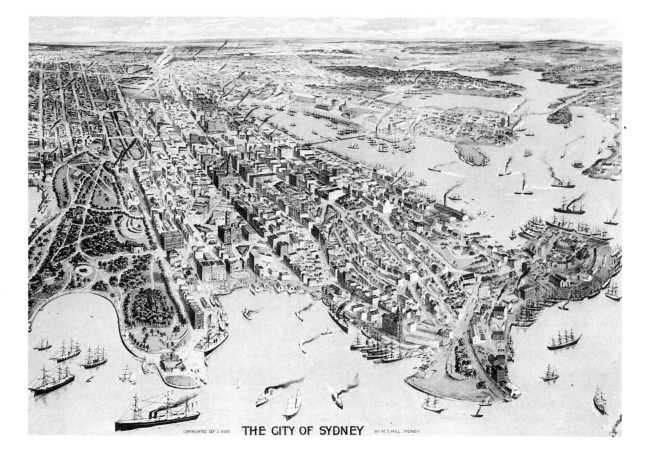

THE CITY OF SYDNEY

M.S. Hill, View of Sydney, *1888.*

between the harbour and Botany Bay, also owes its origins to Macquarie who made land here over to his regiment, the 73rd, whose soldiers cleared the underwood to make a race course. Races were held in the park until the late 1820s when it became a cricket ground. Beneath it convicts laboured on their knees for ten years to make the Busby Bore which brought water to the city from the Lachlan Swamps, yet another of the numerous places in the colony named after the Governor.

After Macquarie's return to England work began, under the direction of a military engineer, Colonel George Barney, on the transformation of Sydney Cove into Circular Quay, a waterfront worthy of the increasingly important city. The last of the major works in Sydney to be undertaken by convict labour, the Circular Quay was completed in 1844 and thereafter for a generation clipper after fast-sailing clipper sailed into Port Jackson between Kirribilli and Bennelong Points to tie up in the wharves beneath the warehouses and the woolstores.

The first Merino sheep had been brought to the area at the beginning of the century, and the highly successful wool industry which had subsequently developed had encouraged a rapid growth in population. The discovery of gold in New South Wales in 1850 stimulated further growth and the expansion of the city both to the north and south of the harbour: within forty years its population rose from sixty thousand to four hundred thousand. Unlike that of most other Australian cities the expansion of Sydney took place haphazardly and piecemeal with no controlling plan. Yet the new suburbs with their rows of terraced houses, each with their balconies and cast iron railings, were attractive places to live, far more so than the crowded Victorian cities from which most immigrants had come. As one settler wrote home, 'From Manchester to Sydney is a journey into another, far more pleasant world.'

The growth of Sydney was checked by an economic crisis in the 1890s; but the halt proved temporary and after the end of the First World War the population rose to over a million. The need for a bridge across the harbour, linking downtown Sydney on the south to the spreading suburbs to the north, became ever more pressing. As long before as 1815 Francis Greenway had proposed such a bridge; and in 1900 the Minister of Works had invited architects and engineers to submit designs and estimates. But it was not until 1923 that work at last began on the famous structure that for years was to be the city's pride and symbol and not until nine years later, and at a cost of over two million dollars a year, that the bridge was finished and the last coat of grey paint – the only colour available in sufficient quantities – was at last applied to the immense structure.

The largest single-span bridge in the world, it soars across the harbour from Dawe's to Milson's Point between massive pylons strongly influenced by those Egyptian models that the recent discovery of Tutankhamen's tomb had made so popular. The opening ceremony took place on 19 March 1932 and proved unexpectedly exciting. As the Labour prime minister, J. T. Lang, stood ready to cut the ribbon with a pair of golden scissors, an eccentric and disgruntled officer, strongly opposed to his policies, charged wildly forward on a horse and slashed through the ribbon with his sword. Spectators stood aghast, the band stopped playing, three women fainted. At length the ribbon was re-tied and Mr Lang made use of his golden scissors.

Cyril Farley, Proposed Sydney Harbour Bridge, *1924.*

West of the bridge's south pylon on Bennelong's Point stands, or appears to float upon the water, that other symbol of the city, the Opera House. Compared to swans, and flowers, to shells and butterflies, to a nautilus or a ship in sail, this extraordinary and dramatic building was designed by the Danish architect, Jørn Utzon, whose plans were selected in 1956 after an international competition. His original estimate of the cost came to some £4,500,000. But this figure was soon exceeded; the cost of the building rapidly rose to £17,000,000 and went on rising; angry protests were voiced in parliament; Utzon resigned in 1966 and three other Australian architects were appointed in his place. Lottery tickets with a first prize of £100,000 were sold to meet the increasing cost which by the time Queen Elizabeth II opened the Opera House in 1973, had eventually come to 102,000,000 Australian dollars. For this huge sum, however, Sydney was provided not only with an opera house but with concert and exhibition halls, a theatre, a cinema, music and reception rooms, two restaurants, rehearsal and recording studios and a shop in a dynamic building of spectacular beauty on a site surrounded on three sides by water, and commanding incomparable views.

Sydney has continued to grow apace since work on the Opera House began. Its population, now well over three million and constituting almost a quarter of the population of Australia, is expected to reach five and a half million by the end of the century. Some eighty per cent of Sydney-siders, as they like to call themselves, are of British

Sydney Harbour as it is today.

descent, many of them proud to acknowledge convicts as their ancestors. Among the rest, in addition to about four thousand aboriginals, all European nationalities are represented and parts of the inner suburbs have a pronounced Greek or Italian flavour. Although there was a violent riot on Circular Quay when six hundred Chinese immigrants vainly attempted to land to work in the sweatshops of Sydney in the 1880s, there are now many Chinese in the city; and since their arrival people from other Asiatic countries and from the Middle East have followed them. The cosmopolitan atmosphere of the city is nowhere more apparent than in King's Cross, the area east of Hyde Park and south of Wooloomooloo Bay, a neighbourhood of strip joints and massage parlours, patisseries and restaurants, prostitutes and tourists; and, to the south of King's Cross, in Paddington, once a slum, now much favoured by the young intelligentsia and distinguished by its terraces of late nineteenth-century houses decorated with delicate traceries of ironwork.

If King's Cross might be said to be Sydney's Soho and Paddington its Chelsea, the city centre is now a kind of Manhattan on a smaller scale; and it shares with Manhattan the problems of urban overdevelopment and the tyranny of the motor car. Yet Sydney is a far more relaxed city than New York. Its people are for the most part genial, easy-going and informal, though eager for their city to be admired and inclined to be resentful if it is not. Disinclined to work harder than they need, they take full advantage of the pleasures offered them by their harbour and beaches, their parks and pleasure grounds, their warm and sunny climate, pleasures which, however fast the city grows, will never be denied them and which so many other modern cities cannot enjoy. Although built, as it has been said, 'on a landscape littered with human bones', Sydney, in rejecting the destiny that was planned for it, has indeed become one of the most pleasant modern cities in the world.

PHOTOGRAPHIC ACKNOWLEDGEMENTS

The publishers would like to thank the following for making photographs available.

H.M. The Queen: p. 53
The Ashmolean Museum, Oxford: p. 144
BBC Hulton Picture Library: pp. 191 (*centre*), 193 (The Bettman Archive, Inc); 203 (*above & below*); 206; 212; 234 (Photo: Lewis Hine)
Bildarchiv Preussischer Kulturbesitz: p. 209
Blackburn Museum and Art Gallery: pp. 196–7 (Lewis Collection)
BPCC/Aldus Archive: pp. 20–1 (British Museum); 26 (Chester Beatty Library, Dublin); 59; 89 (British Museum)
Bridgeman Art Library: pp. 116 (Beit Collection, Ireland); 198 (Private Collection)
The Trustees of the British Museum: pp. 15; 35 (Photo: Michael Holford); 69
Bulloz: pp. 128, 130 (Musée Carnavalet, Paris)
E.T. Archive: pp. 34; 38; 39 (*above; centre right*: German Archaeological Institute, Athens); 40 (Ashmolean Museum, Oxford); 41; 42; 46 (*below*); 49 (*above*: Naples Museum); 58; 61; 62; 70 (*above & below*), 71 (British Museum); 75 (National Palace Museum, Taiwan); 85 (British Library); 92 (Com'era, Florence); 94; 95 (Galleria Accademia); 97 (Galleria degli Uffizi, Florence); 117 (National Gallery); 124–5 (Musée Carnavalet, Paris); 156; 160; 179; 186–7; 195; 200 (Postal Museum, Frankfurt); 228–9; 242 (Royal Commonwealth Society); 244 (*above; below*: Mitchell Library, Sydney); 245 (Eileen Tweedy); 246 (Australia House); 247 (British Steel Corporation)
Mary Evans Picture Library: p. 167
The Fine Art Society, London: p. 183
Werner Forman Archive: pp. 10 (*centre & below*); 16; 19; 58 (*below*); 64 (British Museum)
Sonia Halliday Photographs: pp. 11; 25 (*above*); 28; 29; 44–5; 60
Robert Harding Picture Library: pp. 216–17; 248
Michael Holford: pp. 8–9; 10 (*above*); 12–13; 32–3 (Photo: Gerry Clyde); 35 (British Museum); 37; 50 (British Museum); 90–1, 104–5; 106 (Prado, Madrid); 110, 111 (*above & below*); 114
Peter Jackson Collection: pp. 136–7; 145; 147
Kunsthistorisches Museum, Vienna: p. 109
Mansell Collection: pp. 46 (*above*: Museo Nazionale, Naples); 63; 99 (Museo Nazionale, Florence); 100 (Galleria degli Uffizi, Florence); 129; 171; 243
Metropolitan Museum of Art, New York: pp. 18; 113 (Bequest of Mrs H.O.Havemeyer, 1929. The H.O.Havemeyer Collection)

Tony Morrison South American Pictures: pp. 78–9; 81 (*left & right*); 86 (*above & below*); 87
Museen der Stadt Wien: pp. 174–5
Nationalgalerie, Staatliche Museen Preussischer Kulturbesitz, West Berlin: p. 208 (*below*: Photo: Jörg P.Anders)
National Gallery, London: jacket illustration; pp. 121; 122; 162–3
National Palace Museum, Taiwan: pp. 66–7; 76 (*above*)
National Portrait Gallery, London: p. 138
Nelson Gallery – Atkins Museum, Kansas City, Missouri: pp. 72; 74
Peter Newark's Western Americana: pp. 188; 189; 190; 191 (*below*); 194; 230 (*above*); 231 (*below*: Photo: Jacob Riis); 233; 237 (Photo: Lewis Hine); 238; endpapers
Novosti Press Agency: pp. 218; 219 (*below*); 221; 223; 224; 225; 227
Pierpont Morgan Library, New York: p. 23
Popperfoto: pp. 178, 191, 199 (*above*) (ENA); 199 (*below*); 202 (ENA); 210; 214; 215; 219 (*above*: ENA); 235; 236; 239
Scala: p. 27
SCR Library: pp. 157 (*below*); 220; 222
Stedelijk Museum, Amsterdam: pp. 118 (*above*: Rijksmuseum, Amsterdam); 118
Collection Thyssen-Bornemisza, 204–5
Ullstein Bilderdienst: pp. 207 (*above*); 208 (*above*); 213
The Victoria and Albert Museum, London: p. 201
The Wallace Collection: p. 126
Weidenfeld and Nicolson Archive: pp. 7, 25 (*below*) (Bibliothèque Nationale, Paris); 30 (Private Collection/Photo: Ronald Sheridan); 48 (Alinari); 49 (Anderson, Rome); 51 (Alinari); 76 (*below*), 82 (British Museum); 88 (Dumbarton Oaks, Washington); 98 (Alinari/Palazzo Vecchio, Florence); 102 (Alinari/Pitti Palace, Florence); 103 (Alinari/Volpi Collection); 108; 127 (Photographie Bulloz/Palace of Versailles); 131 (Photographie Bulloz); 133 (Photo: John Freeman & Co.); 134 (Giraudon); 139 (The Fotoman's Index); 140 (Peter Jackson Collection); 142–3 (The Fotoman's Index); 148–9; 150 (*above*: Tate Gallery; *below*: Museum of London); 154; 155 (Photo: John Freeman & Co.); 158; 159; 165 (Museum of Modern Art, New York, Wrightsman Collection); 166 (National Gallery); 169 (*above & below*: Ca'Rezzonico); 170 (Museo Correr, Venice); 173 (Wallace Collection); 177 (Museum of the History of the Army, Vienna); 176 (Kunsthistorisches Museum, Vienna); 180 (Vienna Museum); 181 (Historisches Museum der Stadt, Vienna); 184 (Bildarchiv des Österreichen Nationalbibliothek)
Zefa: pp. 56–7 (© Golebiowski); 152–3 (© Kurt Goebel); 240–1 (© Andrew Baker)

SOURCES

Albright, W.F., *Archaeology of Palestine* (Harmondsworth 1954)

Allen, Frederick Lewis, *Only Yesterday* (New York & London 1931)

Asbury, Herbert, *The French Quarter* (London 1937)

Ashley, Maurice, *Louis XIV and the Greatness of France* (New York 1946)

Auchmuty, James Johnston, *The Voyage of Governor Phillip to Botany Bay* (Sydney & London 1970)

Baedeker's Berlin (Leipzig & Freiburg 1984)

Balsdon, J.P.V.D., *Roman Women: Their History and Habits* (London 1962)
Life and Leisure in Ancient Rome (London 1969)

Barbon, Nicholas, *An Apology for the Builder* (n.p.1685)

Barker, John, *Justinian and the later Roman Empire* (Madison 1966)

Barker, Theodore & R.M. Robbins, *A History of London Transport* (London 1963)

Baudin, Louis, *Daily Life in Peru under the Last Incas* (trans. Winifred Bradford, London 1961)

Bedford, John, *London's Burning* (London 1966)

Beeson, Trevor, *Discretion and Valour* (London 1974)

Bell, Walter G., *The Great Fire of London in 1666* (New York & London 1920)

Besant, Sir Walter, *London in the Time of the Stuarts* (London 1903)

Biagi, Guido, *The Private Life of the Renaissance Florentines* (Florence 1896)

Bluche, François, *La Vie quotidienne au Temps de Louis XIV* (Paris 1980)

Borsook, Eva, *Companion Guide to Florence* (London 1966)

Boulanger, Jacques, *Le Grand Siècle* (Paris 1948)

Bowra, C.M., *Periclean Athens* (Harmondsworth 1974)
The Greek Experience (London 1957)

Breasted, James Henry, *The Conquest of Civilization* (New York & London 1938)

Brett-James, Norman G., *The Growth of Stuart London* (London 1935)

Brion, Marcel, *Daily Life in the Vienna of Mozart and Schubert* (London 1961)
The Medici: A Great Florentine Family (London 1969)
Venice (London 1962)

Brosses, Charles de, *Lettres historiques et critiques sur l'Italie* (3 vols, Paris 1797)

Browning, Robert, *Justinian and Theodora* (London 1971)
The Byzantine Empire (London 1980)

Bruce Lockhart, R.H., *Memoirs of a British Agent* (London 1985)

Bruckner, Gene Adam, *Florence 1138–1737* (London 1984)
Renaissance Florence (New York 1969)

Bullock, Alan, *Hitler: a study in tyranny* (London 1978)

Burke, Peter, *Venice and Amsterdam* (London 1974)

Bury, J.B., *A History of Greece* (London 1952)

Bushnell, G.H.S., *Peru* (London 1957)

Cable, Mary, *Lost New Orleans* (Boston 1980)

Carcopino, Jérôme, *Daily Life in Ancient Rome* (ed. Henry T. Rowell, trans. E.O. Lorimer, London 1941)

Carpenter, Humphrey, *W.H. Auden* (London 1981)

Carr, J.L., *Life in France under Louis XIV* (New York 1966)

Carr, William, *A Description of Holland* (Amsterdam 1701)

Carter, Hodding (et al.), *The Past as Prelude: New Orleans 1718–1768* (New Orleans 1968)

Cassels, Lavender, *Clash of Generations* (London 1973)

Casson, Lionel, *Ancient Egypt* (New York 1965)
Daily Life in Ancient Egypt (New York 1975)

Ceram, C.W., *Gods, Graves and Scholars* (London 1952)

Chadwick, Owen, *The Reformation* (London 1972)

Chamberlain, Basil Hall & W.B.Mason, *Murray's Handbook: Japan* (London 1903)

Chamberlin, E.R., *Everyday Life in Renaissance Times* (London 1905)

Champigneulle, Bernard, *Paris* (Paris 1973)

Chapman, Guy, *The Travel Diaries of William Beckford of Fonthill* (Cambridge 1928)

Charques, Richard, *A Short History of Russia* (London 1959)

Childs, James R., *Casanova* (London 1961)

Cieza de Leon, Pedro, *La Chronica del Peru, 1551* (ed. Clements Markham, London 1883)
The Incas (ed. Victor von Hagen, trans. Harriet de Onis (Oklahoma 1951)

Cobley, John, *Sydney Cove, 1788* (London 1962)

Conquest, Robert, *The Great Terror* (Harmondsworth 1971)

Cooke, Alistair, *Alistair Cooke's America* (London 1973)

Copplestone, Trewin, *Rembrandt* (London 1984)

Cosio, José Gabriel, *El Cuzcohistorico y monumental* (n.d.)

Craig, Gordon A., *The End of Prussia* (London 1984)

Crankshaw, Edward, *The Fall of the House of Hapsburg* (London 1963)
Vienna (London 1938)

Cronin, Vincent, *Louis XIV* (London 1964)
The Florentine Renaissance (London 1967)

De Brice, Germain, *A New Description of Paris* (trans. James Wright, 1688)

Delmer, Sefton, *Weimar Germany* (London 1972)

D'Encausse, Hélène, *Stalin's Order Through Terror* (London 1981)

De Vaux, Roland, *Ancient Israel* (London 1961)

Djilas, Milovan, *Conversations with Stalin* (London 1962)

Döblin, Alfred, *Berlin Alexanderplatz* (trans. Eugene Jolas, Harmondsworth 1978)

Dube, Wolf Diter, *The Expressionists* (trans. Mary Whittall, London 1972)

Dvinsky, Emmanuel, *Moscow and its Environs* (Moscow and London 1981)

Eberhard, Wolfram, *A History of China* (London 1948)

Erlanger, Philippe, *LouisXIV* (Paris 1965)

Evans, Oliver, *New Orleans* (New York 1959)

Evelyn, John, *The Diary of John Evelyn* (ed. E.S. de Beer, 6 vols, Oxford 1955)

Fitzpatrick, Sheila, *The Russian Revolution* (Oxford 1984)

Fodor's New Orleans (London 1984)

Ford, Richard, *Murray's Handbook of Spain* (2 vols, London 1869)

Gage, John, *Life in Italy at the time of the Medici* (London and New York 1968)

Galbraith, J.K., *The Great Crash 1929* (London 1954)

Garcilaso de la Vega, *Royal Commentaries of the Incas* (trans. and ed. H.V. Livermore, Texas 1966)

Gardiner, Sir Alan, *Egypt of the Pharaohs* (Oxford 1961)

Gautier, Théophile, *Voyage en Espagne* (Paris 1906)

Gérnet, Jacques, *Daily Life in China* (London 1962)

Gibbon, Edward, *The History of the Decline and Fall of the Roman Empire* (edition of 1854–5 London)

Girouard, Mark, *Cities and People* (London 1985)

Goldoni, Carlo, *Le Théâtre et la Vie en Italie au XVIIIᵉ Siècle* (Paris 1896)

Gombrich, E.H., *The Story of Art* (London 1950)

Gouaud, Henri & Colette Gouvion, *Egypt Observed* (London 1979)

Graham, Stephen, *Peter the Great* (London 1929)

Grant, Michael, *History of Rome* (London 1978)
   Julius Caesar (London 1969)

Griffin, Thomas Kurtz, *New Orleans* (New York 1961)

Griffis, W.E., *Guide Book of Yedo* (n.d.)
   The Mikado's Empire (n.d.)

Gross, Leonard, *The Last Jews in Berlin* (trans. Arnold J.Pomerans, London 1982)

Grosz, George, *A Small Yes and a Big No, The Autobiography of George Grosz* (London 1982)

Grunfeld, Frederick V., *Berlin* (London 1977)

Guinard, Paul, *Greco* (London 1956)

Hale, J.R., *Florence and the Medici* (London 1977)

Hamilton, G.H., *The Art and Architecture of Russia* (Harmondsworth 1954)

Hare, Augustus, *Wanderings in Spain* (London 1892)

Haslip, Joan, *The Lonely Empress* (London 1965)

Hayward, Arthur L. (ed.), *The London Spy by Ned Ward* (London 1927)

Hemming, John, *The Conquest of the Incas* (London 1970)

Heyworth, Peter, *Otto Klemperer : His Life and Times* (vol. 1, Cambridge 1985)

Highet, Gilbert, *Poets in a Landscape* (New York 1957)

Hughes, Spike, *Great Opera Houses* (London 1956)

Hume, Martin, *Philip II of Spain* (Cambridge 1911)
   Spain, 1479–1788 (Cambridge 1905)

Innes, Hammond, *The Conquistadors* (London 1973)

Isherwood, Christopher, *Goodbye to Berlin* (London 1939)

James, T.G.H., *Pharaoh's People* (London 1984)

Janin, R., *Constantinople byzantine* (Paris 1964)

Jonard, Norbert, *La Vie quotidienne à Venise du XVIII Siècle* (Paris n.d.)

Jones, Ernest, *Sigmund Freud* (Harmondsworth 1965)

Jones, Arnold H.M., *Athenian Democracy* (Oxford 1959)

Keller, Werner, *The Bible as History* (London 1956)

Kelly, Laurence, *Moscow : A Traveller's Companion* (London 1983)
   St Petersburg : A Traveller's Companion (London 1981)

Kemp, Peter, *The Strauss Family* (Tunbridge Wells 1985)

Kendall, Ann, *Everyday Life of the Incas* (London 1973)

Kennett, Victor and Audrey, *The Palaces of Leningrad* (London 1973)

Keyes, Frances Parkinson, *All This is Louisiana* (London 1950)

Krautheimer, Richard, *Three Christian Capitals : Topography and Politics* (Berkeley & London 1983)

Lang, Jane, *Rebuilding St Paul's after the Great Fire* (London 1956)

Lavedan, Pierre, *Histoire de l'Urbanisme à Paris* (Paris 1975)

Leapman, Michael, *The Companion Guide to New York* (London 1983)

Lee, Vernon, *Studies of the Eighteenth Century in Italy* (London 1880)

Lewis, W.S. (ed.), *The Correspondence of Horace Walpole* (39 vols, London 1937–79)

Loth, David, *Philip II of Spain* (London 1932)

Lucas-Dubreton, J., *Daily Life in Florence at the time of the Medici* (trans. A. Lytton Sells, London 1960)

Maly, Eugene H., *The World of David and Solomon* (New Jersey 1965)

Marañón, Gregorio, *Elogio e Nostalgia de Toledo* (n.p.1941)

Marsden, Christopher, *The Palmyra of the North* (London 1943)

Mason, J. W., *The Ancient Civilizations of Peru* (New York 1957)

Massie, Robert K., *Peter the Great : His Life and World* (London 1981)

Masson, Georgina, *The Companion Guide to Rome* (6th edn, London 1980)

Mawdsley, Evan & Margaret, *Moscow and Leningrad* (Blue Guide, London 1980)

McKenzie, J.L., *Dictionary of the Bible* (London 1965)

Means, P.A., *Fall of the Inca Empire and the Spanish Rule in Peru* (New York & London 1932)

Merriman, Roger B., *The Rise of the Spanish Empire* (vol. 2, New York 1925)

Meyer, Jean, *Colbert* (Paris 1981)

Millingen, Alexander van, *Byzantine Constantinople : The Walls of the City adjoining the Historical Sites* (London 1899)
   Constantinople (London 1906)
   Byzantine Churches of Constantinople (London 1912)

Mitchell, J.R. & M.D.R. Leys, *A History of London Life* (London 1958)

Mongrédien, Georges, *La Vie Quotidienne sous Louis XVI* (Paris 1948)
   Colbert (Paris 1963)

Monnier, Philippe, *Venise au XVIII Siècle* (Paris 1907)

Morrell, Elizabeth, *A Visitor's Guide to China* (London 1983)

Morris, Edmund, *The Rise of Theodore Roosevelt* (London 1979)

Morris, Jan, *The Venetian Empire : A Sea Voyage* (London 1980)

Morse, E.S., *Japan Day by Day* (Tokyo 1936)

Motley, J.L., *The Rise of the Dutch Republic* (London 1882)

Muggeridge, Malcolm, *Chronicles of Wasted Time*, Vol. 1: *The Green Stick* (London 1972)

Mumford, Lewis, *The City in History* (London 1961)

Nash, Ernest, *Pictorial History of Ancient Rome* (2 vols, London 1961)

Neill, William, *The Bible Story* (London 1973)

Norwich, John Julius, *Venice : The Greatness and the Fall* (London 1981)
   Venice : The Rise to Empire (London 1977)

Nugent, Mr [Sir Thomas], *The Grand Tour containing an Exact Description of most of the Cities, Towns and Remarkable Places of Europe* (4 vols, London 1749)

Obolensky, Dimitri, *The Byzantine Commonwealth* (London 1974)

Owens, R.J., *Peru* (London & Oxford)

Page, Thomas, *New York* (Geneva 1976)

Parker, Geoffrey, *Philip II* (London 1979)

Park, Ruth & Cedric Emanuel, *The Sydney We Love* (Sydney 1983)

Parry, J.H., *The Age of Reconnaissance* (London 1973)
   The Discovery of South America (London 1979)

Pepys, Samuel, *The Diary of Samuel Pepys* (ed. Robert Latham and William Matthews (11 vols, London 1970–83)

Perowne, Stewart, *The Life and Times of Herod the Great* (London 1956)

Petrie, Sir Charles, *Philip II* (London 1963)

Petrie, Sir Flinders, *Social Life in Ancient Egypt* (London 1923)

Pierson, Peter, *Philip II of Spain* (London 1975)

Poëte, Marcel, *Le Promenade à Paris au XVIIe Siècle* (Paris 1913)

Polo, Marco, *Travels* (edn of 1982, London)

Posener, Georges, *Dictionary of Egyptian Civilization* (London 1962)

Prescott, W.H., *History of the Conquest of Peru* (ed. J.K. Kirk, London 1901)

Prittie, Terence, *Konrad Adenauer* (London 1972)

Pryce-Jones, David, *Vienna* (n.p.1978)

Quennell, Peter, *The Colosseum* (London 1971)

Ranum, O.A., *Paris in the Age of Absolutism* (New York 1968)

Reddaway, T.R., *The Rebuilding of London after the Great Fire* (London 1940)

Reider, Frederic, *The Order of the S.S.* (London 1981)

Rich, Alan, *The Listeners' Guide to Jazz* (Poole 1980)

Richter, Hans, *Dada* (London 1966)

Robinson, Cervin & Rosemarie Haag Bletter, *Skyscraper Style : Art Deco New York* (New York 1975)

Romer, John, *Ancient Lives : Daily Life in the Egypt of the Pharaohs* (London 1985)

Roover, Raymond de, *The Rise and Decline of the Medici Bank* (Cambridge, Massachusetts 1963)

Rossiter, Stuart, *Greece* (London 1981)

Rowdon, Maurice, *The Silver Age of Venice* (London 1970)

Ruskin, John, *The Stones of Venice* (London 1851–3)

Savage, George, *Porcelain through the Ages* (Harmondsworth 1963)

Scaife, Walter, *Florentine Life during the Renaissance* (Baltimore 1893)

Schevill, Ferdinand, *History of Florence* (London 1937)
The Medici (London 1950)

Schonberg, Harold, *The Lives of the Great Composers* (London 1981)

Seidensticker, Edward, *Low City, High City : Tokyo from Edo to the Earthquake* (New York 1983)

Serna, Gaspar Gomez de la, *Castille la Nueva* (n.p.1964)

Sherrard, Philip, *Byzantium* (London 1966)

Shirer, William L., *The Rise and Fall of the Third Reich* (London 1960)
20th Century Journey, vol. II: *The Nightmare Years* (London 1984)

Simons, Joannes, *Jerusalem in the Old Testament* (Leiden 1952)

Slive, Seymour & H.R. Hoetink, *Jacob van Ruisdael* (Amsterdam 1981)

Smith, Robin & Betty Roland, *Sydney* (London 1964)

Smollett, Tobias, *Travels through France and Italy* (London 1766)

Solzhenitsyn, Alexander, *The Gulag Archipelago* (London 1974)

Souter, Gavin & Quinton Davis, *Sydney* (Sydney 1965)

Squier, E.G., *Peru : Incidents of Travel and Exploration in the Land of the Incas* (London 1877)

Stewart, Desmond, *The Pyramids and Sphinx* (London 1972)

Summerson, John, *Sir Christopher Wren* (London 1953)

Sumner, B.H., *Survey of Russian History* (London 1966)

Sutcliffe, Anthony (ed.), *Metropolis* (London 1984)

Talbot Rice, David, *Byzantine Art* (Oxford & London 1935)

Talbot Rice, Tamara, *A Concise History of Russian Art* (London 1963)
Everyday Life in Byzantium (London 1967)

Tapié, Victor-L., *Vienne au Temps de François-Joseph* (Paris 1970)

Tauranac, John, *Essential New York* (New York 1979)

Terry, Philip, *Guide to the Japanese Empire* (London 1920)

Thomson, David, *Renaissance Paris : Architecture and Growth 1475–1660* (London 1984)

Thrale, Hester Lynch, *Glimpses of Italian Society* (London 1892)

Tirro, Frank, *Jazz : A History* (New York 1977)

Tregear, Mary, *Chinese Art* (London 1980)

Ure, P.N., *Justinian and His Age* (London 1951)

Varner, John Grier, *El Inca* (Austin and London 1968)

Vasari, Giorgio, *The Lives of the Artists* (trans. George Bull, Harmondsworth 1965)

Vaussard, Maurice, *Daily Life in Eighteenth-Century Italy* (trans. Michael Heron, London 1962)

Vincent, L.A. & M.A. Steve, *Jérusalem de L'Ancien Testament* (n.p.1954)

Webster, T.B.L., *Everyday Life in Classical Athens* (London & New York 1969)

White, John Manchip, *Everyday Life in Ancient Egypt* (London & New York 1963)

Wiethoff, Bodo, *Introduction to Chinese History* (trans. Mary Whittall, London 1979)

Wilhelm, Jacques, *La Vie quotidienne des Parisiens au Temps du Roi Soleil* (Paris 1977)

Willett, John, *The Theatre of Bertolt Brecht* (London 1967)

Wolf, John B., *Louis XIV* (London 1968)

Woodham-Smith, Cecil, *The Great Hunger* (London 1962)

Youde, Pamela, *China* (Hong Kong & London 1982)

Zárate, Augustin de, *The Discovery and Conquest of Peru* (trans. J.M. Cohen, Harmondsworth 1968)

Zorzi, Alvise, *Venice, 697–1797* (trans. Nicoletta Simborowski & Simon MacKenzie, London 1983)

Zumthor, Paul, *Daily Life in Rembrandt's Holland* (trans. Simon Watson Taylor, London 1962)

Zweig, Stefan, *The World of Yesterday* (London 1943)

INDEX

Abraham, Patriarch, 19, 31
Adler, Alfred (1870–1937), 182
Alberti, Leon Battista (1404–72), Renaissance man, 96, 100
Albizzi, Rinaldo degli, 97–8, 99
Alfonso V of Castile, 106, 107
Algarotti, Francesco (1712–64), 152
Alonso de Berruguete (c.1468–1561), 112
Amsterdam, 157, 160, 161; merchant fleet, 115, 117–18; 119–20, 122; Dutch East India Company, 117, 230
Angelico, Fra (1387–1455), 101
Antoninus Pius, Emperor (AD 86–161), 55
Archenholz, Baron von, on Venice, 167
architecture, 38; American High Rise, 237–8; Baroque, 176, 179, 195, 218; Bauhaus and Art Deco, 215, 237; Dutch, 155–6, 158; Gothic, 112, 127
Ark of the Covenant, 21, 22, 24, 25–6; Holy Place and Holy of Holies, 25, 26, 27, 29, 31
art movements, Art Deco, 237; Art Nouveau, 180; Constructivism, Cubism, 223; Dada, 208–9; Expressionism, 209; Futurism, 225; Weiner Sezession, 180
arts, the, Egyptian, 15, 16, 17, 51; Chinese, 76–7; Greek, 34, 38–9, 40
Atahualpa (d.1533), ruler of the Incas, 80, 81, 82, 83–4, 87–8
Athens, ideal city state, 31, 34–5; building programme, 34–5; athletic contests, 35, 39; Council of the Areopagus, 35, 37; debt to Pericles, 36–40; Dionysiac festival, 39; buildings, Acropolis, 33, 34, 35, 36, 38, 39, 40; Agora, 34, 35, 37, 39; Ditylon, 34; Erechtheum, 34; Hekatompedon, 34; Hephaisteion, 40; Odeion, 39; Painted Colonnade, 37; Parthenon, 34, 38; Propylaea, 38; Stoa, 37, 40; Temples, 38–9, 40; Theatre of Dionysios, 39; Tholos, 37
Auden, W.H. (1907–72), in Berlin, 210
Augustin di Zárate, on Incas, 84
Augustus, Emperor (63 BC–AD 14), 43, 44, 47; Porta Prima Villa, 49
Aurelius, Marcus, Emperor (121–180), 55, 127
Aztec Civilization, 77

Bakst, Leon (1866–1924), 221
Bartholdi, Frédéric-Auguste (1834–1904), Statue of Liberty, 232
bathrooms and lavatories, Chinese, 72; Constantinople, 64; Egyptian, 17; Greek, 40, 42; Roman, 52
Bazhenov, Vasily (1737–99), 219
Beckford, William Thomas (1760–1844), on Venice, 165, 167, 171
Becket, Thomas à (1118–70), 136
Bedford, Duke of, 146
Beethoven, Ludwig van (1770–1827), 177, 184
Benois, Alexander (1870–1960), 221
Berg, Alban (1885–1935), *Wozzeck*, 209
Berlin, post World War I, 206, 207; population, 206, 207; architecture, 207; political and artistic turmoil, 207; Dada movement, 208–9; theatrical productions, 209–10; film industry, 210; night clubs, 210; transvestites, 210, 211; and Hitler,

211–12; Olympic Games, 1936, 213–14; Sommerfield House, 215; Allied bombing, 215 *see also* Germany
Bismarck, Prince Otto von (1815–98), 207
Bligh, Capt. Wm (c.1753–1817), 243
Boileau-Despréaux, Nicolas (1636–1711), 135
Bolsheviks, 217, 218, 223
Boncompagni, Cardinal Ugo (1502–85), 172
Bond, Sir Thomas, 145, 146
Botticelli, Sandro (1444–1510), 101, 103
Boulle, Charles André, (1642–1732), 135
Bove, Osip (d.1834), architect, 219
Brahms, Johannes (1833–97), 184
Brecht, Bertolt (1895–1956), 209, 215
Brisbane, Sir Thomas (1773–1860), 244
Brosses, Charles de (1709–77), 166, 168, 173
Bruce Lockhart, R.H., 222–3
Brunelleschi, Filippo (1337–1446), and Florence, 91–2, 99, 100
Byzantium, 57, 58, 161; architecture, 62, 63; Golden Horn, 57, 58; Hippodrome, 14, 58, 60, 61

Caesar, Gaius Julius (100/102 BC–44 BC), 43, 44, 52
Cajamarca, Inca town, 80, 83, 84
Canaan, (later Palestine), 19, 21, 24, 31
Canaletto (Antonio Canale; 1697–1768), 173
Carlos, Don (1545–68), 109–10
Casanova, Giovanni Jacopo (1725–98), 161, 166, 172
Catherine I, Empress Consort, 155, 158–9
Cervantes, Miguel de (1547–1616), 104
Chalcuchima, Inca general, 84
Chaliapin, Fedor (1873–1938), 221
Charles II (1630–85), 139, 140, 232
Charles III, King of Spain, 188
Charles V, Emperor, 80, 103, 107, 115
Charles V, King of France, 128
Charles IX, King of France (1530–74), 128
Charles XII, King of Sweden, 157
Christians, Christianity, death in the arena, 54–5; Constantine and, 55; reconquista of Spain, 106, 107
China, Civilization, 66, 75, 77, 197; Period of Disunion, 66; Hwang-Ho (Yellow River), 66, 68; Great Wall, 66; monasteries, 69; dynasties, Chow, 'Sons of Heaven', 66; Han, 66; Shang, 66; Sui (Yang Chien), 66; Sung, (Chao Kuang), 66; Kao-Tsung, 68
Cicero, Marcus Tullius (106–43 BC), 47
Cimabue, Giovanni (c.1240–c.1302), 91
clothing, Chinese, 73; Constantinople, 59–60, 64; Egyptian, 18; Florentine, 94; Japanese, 204; Jewish, 29, 30–1; New Orleans, 189; Parisian, 134; Roman, 49–50; Sydney convicts, 244, 245
Colbert, Jean-Baptiste (1619–83), and Paris, 128–9, 130
Commodus, Emperor (AD 161–92), 55
Communist Party, German, suppression in 1918, 207–8, 210; Russian, 223
Conder, Josiah, 201–2
Constantine I, the Great (c.274–337), and Christianity, 55; and a New Rome, 55, 57–9

Constantinople, 57, 64, 164; construction, 58–9; socio/religious factions, 59; Nika Riots, 60–1, 62; work on Cathedral, 62; buildings, churches, 62, 65; Haghia Sophia, 62, 65; Hall of Tribunals, 61; Hippodrome, 14, 58, 60, 61–2; Palace of Byzantium, 61
Cook, James (1728–79), 240, 242
Cooke, Alistair, on N.Y. immigrants, 236
Cortés, Hernándo (1485–1547), conquest of Mexico, 80
Coryat, Thomas (1577–1617), on Venetian Courtesans, 166
Coysevox, Antoine, sculptor, 132
Crassus, Marcus Licinius, Roman General, 27
Crete, Minoan Civilization, 31, 66; fall of, 1669, 168; Palace of Knossos, 31
Cuzco, Inca capital, 80, 83, 84; construction, 84, 87; Cusipata (Place of Joy), 84, 87; Huacapata (Holy Place), 84; palaces, 87–8; Sacsahuaman fortress, 88, 89; Temple of the Sun (Coricancha), 82, 88–9

David, King of Israel and Judah, 22, 24–5
Dante (1265–1321), 91, 95
Delphi, oracle at, 33
Diaghilev, Sergei (1872–1929), 221
Diocletian, Emperor (245–313), 55; removes his capital to Izmir, 55
diseases, malaria, 188; plague, 26, 43; Great Plague, 141; yellow fever, 188, 190
Dolgorusky, Prince Yuri, and Moscow, 218
Donatello (c.1386–1466), 92, 99; *David*, 100

Ebert, Friedrich (1871–1925), 208
Egypt, ancient, pharaonic civilization, 10–12, 66; Theban influence, 12; eras of disruption, 12–13; Asiatic invasion, 13; expansion, 13–14; Temples, 14, 15, 16; prosperity, 16
Egyptians, ancient, mummification, 14, 17, 19; living conditions, 16; embalming process, 17; toiletry, 18
Ehrenburg, Ilya, Moscow apartment, 226
Einstein, Albert (1879–1955), 215
Eisenstein, Sergei (1898–1948), 225
Elizabeth Petrovna, Empress (1709–62), 158, 160
Elizabeth of Valois, Queen of Philip II, 108–9; and Don Carlos, 109–10
England, 155; wool exports, 115; hostelries, 122; Civil War, 135, 140, 146; and France, 128; growth as world power, 135; claims on America, 232
entertainment, Chinese, 75; Greek symposium, 42; London, gaming houses, 147; Tower of London, 151; Moscow, 222–3; New Orleans, quadroon balls, 189–90; Mardi Gras, 191; Roman, 52–4; Russian debauched assemblies, 158–9; dance houses, 192
Erlach, Johann Bernard von (1606–1723), 176
Etruscans, 43, 47, 54
Eugene, Prince of Savoy (1663–1736), 176

Euphranor, Greek painter, 40
Evelyn, John (1620–1706), and Louis
    XIV, 124; and Great Fire, 140, 141;
    rebuilding plan, 141; visited by Peter
    the Great, 155; on Venice, 164, 170–1

Ferdinand I, Emperor of Austria, 174
Ferdinand II of Aragon, 103, 107, 112
Ferdinand III, King of Castile and
    Léon, 107
Fioravanti, Aristotele, architect, 218
First World War, 206, 207, 208
Florence, artistic renown, 91–2;
    population, 92, 95; streets and houses,
    92, 93; Arno bridges, 92–3; *quartiere*
    and wards, 93; trade guilds, 93, 95, 96,
    99; festival of *Calendimaggio* (May
    Day), 93; sumptuary laws, 94, 95;
    social hierarchy, 95, 96; constitution,
    96; Signoria, 96; rich merchants,
    96–7; buildings, Baptistry, 99;
    Bargello, 92, 101; churches, 92, 96,
    99, 101; Medici Palace, 100, 101;
    Mercato Vecchia, 93; Orsan Michele,
    99; Ospedale degli Innocenti, 99;
    Palazzo della Signoria, 96; Pitti
    Palace, 101; Santa Maria del' Fiore
    Cathedral, 91, 100, 101, 102;
    campanile, 91, 92; Santissima
    Annunziata choir, 99–100, 101
food and drink, Chinese, 69–72;
    Constantinople, 64; Dutch, 120–1;
    Egyptian, 16, 18–19; Florentine, 95,
    96; French (gastronomy), 134; Greek,
    40–2; Inca, 88; Japanese, 204; Jewish,
    29–30; London, (Pepys), 147;
    Moscow, 222; New Orleans, 192;
    Roman, 51–2, 53; Russian, 159, 160;
    Venetian, 164; Viennese, 185
Francis I, King of France (1494–1547),
    128
Franz Josef, Emperor (1830–1916), 77
Frederick the Great (1712–86), 206–7
Frederick William, Great Elector
    (1640–88), 206
Freud, Sigmund (1856–1939), 182, 184
furniture, Chinese, 73; Dutch, 119–20;
    Egyptian, 17; Florentine, 93–4;
    Greek, 41, 42; Inca, 87–8; Jewish, 29;
    Roman, 48; Russian, 158
Furtwängler, Wilhelm (1886–1954), 210
Fuseli, Henry (1741–1820), *The
    Nightmare*, 181, 182

Garcilaso de la Vega (1503–36), 104; on
    Incas, 82, 87
Garde, Count de la, on the waltz, 176
Ghiberti, Lorenzo (1378–1455),
    Baptistry, 99
Ghirlandaio, Domenico (1449–94), 103
Giotto di Bondone (1267–1337),
    frescoes, 91
Girard, Dominique, gardener, 176
Girardon, François (1630–1715), 135
Giza, pyramids, 11; Great Sphinx, 11
gods and goddesses, Egyptian, Amun,
    14, 15; Anubis, 19; Isis and Osiris,
    19; Greek, Apollo, 42; Athena, 33, 35,
    38; Dionysus, 41; Hephaistos, 39,
    Heracles, 42; Zeus, 40; Persian,
    Ahura Mazda, 33
Goebbels, Josef (1897–1945), 213
Goering, Hermann (1893–1946), 212
Goethe, Johann Wolfgang von
    (1749–1832), and Venice, 168, 170
Goldoni, Carlo (1707–93), 167
Goldsmith, Oliver (1728–84), on
    Dutchmen, 120
Gozzoli, Benozzo (1420–98), 101
Greco, El (1541–1614), 115

Greenway, Francis, and Sydney, 245, 247
Griffis, W.E., *Ginza Book of Yedo*, 199
Gropius, Walter (1883–1969), 214–15
Grosz, George (1893–1959), 215; on
    Berlin, 206, 207, 211; and Dada, 209
Guardi, Francesco (1712–93), *Il
    Parlatorio*, 173
gymnasia, Greek, Academy, Lyceum,
    Kynosarges, activities, 42

Habsburgs, 103, 117, 173, 174, 176
Hadrian, Emperor (76–138), 55
Hangzhou (Kinsai), capital of Sung
    dynasty, 68–9; population, 68; daily
    life, 68–9; imports, 69; food markets,
    71; restaurants, 71–2; home meals,
    72; drunkenness, 72; tea houses, 72;
    courtesans, 72, 75; prostitution, 72;
    works of art, 76–7 *see also* China
Haussmann, Baron Georges, and Paris,
    177
Haydn, Franz Joseph (1732–1809), 177,
    184
Hecht, Ben (1894–1964), 209
Henry III, King of France (1551–89), 128
Henry IV, King of France (1553–1610),
    123, 128, 130
Herod, the Great, King of Judea, 27, 29;
    rebuilding of Jerusalem, 28; Temple
    and palace, 28–9, 31
Herodotus, tour of Egypt, 9, 11; on
    embalming, 17; and Persian army, 33;
    on invasion of Athens, 34
Himmler, Heinrich (1900–45), SS, 212
Hindemith, Paul (1895–1963), 215
Hindenburg, Field Marshal von, 211, 212
Hitler, Adolf (1889–1945), 227; Storm
    Troopers, 208, 211, 212; and Olympic
    Games, 214; architectural plans, 215;
    death, 215
Hobbes, Thomas (1588–1679), 124
Hohenzollern Dynasty, 206–7
Holland, 115, 140, 155
housing, Amsterdam, 118; interior,
    119–20; Berlin, 207–8; Chinese, poor
    and rich, 73; Constantinople, 63–4;
    Florentine, 93; French, 130; Greek
    (Athens), 35, 40; Inca, 82, 84; Israel-
    ite, 24, 29; Japanese, 198, 200, 201;
    Moscow, 219; New Orleans, 188, 195;
    Roman, 47; interior, 48–9, 51; Russian,
    157, 158, 219; Spanish (Toledo),
    106, 112, 115; Theban, poor and rich,
    16, 17; Viennese proletariat, 182
Hübner, Baron, on Viennese women, 180
Hudson, Henry (d.1611), 229–30, 232

Imhotep, architect, 11
Incas, human sacrifices, 77, 83; Spanish
    discovery, 79–80; advanced civilization,
    80; legendary foundation, 80; vast
    empire, 80–1, 89; authoritarian
    rule, 80–1, 84; internal communication
    system, 81; social hierarchy, 81, 82;
    Virgins of the Sun, 81–2, 83, 88; govern-
    ment, 82; natural resources, 82; farm-
    ing, 82; punishments, 83; peasant
    children, 83; feast of Raymi, 83; use
    of gold *passim*
Isherwood, Christopher (b.1904), 210
Ivan III, Grand Prince, 'the Great'
    (1440–1505), and Ukraine, 151; and
    Moscow, 218
Ivan IV, 'the Terrible' (1530–84), 151

Jeroboam, labour prefect, 26
Jefferson, Thomas (1743–1826),
    Louisiana Purchase, 188
Jerusalem, capital city of Israelites, 24;
    royal palace and houses, 24, 26;

Solomon and temple, 25–6; moral and
    physical disintegration, 26; return of
    the Jews, 26, 27; rebuilding and
    fortification, 26–7; captured by
    Alexander, 27; and Ptolemy, 27;
    Roman dominance, 27–8; Temple of
    Herod, 28–9; Roman conquest, and
    destruction, 31; Mosque of Oman, 25
Jews (Israelites), exodus into Egypt, 19;
    enslavement, 19; belief in their return
    to 'Promised Land', 19; in Palestine, 21;
    and Philistines, 22, 24; under David
    and Herod, 22, 24–31; restoration
    of religious customs, 27; anti-Roman
    rebellion, 31; Roman massacre, 31;
    immigrants from pogroms, 236
Jones, Inigo (1573–1652), 144
Joseph II, Emperor of Austria, 177
Justinian I (482–565), Emperor, and
    Constantinople, 59; and Roman Law,
    59; opposition to, 60, 61; churches, 62;
    and Haghia Sophia, 63; theatre, 65
Juvenal, Decimus Junius (c.55–140),
    Roman life, 47, 48, 52; 'bread and
    circuses', 54

Kamenev, Lev (1883–1936), 219
Karamzin, Nikolai (1766–1826), 132
Kazakov, Matvei (1738–1813), 219
Ketteler, Freiherr von, defines
    Borussismus, 206
Kidron Valley, Gihon spring, 24, 26
Klee, Paul (1879–1940), 215
Kleiber, Erich (1890–1956), 209, 215
Klemperer, Otto (1885–1973), 209, 215
Klimt, Gustav (1862–1918), *Nude
    Veritas*, 180

La Fayette, Marie, Comtesse de
    (1634–93), 135
Lake Pontchartrain, 187–8, 193
Landsteiner, Karl (1868–1943), 181
La Rochefoucauld, François, Duc de
    (1613–80), 135
Leapman, Michael, and New York, 239
Le Blond, Jean Baptiste, 159–61
Lenin, Vladimir Ilyich (1870–1924),
    217, 223
Le Nôtre, André (1613–1700), 129, 159
Leonardo da Vinci (1452–1590), 103
Liebknecht, Karl (1871–1919), 208
Lippi, Filippo (1457–1504), 92, 103
Lippi, Fra Filippo (Lippo, 1406–69), 101
London, 14, 136, 198; financial and
    commercial pre-eminence, 135; Great
    Fire, 1666, 138–41, 144; streets, 136,
    138, 141–3, 147; housing, 136, 142,
    144–6; reconstruction, 140–2; City
    Livery Companies, 140–1; suburban
    expansion, 144–5; property develop-
    ers, 145–6; areas and buildings,
    Bethlehem Hospital, 151; Bloomsbury,
    144, 146; Covent Garden, 146;
    Customs House, 139, 144; Guildhall,
    139, 143–4; London Bridge, 136, 138,
    141, 151; Pall Mall, 145; Piccadilly,
    145, 146; Royal Exchange, 139, 141,
    143; St James's and Palace, 144–5,
    146; St Paul's Cathedral, 141, 142,
    144; fires, 136, 138, 139; Soho, 146;
    Tower, 151; Westminster, 144;
    Whitehall Palace, 138, 141
Longhena, Baldassare (1598–1682), 173
Longhi, Pietro, 168
Lope di Vega (1562–1635), 104
Loti, Pierre (1850–1923), 199, 201
Louis IX, St King of France (1215–70),
    127–8
Louis XIII, King of France (1601–43),
    128

Louis XIV, King of France
(1638–1715), 123, 124, 126, 159, 187;
and the arts, 123, 127, 135, 140;
influence on fashion, 135
Louisiana, 187; Purchase of, 1803, 188,
195; Superdrome (1970s), 190;
secedes from the Union, 1861, 192
Luxemburg, Rosa (1871–1919), 208
Luxor, 9, 15, 16

McGee, Thomas D'Arcy, 234
Macquarie, Lachlan, in Sydney, 243–4;
treatment of convicts, 244;
eponymous areas, 245, 246; building
programme, 245–6
Madrid, 104, 106; Escorial, the, 112
Mamontov, Sava, art school, 221–2
Mann, Heinrich (1871–1950), 215
Mansart, Jules Hardouin (1645–1708),
129
Marie Antoinette, Queen (1755–93), 176
marriage customs, Chinese, 66, 75–6;
Egyptian, 13; Inca, 81–2; Jewish, 27,
31, 214; New Orleans (quadroons),
189–90
Martial, Marcus Valerius
(c.AD 40–c.104), 52
Martineau, Harriet (1802–76), in New
Orleans, 189
Masaccio (1401–28), 92
Mazarin, Cardinal (1602–61), 129, 130;
and Louis XIV, 124, 126
Maximilian, Emperor of Mexico
(1832–67), 177
Maria Theresa, Empress, 176
Medici, Cosimo de' (1389–1464),
Renaissance man, 97–8, 100–1; ruler
of Florence, 99; death, 101, 103
Medici, Lorenzo de', the Magnificent
(1449–92), 102–3
Medici, Piero I de' (1414–69), 101
Memphis, necropolis, 11
Mendelsohn, Erich (1887–1953), 215
Menshikov, Alexander Danilovich
(1660–1729), 155, 160
Menshikov, Prince, 158, 161
Michelangelo (1475–1564), 99, 103;
Cordonata to the Capitol, 35
Michelozzo (1396–1472), 99–100
Micon, Greek painter, 37
Mies van der Rohe, Ludwig
(1886–1969), 215
Milan, 55, 89, 92, 103, 162
Minuit, Peter, 230, 232
Mississippi River, 150, 187, 188;
boatmen, 190; steamboat luxury,
190–1, 193
Mnesicles, Greek sculptor, 38
Montagu, Lady Mary Wortley
(1689–1762), on Venice, 164
Moscow, as capital of Russia, 151, 152,
218; physical conditions, 151, 218,
222; architects, 218, 225; population,
218, 219, 225; trading centre, 218–19;
noblemen's houses, 219; theatre and
music, 221–2; primitiveness/
decadence, 223; reaction to Revolution, 223–4; and Stalin's purges, 224–5;
socio/economic reforms, 225;
reconstruction, 225, 227; foreign
opinions, 226; reaction to German
advance (1941), 226–7; buildings,
Bolshoi Theatre, 219, 221; Tsar Cannon and Bell, 219, 221; Cathedral of the
Archangel Michael, 218; of the Assumption, 218; of Christ the Redeemer,
219; churches, 218; Club of the Nobility, 222; Kremlin, 151, 154, 218, 219,
227; Lubyanka, Butyrka gaols, 224;
Manezh (Riding School), 222; Trade

Union House, 217; Triumphal Arch,
219; university, 225
Moses, 19, 21, 22, 27
Mozart, Wolfgang Amadeus (1756–91),
177, 184
Muggeridge, Malcolm, in Moscow, 226
music, in Berlin, 1920s, 209, 211;
ancient Egyptian, 19; Japanese, 204;
jazz and ragtime, 193; in Moscow,
221–2; in Paris, 135; Viennese, 175–6,
184, 185
Mycenaean civilization, 31

Napoleon I (1769–1821), 176, 188, 207,
218
Napoleon III (1808–73), 177
Nebuchadnezzar, King of Babylon, 26
Nehemiah, 27
Nero, Emperor (AD 37–68), 47, 54
Neva, the, Fortress of SS. Peter and
Paul, 155, 157; Kronstadt naval base,
156, 160, 223
New Orleans, foundation, 187–8;
rebuilding after fire, 188, 195; refugee
and immigrant arrivals, 188–9, 190,
195; racial/social divisions, 189–90;
population growth, 190, 191; advent
of steamboat, 190–1; economic and
commercial prosperity, 190–1; city of
pleasure, 191–2; carpet-baggers,
191–2; Civil War and, 192; era of
violence, 192, 193; areas of brothels,
barrel-houses and dance houses,
192–3; Mafia activity, 192–3; causes
of decline, 194–5; architectural
features, 194–5; Algiers, 195; creole
faubourgs, 195; Districts, 195;
national enclaves, 192, 195;
Storyville, 192, 193; the Swamp, 190
New South Wales, convict settlement,
240, 242–3; governors of, 240–1;
treatment of convicts, 243–6; gold
mining, 246; wool industry, 246
New York, 118; first US capital, 229,
232; multi-national culture, 232;
immigrants, 232, 234, 236; boarding
houses, 234, 235; sanitary conditions,
235–6; neighbourhood politicians, 236;
US financial centre, 237; millionaire
art patrons, 237; Wall Street Crash,
238–9; national enclaves, 239; areas
and buildings, Brooklyn Bridge, 229;
Ellis Island, 236; Greenwich Village,
236; skyscrapers, 237–8; Long Island
Sound, 230, 239; Manhattan Island,
118, 229, 230, 232, 248; Tammany
Hall, 194, 236–7; UN Centre, 239
Nile, the, 16, 44; source of Egyptian
civilization, 9, 12
Nubia, 12, 14, 15, 16
Nugent, Sir Thomas, 121–2; The Grand
Tour, 165, 166

Olbrich, Josef (1867–1908), 180
Oldenburg, Henry, FRS, 141
Ossner, Hans Konrad, 160

painting, Egyptian, 16, 17; Greek, 37,
40; Roman frescoes, 52; Venetian, 173
Palestine, 19; Egyptian influence, 12,
13; arrival of Israelites, 21
Palladio, Andrea (1518–80), San Giorgio
Maggiore, 173
Papacy, 92, 98, 99, 102, 103; at Avignon,
92
Paris, 92, 140, 142, 177, Louis XIV and,
124, 127, 128, 140; Roman occupation,
127; development in classical style,
127–9; water supply and drainage,
130; foreign opinions, 130, 132; ab-

sence of sanitation, 131, 132, 147; crime,
132, 133; the poor, 133–4; places of
enjoyment, 134; centre of fashion and
culture, 134–5; academies, 135; buildings, Bastille, 128, 132; Church of the
Invalides, 129; College of the Sorbonne,
127; Faubourgs, St Antoine, 129; St
Germain, 129, 134; St Honoré, 128;
Hôtels, 128, 129, 130, 135, 159; Ile de
la Cité, 127, 130; Invalides, Hospital,
129; Louvre palace, 127, 128, 129,
135; Luxembourg, 128; Notre Dame,
127; Palais Royal, 128; Place des Victoires, 129, 131; Pont-Neuf, 128; Salt-
petrière, 129, 134; Tuileries, 128, 129,
135; Versailles, 127, 130, 135, 159, 160
Pepys, Samuel (1663–1703), 136, 138,
147; on Great Fire, 1666, 138–9;
London houses, 146–7
Pericles (c.490–c.429 BC), democratic
reforms, 35–6; character and
appearance, 36; as orator, 36;
beautifies the city, 36–40;
civilization's debt to, 43
Perrault, Claude (1628–1703), 129
Persia, Persians, 26, 59; invasion of
Greece, 33–4, 36; defeat at Marathon,
37
Peter, the Great, Tsar of Russia
(1689–1725), 152, 155, 156–61;
character and appearance, 152, 154,
155; dual Tsar with brother Ivan, 154;
marriages, 154, 155; westernization
ideas, 154; use of naval power, 154–5;
treatment of workmen, 155, 157; housing, 155–6, 156–7, 159–60; shipbuilding, 156; military exploits, 157–8;
entertaining visitors, 160
Petronius Arbiter (1st century AD),
Trimalchio, 46
pharaohs, unification of Egypt, 10;
Dynasties, 11, 12, 15; diminution of
godhead, 14, 15; enslavement of the
Israelites, 19; Ahmose I, 13;
Amenophis I, 13; Amenophis III, the
Magnificent, 15, 16; Djoser, 11;
Hatshepsut, 13–14; Khafre, 11;
Khufu, 11; Menkaure, 11; Rameses
II, 15, 16, 19; Seti I, 15; Shishak, sack
of Jerusalem, 26; Tutankhamen, 13,
16; Tuthmosis I, 13, 16; Tuthmosis
II, 13; Tuthmosis III, 14–15
Phidias, Greek sculptor, 38, 58
Philip II, Augustus (1180–1223), 127
Philip II, King of Spain (1527–98),
marriages, 107, 108, 109; accession,
108; transfers capital to Madrid, 112;
death, 112; vast empire, 115; and the
Netherlands, 115, 117
Phillip, Capt. Arthur, Gov. New South
Wales (1738–1814), 240, 242, 243,
244, 245
Piccolomini, Aeneas Silvio de (Pius II),
99
Pierozzi, Antonio (1389–1459),
Archbishop of Florence, 100
Pilate, Pontius, 28, 54
Pisistratus, tyrant, 34, 35
Pizarro, Francisco (1478–1541), and the
Incas, 80, 81, 84, 88
Plato, 42
Plutarch, 36
Poelzig, Hans, 209
Pollaiuolo (1429–98), 101, 103
Polo, Marco (1254–1324), 68, 71, 72
Polygnotos of Thasos, 37
Pompey (106–48 BC), 27, 43
Procopius (c.AD 499–565), and
Constantinople, 59–60, 61, 62;
profligacy of Theodora, 65

Prussia, 206, 207
Ptolemy XIII, the Great, 27, 43
Pulitzer, Joseph (1847–1911), 232
pyramids, of the Pharaohs, 11–12, 14

Rathenau, Walther (1867–1922), 210
Reinhardt, Max (1873–1943), 209, 215
religion, Aztec, 77; Inca, 80, 81–2, 83;
    Judaism, 21, 24–7 passim;
    Protestantism, 115, 117, 123
Rembrandt (1606–69), 117, 118, 123
Rerberg I.I., architect, 225
Reynie, Nicolas-Gabriel de la, 132
Robbia, Luca della (c.1400–82), 101
Richelieu, Cardinal (1585–1642), 128,
    135
Rohm, Ernst (1887–1934), 212
Rolle, Rev. Samuel, 142
Roman Empire, 27–31, 43–4, 55, 59, 92
Romans, rights of citizenship, 43, 44;
    clothing, 49–50; social rank, 50, 54;
    prostitution, 50, 52; role of aediles, 52;
    Vestal Virgins, 54; massacre of
    Christians, 54–5; pagan beliefs, 55;
    barbarian assaults, 174
Rome, Caput mundi, 43; the Senate, 44;
    population, 46; public services, 47;
    street life, 47–8; baths and brothels,
    52; as capital city, 55; buildings,
    Basilicus Nova, 55; Capitol, 31, 35;
    Circus Maximus, 14, 52–3;
    Colosseum, 44, 54; Egyptian Obelisk,
    14; 'Subura', 52; Temple of Jupiter
    Capitolinus, 31; Trajan's Column, 44
Roosevelt, President Theodore, 229, 232
Rubinstein, Anton (1829–94), 221
Rudolf of Habsburg, Count (1218–91),
    175
Russia, 115; isolationism, 151, 218;
    debauched parties, 159, 223; Russo-
    Japanese War, 223; Orthodox
    Church, 218; October Revolution,
    223, 227; Kronstadt insurrection,
    223; resistance to Communism, 223;
    New Economic Policy, 223, 225 see
    also Moscow; St Petersburg

St Petersburg, becomes capital of
    Russia, 152; building of St Peter and
    St Paul Fortress, 155–7; socio/econom-
    ic conditions, 156–7; housing, 156–7,
    158; achieves Emperor's dream, 161;
    buildings, Admiralty, 155, 159; Alex-
    ander Nevsky Monastery, 158, 159;
    Church of the Holy Trinity, 158;
    Nevsky Prospect, 159; St Peter and
    St Paul Cathedral, 158; Summer
    Palace, 158, 159; Trinity Square, 158;
    Triumphal Osteria of the Four
    Frigates, 158; Winter Palace, 158
Salamis Island, 33, 38
Sartre, Abbé, Dutch food, 120
Saul, first King of Israel, 22
Sauval, Henri, on Paris, 133
Schubert, Franz Peter (1797–1828), 177,
    184
Schönberg, Arnold (1874–1951), 215
Senmur, architect, 14
Sennacherib, King of Assyria, 26
Severus, Septimus (146–211), 58
Sévigné, Marie de (1626–96), 135
Shigure, Hasegawa, 203
Shostakovich, Dimitri, 226
Sitte, Camillo, architect, 179–80
slaves, slavery, 26; Egyptian, 11, 17; of
    the Israelites, 19; Greek, 40; Roman,
    43, 46; in Florence, 95; in New
    Orleans, 188–9, 190; Santa Domingo
    revolution, 190
Solzhenitsyn, Alexander, 224

Soderini, Niccolò, orator, 101
Solomon, character and economic
    achievements, 25; his Temple and
    Palace, 25–6; and decline, 26
Southampton, Earl of (d.1677), 146
Spartans, 36
Stalin (1879–1953), rise to absolute
    power, 218, 223, 224; purges, 224;
    and defence of Moscow, 227
Stanislavsky, Konstantin, 226
Stresemann, Gustav (1878–1929), 211
Stuyvesant, Peter (1590–1672), 232
Suetonius, Gaius (AD 73–160), 211
Suleiman I, the Magnificent
    (1494–1566), 176
Sydney, expansion, 245–8; Hyde Park
    Barracks, 245–6, 248; Bushy Bore,
    246; Circular Quay, 246, 248; popu-
    lation, 247–8; Bridge, 247; Opera
    House, 247; Sydney Harbour, early
    settlement, 240, 242; state of convicts,
    242; subsidized settlers, 243, 244; condi-
    tions in, 243–5; The Rocks, 244; Argyle
    Place, 244; Holy Trinity Church, 244;
    later development, 245–8
Syria, 12, 13, 19, 25, 27, 43

Tacitus, Publius (c.55–150), 54
Taharqa, King of Nubia, 15
Tenochtitlan, Aztec capital, 77
Thames, the, 141, 151
theatres and opera houses, in Berlin,
    209; Constantinople, 65; Paris, 135;
    Venice, 164, 170
Theodora, Empress, (c.500–547), 61, 65
Thrale, Mrs Hester, on Venice, 167
Thucydides (c.460–c.400 BC), and
    Pericles, 36; on 430 BC plague, 43
Tiberius, Emperor (42 BC–AD 37), 54
Tiepolo, Giovanni Battista (1696–1770),
    164
Titus, Emperor (AD 39–81), 54
Thebes, influence on Egyptian
    civilization, 12–13; mortuary temples,
    15, 16; decorated tombs see also
    Egypt; Pharoahs
Thermopylae, Pass of, Greek defeat, 33
Thon, Konstantin (1839–83), 219
Tokyo (Edo), High and Low Cities, 198,
    199, 201, 204; housing, 198; and
    foreigners, 198, 199, 204; brothels and
    tea-houses, 198–9, 203; new capital city,
    198; Westernization, 199, 202, 203,
    204; street life, 199, 201; the rickshaw,
    201; foreign architects, 201–2; depart-
    ment stores, 202; old Edo, 202–3;
    changed appearance of its people, 203,
    204; public services, 204; areas and buil-
    dings, Ginza district, 199, 201; Hoter-
    ukan, 198; New Shimabara, 198–9;
    Nikolai Cathedral, 202; Rokumeikan,
    the, 201, 204; Ryōunkaku, 202
Toledano, Roulhac, on New Orleans,
    195
Toledo, 103; siting and ethos, 104;
    pesadumbre, 104; cigarrale estates,
    104, 106; foreign occupations, 106;
    Mozarah community, 106; Muwallads,
    106; Arab and Jewish students, 106;
    French influence, 106–7; archbishop-
    ric, 107; Arab/Jewish/Christian
    culture, 107, 112; Gothic architecture,
    112; Civil War and, 112; commercial
    and ecclesiastical activity, 112;
    buildings, Alcazar, 108, 109, 112;
    Cathedral, 106, 112, 115
Trajan, Emperor (AD 53–117), 43, 44, 55
Trezzini, Domenico, architect, 158
Trotsky, Leon (1879–1949), and Lenin's
    funeral, 217–18; murder, 218

Turkey, Turks, 39, 62, 63, 176

Uccello, Paolo (1397–1475), 101
Utzon, Jøern, Sydney Opera House, 247
Uzzano, Niccolò de, 96

Valley of the Kings, tombs of the
    pharaohs, 16
Vasari, Giorgio (1511–74), on
    Michelangelo, 91
Venice, 89, 92, 97, 155, 160; city of
    pleasure, 161, 162, 164, 165, 171, 173;
    amorous adventures, 165; gondola as
    'love-nest', 165; courtesans, 165–6,
    173; 'the brothel of Europe', 166;
    insanitary state, 166, 168; political
    activities, 168; fall of Crete and, 168;
    street activities, 168, 170, 171;
    Murano glass factory, 170; arsenal,
    170–1; behaviour in church, 172;
    convents as finishing schools, 173;
    architectural features, Academia, 173;
    Basilica, 168; Campanile, 164, 168;
    Doge's Palace, 167, 172–3; the
    Giudecca, 164; Grand Canal, 168,
    171, 173; Rialto Bridge, 168, 173;
    S. Francesco della Vigna, 164; St
    Mark's Square, 162, 164, 173
Verrazano, Giovanni de (1485–1528),
    229
Veronese, Paolo (1528–88), 173
Verrocchio, Andrea del (1435–88), 101
Victoria, Queen, and Franz Josef, 177
Vienna, city of pleasure, 173, 176, 185;
    development, 175–6, 182; occupied
    by Napoleon, 176; 1814–15 Congress,
    176; music and dancing centre, 176–7,
    184–5; Biedermeier age, 180, 181;
    class segregation, 181–2; sanitary sys-
    tem, 182; buildings, Belvedere, 179,
    the Börse, 179; Burgtheater, 176; Hof-
    burg, 176, 180, 181, 185; City Hall (Rat-
    haus), 179; Justiz Palast, 179; Opera
    House, 177; Ringstrasse, 177, 179, 180;
    Schönbrunn, 176, 181; Votivkirche, 179
Vincent de Paul, St (c.1580–1660),
    133–4

Wagner, Otto (1841–1918), 179–80
Walpole, Horace (d.1797), on Paris, 132
Walter, Bruno (1876–1962), 209, 215
Waters, Thomas, and Ginza District,
    199, 201
Weber, Frederick Christian on a
    Russian debauch, 159
Weill, Kurt (1900–50), 209, 215
Williams, Tennessee, 195
women, Chinese, 72, 75–6; Dutch, 120,
    121, 122; French, 122; Greek, 39, 42;
    Inca, 82–3, 88; Japanese, 203–4;
    Jewish, 30; New Orleans (half-castes
    and prostitutes), 189–90, 192–3;
    Roman, 50–2; Russian, 158–9; nuns
    as lovers, 172; Viennese society, 180
Wren, Sir Christopher (1632–1723), and
    re-building of London, 141, 144;
    churches, 142, 144, 135
Wright, Frank Lloyd (1869–1959), 204,
    238

Young, John R., and Tokyo, 202–3

Zanardelli, Giuseppe, Italian PM, 236
Zeno, Greek philosopher, 40
Zinoviev, Grigori (1883–1936), 218
Zion, City of David, 24, 26
Zweig, Stefan (1881–1942), 181; on
    Germany's financial and moral
    collapse, 210, 211